Part-time Working in General Practice

Isobel Allen

Policy Studies Institute, London

The publishing imprint of the independent
POLICY STUDIES INSTITUTE
100 Park Village East, London NW1 3SR
Telephone: 071-387 2171; Fax: 071-388 0914

ISBN 0 85374 550 1

A CIP catalogue record of this book is available from the British Library.

1 2 3 4 5 6 7 8 9

How to obtain PSI publications
All bookshop and individual orders should be sent to PSI's distributors:

BEBC Distribution Ltd, P O Box 1496, Poole, Dorset, BH12 3YD

Books will normally be despatched in 24 hours. Cheques should be made payable to BEBC Distribution Ltd.

Credit card and telephone/fax orders may be placed on the following freephone numbers:

FREEPHONE: 0800 262260 FREEFAX: 0800 262266

Booktrade Representation (UK & Eire)
Book Representation and Distribution Ltd
244a London Road, Hadleigh, Essex, SS7 2DE

PSI Subscriptions
PSI Publications are available on subscription.
Further information from PSI's subscription agent:
Carfax Publishing Company, P O Box 25, Abingdon, Oxon, OX14 3UE

Laserset by Policy Studies Institute
Printed in Great Britain by BPCC Wheatons Ltd, Exeter

Acknowledgements

This study was initiated and funded by the Department of Health. Several members of staff at the Department gave support and guidance at various stages of the research and the author of the report greatly appreciated their help.

Special thanks are due to officers and staff of the Royal College of General Practitioners and the Joint Committee on Postgraduate Training for General Practice (JCPTGP) for facilitating and arranging the sampling of doctors from the records of those holding vocational training certificates issued by the JCPTGP, and for supervising the dispatch of the questionnaires. This study could not have taken place without their help and cooperation.

Staff at the General Medical Council also played an important role in supplying addresses for the selected doctors, and the researchers are particularly grateful to Carol Stone for all her help and interest in the study.

The study was designed and directed by Isobel Allen, who wrote the report. Annette Walling assisted on the design of the questionnaire and was responsible for supervising the organisation of the postal survey and for initiating the coding and analysis of the data. Sally Walker and Mary Haydon were responsible for the coding and selection of material from most of the questionnaires, and additional coding was carried out by Katy Fidler, Cory McCracken and Christian Schroeder.

Karen MacKinnon was responsible for the computing and preparation of tables. Karin Erskine prepared the text for publication.

Finally, our major thanks go to the 1263 doctors who responded to this survey. The questionnaire was long, in spite of our encouraging notes to respondents that it was not as long as it looked. We asked doctors to give us their views and experience as well as to ring codes and tick boxes. The responses were full and detailed, and we express our gratitude to all those doctors who took the time and trouble to fill in the questionnaires. All their responses received detailed attention, as they can see from the resulting report.

Contents

Tables

1　Introduction

The aim of this study was to look at the factors affecting the demand for part-time training and part-time career posts in general practice. The Department of Health, which initiated and funded the report, was interested not only in establishing an indication of the actual and potential demand for such part-time posts, but also in gaining an insight into the nature of the demand.

The research was designed to give the Department more information on the nature of the demand, including the numbers of hours or sessions required and the length of time needed in part-time employment. It was also designed to explore the extent to which there were any factors which prevented doctors from achieving part-time training or part-time career posts in general practice. It was recognised that 'part-time' working in medicine was open to a wide variety of interpretations, and particular attention was paid to exactly what was meant by 'part-time' in the context of general practice.

The problems of definition of part-time working in medicine arise throughout this report and are discussed in more detail in Chapter 11. Although 'less than full-time' working would be a more accurate description of much of the activity recorded, we have tended to use the phrase 'part-time' for the sake of brevity. The reader should, however, be aware that 'part-time' working in medicine covers a very broad range, and may sometimes entail more hours than full-time working in other occupations.

Vocational training in general practice

Since February 1981, those wishing to work as general practitioners have had to hold a certificate of prescribed or equivalent experience, or to have been exempted by the vocational training regulations from the need to have either of these certificates. The Secretary of State prescribed the Joint Committee on Postgraduate Training for General Practice (JCPTGP) as the body for issuing certificates under the National Health Service (Vocational Training) Regulations 1979 (SI 1979 No 1644), and issued information and guidance on the effect of the regulations in a Health Circular in February 1980 (DHSS, HC(FP)(80)1, 1980). These certificates of prescribed and equivalent experience are usually referred to as vocational training certificates and this practice has been followed in this report.

The regulations and guidance are complicated, but a brief summary is given here, since an understanding of the requirements of vocational training in general practice is useful in reading this report.

A certificate of prescribed experience can be issued by the JCPTGP only to a doctor who has completed a period of training amounting to at least three years whole-time employment or its equivalent, of which at least 12 months full-time or its equivalent is spent as a trainee in general practice and the remainder is spent training in educationally approved posts, including not less than six months full-time or equivalent in two of certain prescribed specialties.

A certificate of equivalent experience can be issued when the Joint Committee is satisfied that the applicant's experience is equivalent to the prescribed experience (SI 1979 No 1644). A certificate of equivalent experience is of equal value in every respect to a certificate of prescribed experience (DHSS, HC(FP)(80)1, 1980).

The training required for certificates of prescribed experience must be completed within seven years, whether undertaken whole-time, part-time or partly whole-time and partly part-time. Any periods of part-time training must not be less than half-time. However, part-time training undertaken for less than half-time, or training spread over a period of more than seven years, may be considered for certificates of equivalent experience.

It should be noted that the regulations were implemented in two stages. From 16 February 1981 until 15 August 1982, the prescribed medical experience was 12 months whole-time or its equivalent as a trainee general practitioner. It was not until 16 August 1982 that the requirements for prescribed experience of three years whole-time employment or its equivalent as outlined above were fully implemented.

The circumstances in which a doctor is exempt from the need to have acquired either prescribed or equivalent experience are laid down in the regulations, but refer mainly to doctors who were on a medical list as providing the full range of general medical services on 15 February 1981, and to a limited range of doctors of similar status.

Table 1.1 shows the breakdown of certificates issued by the JCPTGP between 1981 and 1991. It can be seen that the 1981 total of 2562 certificates and the 1982 total of 2433 certificates were relatively high compared with later years, no doubt reflecting a certain 'catching up' and a desire on the part of some doctors for recognition of the completion of their vocational training before certificates were first issued in 1981. The total figure fell sharply in 1983 to 1716, and then climbed to a peak of 2237 in 1987, since when it has declined gradually to 2112 in 1990, with a slight upturn in 1991 to 2128.

The proportion of certificates of prescribed experience has been steadily rising since 1985, as Table 1.1 shows, and has hovered around the 90 per cent mark since 1987. There is, perhaps not surprisingly, a difference between UK-qualified doctors and others in the proportion holding the two types of certificates. In 1990, overseas and European Community qualified doctors accounted for just under 10 per cent of those issued with prescribed experience

Table 1.1   Number of certificates issued by JCPTGP between 15 February 1981 and
31 December 1991

Year	Total	Prescribed	Equivalent	Ratio Prescribed: Equivalent
1981	2562	2376	186	93:7
1982	2433	2083	350	86:14
1983	1716	1426	290	83:17
1984	1872	1415	457	76:24
1985	2041	1518	523	74:26
1986	2196	1835	361	84:16
1987	2237	2014	223	90:10
1988	2198	1935	263	88:12
1989	2186	1983	203	91:9
1990	2112	1895	217	90:10
1991	2128	1815	313	85:15
Total	23681	20295	3386	86:14

Source: Report on the work of the Joint Committee on Postgraduate Training for General
Practice 1991

certificates but 42 per cent of those issued with equivalent experience certificates
(JCPTGP, 1990).

The proportion of overseas qualified doctors gaining vocational training
certificates has been steadily falling over the past ten years, as Table 1.2 shows.
In 1981 they accounted for 19 per cent of those issued with certificates, but this
proportion had fallen to 8 per cent in 1990 and 9 per cent in 1991. There are a
number of reasons for this, perhaps the most important being the tightening up
of the qualifications required for full registration in this country by the General
Medical Council. (Full registration is required in order to become a GP trainee.)
In addition, the change in the immigration rules in 1985 made it very difficult in
effect for overseas qualifiers to gain a place as a vocational trainee in general
practice if they did not have a right to remain within the United Kingdom on
completion of training.

The proportion of EC qualifiers was 3 per cent in 1981, 4 per cent in 1990
and 5 per cent in 1991, with only minor fluctuations in the intervening years. It
should be noted that doctors who qualify in another EC country are not required
to have a vocational training certificate to practise as a GP in this country. This
will change in 1995, and may well lead to an increase in the numbers and
proportion of EC qualifiers taking vocational training certificates after that date.

Table 1.2 Analysis of certificates issued by the JCPTGP between 15 February 1981 and 31 December 1991 by sex and place of qualification

Year	Total	UK Male	UK Female	Overseas Male	Overseas Female	EC Male	EC Female
1981	2562	1093	890	398	95	61	25
1982	2433	1134	828	336	69	42	24
1983	1716	920	489	196	33	55	23
1984	1872	956	567	213	59	52	25
1985	2041	1073	631	223	49	45	20
1986	2196	1119	757	187	61	48	24
1987	2237	1107	790	178	71	56	35
1988	2198	1101	798	140	47	78	34
1989	2186	1041	857	153	40	62	33
1990	2112	947	892	146	33	54	40
1991	2128	960	862	147	55	62	42
Total	23681	11451	8361	2317	612	615	325

Source: Report on the work of the Joint Committee on Postgraduate Training for General Practice 1991

It can be seen from Table 1.2 that women accounted for a much lower proportion of overseas qualifiers gaining certificates and a rather lower proportion of EC qualifiers than found among UK qualifiers. This will be discussed in the next section.

Women doctors and vocational training

The proportion of women as entrants to general practice has been rising steadily over the past 15 years, and, indeed the proportion of women GP trainees rose from 31 per cent to 40 per cent between 1977 and 1986, while the proportion of women unrestricted GP principals rose from 14 per cent to 20 per cent over the same period. By 1990, 47 per cent of GP trainees and 24 per cent of unrestricted GP principals were women, as Table 1.3 shows. Women will shortly account for 50 per cent of those entering general practice, and there is clearly an imperative both for the profession and for the health service that the best possible use is made of the talents of half our new GPs.

The proportion of women gaining GP vocational training certificates issued by the JCPTGP was somewhat higher than the proportion of women GP trainees at the beginning of the 1980s, with 39 per cent of the certificates issued in 1981 being gained by women (JCPTGP, 1991). The evidence in this survey suggests that there was some 'catching up' by older women GPs who wished to gain their

Table 1.3 General Medical Practitioners in post in England and Wales: by grade showing females as percentage of total at 1 October each year

Year	All practitioners		Unrestricted principals		Restricted principals		Assistants		Trainees	
	Total	Percentage female	Total	Percentage female	Total	Percentage female	Total	Percentage female	Total	Percentage female
1979	24510	16.6	22696	15.1	255	33.3	323	54.2	1236	30.8
1980	25160	17.3	23184	15.7	236	35.2	284	56.3	1456	32.3
1981	25906	18.0	23701	16.2	217	35.9	286	54.9	1702	34.3
1982	26414	18.6	24217	16.9	208	38.5	269	58.7	1720	34.4
1983	26962	19.2	24719	17.4	188	39.4	286	58.0	1769	37.0
1984	27449	20.0	25132	18.1	180	39.4	275	56.0	1862	37.6
1985	27889	20.6	25558	18.7	171	39.8	236	57.6	1924	40.1
1986	28248	21.4	26009	19.6	163	37.4	262	58.0	1814	40.4
1987	28793	22.4	26509	20.6	162	37.0	246	57.3	1876	41.8
1988	29196	23.5	26921	21.5	161	37.3	264	61.7	1850	44.7
1989	29556	24.5	27239	22.5	166	37.3	251	62.5	1900	48.1
1990	29323	25.2	27257	23.5	151	36.4	205	59.0	1710	47.2

Source: Department of Health National Tables, 1990

Table 1.4   Number of certificates issued by JCPTGP between 15 February 1981 and
31 December 1991 by sex

Year	Total	Male	Female	Percentage Female
1981	2562	1552	1010	39
1982	2433	1512	921	38
1983	1716	1171	545	32
1984	1872	1221	651	35
1985	2041	1341	700	34
1986	2196	1354	842	38
1987	2237	1341	896	40
1988	2198	1319	879	40
1989	2186	1256	930	42
1990	2112	1147	965	46
1991	2128	1169	959	45
Total	23681	14383	9298	39

Source: Report on the work of the Joint Committee on Postgraduate Training for General
Practice 1991

vocational training certificates, even if they might have been exempt from the
requirement to do so. The proportion of women dropped to 32 per cent in 1983,
but gradually climbed to 40 per cent in 1987. By 1990 the proportion had risen
to 46 per cent, but dropped slightly to 45 per cent in 1991, as Table 1.4 shows.

There are some interesting differences between qualifiers from UK medical
schools and those from the EC and overseas, as Table 1.2 shows. In 1981, in
fact, women accounted for 45 per cent of the vocational training certificates
issued to UK qualifiers, compared with only 19 per cent of the certificates issued
to overseas qualifiers. By 1990, women accounted for 48 per cent of the UK
qualifiers gaining vocational training certificates compared with only 18 per cent
of the overseas qualifiers. Comparable proportions in 1991 were 47 per cent of
UK qualifiers and 27 per cent of overseas qualifiers. The highest proportion of
women among the overseas qualifiers was in 1987, when they accounted for 29
per cent of the certificates gained by graduates from overseas. The proportion of
women among the EC qualifiers has fluctuated considerably over the last ten
years or so, from 29 per cent in 1981 to 35 per cent in 1989 and then to 40 per
cent in 1991, but the numbers are small, and it is difficult to discern a real trend.

Women doctors and general practice
These statistics of an increasing proportion of women doctors entering general
practice are not, however, as simple as they might appear to be. The nature of

the contribution of women GPs is rather different from the contribution of men GPs and this has important implications for the future organisation of general practice.

One of the major findings of *Doctors and their Careers* (Allen, 1988), which looked at the careers of equal numbers of men and women qualifying as doctors in 1966, 1976 and 1981, was the extent to which women doctors worked part-time or less than full-time in medicine. It confirmed the indications from previous research on women doctors' careers that the vast majority of medically qualified women remain active in medicine and that the proportion of women doctors not working at all is very low, particularly among more recent cohorts of qualifiers. In *Doctors and their Careers*, we found that only 5 per cent of each cohort of women doctors were not working at all at the time of the survey, and that a high proportion of women were working less than full-time in medicine, particularly among the two older cohorts of qualifiers, who were aged, on average, 43 and 33 at the time of the study, compared with the youngest cohort who were aged 28 on average.

That study showed that women doctors were more successful in obtaining career posts in general practice as GP principals than in hospital medicine as consultants. It also found that women in career posts in general practice were much more likely to be working or to have worked part-time than those in hospital medicine. Just over half the women GP principals were working less than full-time in general practice (including the 20-hour a week principals who were regarded as full-time to attract the full Basic Practice Allowance before the introduction of the new GP contract in April 1990). However, there was no real evidence of whether this was meeting the demand for part-time career posts or whether it was a greater availability of part-time career posts which attracted women to enter general practice rather than go into hospital medicine.

Design of the present study

The present study was concerned with three cohorts of doctors who had been issued with vocational training certificates in general practice by the JCPTGP in 1981, 1985 and 1988. The study concentrated on the experience of relatively recent entrants to general practice, since one of the main purposes of the research was to look at the question of part-time or less than full-time working in general practice. The steady increase in the proportion of women entering general practice over the past ten years is clearly an important factor in this, and we decided to restrict the study to those entering general practice during the 1980s. We were mainly interested in doctors in their late twenties and in their thirties. The experiences of older doctors, although interesting, are of more limited value in predicting future trends.

We wanted to use a cohort approach, which had proved a useful approach in *Doctors and their Careers* in showing trends and allowing careers and experience to be compared within one cohort and across cohorts. It also provided a data base for building on for further exploration. In addition, we wanted to have a sampling frame in which comparability was possible. For this reason, in consultation with the Department of Health, we decided to seek collaboration with the JCPTGP with a view to using their records of doctors to whom they had issued vocational training certificates as our sampling frame. Our point of departure was determined by the fact that they first issued certificates in 1981.

Methods

The main evidence collected in this study came from responses to semi-structured postal questionnaires, completed by samples of doctors selected at random from the men and women gaining vocational training certificates from the JCPTGP in 1981, 1985 and 1988.

The study was designed to achieve responses from 1200 doctors, 200 men and 200 women from each of the three cohorts. To this end we arranged with the JCPTGP for the sampling of 1800 names, 300 men and 300 women from each cohort, in the expectation of a 66 per cent response rate. In the event, we received completed questionnaires from 1263 doctors – a response rate of over 70 per cent of the 1800 names sampled. We received responses from 204 men and 221 women of the 1981 cohort, 195 men and 218 women of the 1985 cohort and 179 men and 246 women of the 1988 cohort. The breakdown is analysed in Chapter 2, and the detailed response rates analysed in the Appendix. Details of the sampling from the lists of doctors awarded their vocational training certificates in the selected years are also given in the Appendix, but some comments should be made on the sample here.

Among the 1263 respondents, there were rather more women than would be expected in a true cross section of all certificated doctors in those years. Therefore caution must be exercised in generalising from the results of this survey to all members of the cohorts. However, within each of the six groups, the doctors responding form an unbiased and representative sample.

Although the study is about six separate samples, it is clearly useful to refer to the doctors as a whole, or to refer to men and women separately or to the three cohorts separately. The tables are always presented with the total 'average' response of the 1263 doctors in the first column, and in the text this response is sometimes presented as a point of departure. Where there is homogeneity in the response, this is an acceptable shorthand way of presenting the material. More often, the responses of men and women are used as a starting point, since there were interesting differences between them. Again, it should be recognised that, strictly speaking, the six samples should be regarded as separate entities, but this approach is permissible. The responses of men and women from each of the cohorts are always presented in the tables, and the text comments on similarities and differences among them. The report draws attention to differences only where the probability was less than 5 per cent that they could have arisen by chance.

This description of the nature of the sample underlines the need for caution in making statements about the doctors as a whole. It should be stressed that it can be misleading to assume that a response recorded by perhaps 20 or 30 per cent of the total sample is of little account. The question is not only *who* responded in this way, but how these responses fitted into the general picture. There were important differences between men and women, and there were also important trends. The report looks closely at these trends. Doctors from the 1988 cohort had different views and experience from those in the 1981 cohort, and men and women within these cohorts also held different views. The report goes to great lengths to represent this complex scene which represents a snapshot of a group of doctors in their thirties from varied backgrounds, with varied experience and with very different aspirations.

The sample included doctors who were living overseas at the time of the research. It also included doctors who were not on the Medical Register at the time, although it was not possible to find an address for all of those who were no longer on the register (see Appendix). Questionnaires were not sent to these doctors, and similarly were not sent to those who were known to have died.

The questionnaire was sent out in January 1990 from the JCPTGP, with an explanatory letter from Policy Studies Institute and a covering letter from the Joint Committee endorsing the research. Reply-paid envelopes were enclosed, and those doctors known to be overseas were sent an additional letter asking them to claim reimbursement for their postage. A reminder letter was sent a month later and a further reminder letter with another copy of the questionnaire was sent a month after this. Detailed responses were received in many cases within a week, and in some cases within a day. The interest engendered by this survey surprised the researchers, who had been warned by doctors and other researchers alike that doctors would not be prepared to fill in such a long questionnaire.

The questionnaire was developed in close collaboration with the Department of Health and was piloted in two stages. The questionnaires were fully structured, in that the exact wording of each question was specified and the questions were in a predetermined sequence. A fairly high proportion of questions allowed for an open-ended response, with the respondent being invited to write as much as they liked, within space limitations. The extent to which doctors took advantage of this invitation was striking, and, indeed, many doctors wrote detailed accounts of their experience, spilling over onto the back of the questionnaire and even using additional paper.

Data analysis
The analysis of the type of data generated in a study of this kind is complicated. The questionnaires were analysed using the predetermined codes on the questionnaires, as well as coding frames developed from detailed textual analysis of the 'open-ended' questions. There was no doubt that some doctors wrote less than others, but open-ended questions were almost invariably answered, if only briefly, and provided a rich source of data, not only for quantitative analysis but also for illustration. Verbatim quotes were extracted from the questionnaires and selected for inclusion in a rigorous manner in proportion to the numbers making

such comments. These quotes are used in the report to illuminate the material gathered from the questionnaires.

There is, of course, a potential problem in using quotes from self-completed questionnaires, compared with using quotes from questionnaires completed by experienced interviewers. With postal questionnaires, the researchers are more dependent on how much the respondent is prepared to write in answer to the 'open-ended' questions, whereas an interviewer can usually guarantee a more uniform level of response. However, our use of quotes related to the proportions of doctors making the points should ensure that we have not allowed the more articulate, or perhaps more literate, doctors to dominate the study.

We received responses from nearly 1300 doctors, and we present our material both quantitatively and qualitatively. However, we have used our quantitative material mainly in a descriptive manner rather than as a means of demonstrating differences. We have applied standard tests of statistical significance where we wish to draw attention to differences, as noted above, but there were many instances where significant differences were not perhaps as important as trends or cumulative evidence or strong associations. We have concentrated on trying to illustrate and explain these. This method of analysis entails close knowledge of the completed questionnaires and the interlocking use of quantitative and qualitative data.

The structure and presentation of the report

The report takes a thematic approach to the study, with the exception of Chapter 2, which outlines in detail the main characteristics of the responding doctors. This chapter contains a large number of tables to illustrate the text. Although this type of material is often included in an Appendix, we thought it necessary to place it at the beginning of the report, since so much of the ensuing material can be understood only if the reader has a fairly comprehensive knowledge of the characteristics, qualifications and experience of the doctors who responded.

Chapter 11 summarises the report and presents an overall discussion of the findings of the research. Chapter 12 brings together the main policy implications of the key findings.

We have made a deliberate decision to restrict the references to other studies to those which we feel to be essential. This study was designed and funded as a piece of empirical research to aid policy makers, and, given the resources available, we have concentrated on presenting the findings of our survey, rather than relating it to the literature.

The report suggests that the subject matter of the survey touched a chord with many of the respondents, both men and women, and the comprehensive quality of their responses furnished a great deal of material to indicate that not everything was happy in the world of general practice. The focus of the research was part-time working in general practice, but, as the ensuing chapters show, the context of careers in medicine and the medical profession in general was of overwhelming importance.

2   Who were the doctors?

The study was designed to achieve responses from 1200 doctors who had received their vocational training certificates (VTCs) from the Joint Committee on Postgraduate Training for General Practice (JCPTGP) in the years 1981, 1985 and 1988. We were aiming at responses from 200 men and 200 women sampled from each of these three years. In the event, we received completed questionnaires from 1263 doctors – 425 who gained their vocational training certificates in 1981 (204 men and 221 women), 413 who gained their certificates in 1985 (195 men and 218 women), and 425 who gained their certificates in 1988 (179 men and 246 women). Table 2.1 shows the breakdown.

Table 2.1   Year in which vocational training certificate granted by sex

	Total		Male		Female	
	No.	%	No.	%	No.	%
Year of VTC						
1981	425	33.7	204	35	221	32
1985	413	32.6	195	34	218	32
1988	425	33.7	179	31	246	36
Base: all respondents	*1263*	*100*	*578*	*100*	*685*	*100*

The doctors were sampled from lists held by the Joint Committee of those who received their vocational training certificates in the three years selected for study. However, as a check, we asked the doctors to record the year in which they received their vocational training certificate. Although the majority of doctors reported gaining their certificates in the year from which they had been sampled, there were some discrepancies. This arose in particular among the 1981 cohort, where 5 per cent of the men and 10 per cent of the women reported gaining their certificates in a different year – most of them in 1980 or before.

There was clearly some misunderstanding on the part of these doctors, since vocational training certificates were not issued by the Joint Committee until 1981. It is probable that these doctors were referring to other certificates issued before the vocational training certificates were introduced, and, indeed, some of the respondents stated specifically that they had not gained a vocational training

Table 2.2   Year in which vocational training certificate granted by country of qualification and sex

column percentages

| | Total | UK | | | Country of qualification | | | | | | All other countries | | | |
| | | | | | Ireland | | | Indian sub-continent | | | | | | |
		Total	M	F	Total	M	F	Total	M	F	Total	M	F	n.a.
1981	34	33	33	32	32	37	21	47	48	45	32	50	13	41
1985	33	33	35	31	27	23	36	32	31	32	42	25	60	24
1988	34	34	31	37	41	40	43	21	20	23	26	25	27	35
Base: all respondents	1263	1095	469	626	44	30	14	76	54	22	31	16	15	17

certificate, but certificates of equivalent experience or some other certificate. Some were adamant that they had never gained a vocational training certificate.

Although overall the responses from doctors of both sexes were roughly equally divided among the three years sampled for this study, there were some differences according to the country of qualification of the doctors, as Table 2.2 indicates.

The UK qualifiers, who represented 87 per cent of respondents, were divided fairly equally among the three years, as might have been expected, given their preponderance in the overall figures. However, there were rather more Irish qualifiers among the 1988 respondents than might have been expected and rather fewer among the 1985 respondents.

The most striking difference was among the doctors qualifying in the Indian sub-continent, of whom nearly 50 per cent of both the male and female respondents had gained their vocational training certificate in 1981. There was a clear indication here, reinforced by further evidence, that our sample included a number of doctors from the Indian sub-continent who had been working in general practice for some time in the UK in 1981, who wished to gain their vocational training certificate, even if they might have been exempt from the necessity of doing so by virtue of their previous experience in this country. The relative decline in numbers between 1981 and 1988, particularly among male doctors from these countries, suggests that this factor played a part, but the change in the GMC requirements for full registration and the change in the immigration rules in 1985 referred to in Chapter 1 were probably more important reasons for the decline.

The proportion of doctors from all other countries was rather higher in 1985 than in the other two years, but the overall number of such doctors was small (31) and chance could have accounted for the difference.

Country of qualification and medical school

Qualifiers from British medical schools accounted for by far the highest proportion of respondents in all three cohorts and between both sexes, as Table 2.3 shows.

Among the sample as a whole, UK qualifiers accounted for 87 per cent of respondents, but there was a difference between the sexes, with 81 per cent of the men and 91 per cent of the women respondents qualifying from British medical schools. Six per cent of the sample qualified in the Indian sub-continent, representing 9 per cent of the men and 3 per cent of the women respondents. Three per cent qualified in Ireland, representing 5 per cent of the men and 2 per cent of the women respondents. Two per cent of the respondents qualified in other countries of the world, with equal proportions of men and women, and no information was given on medical school by 1 per cent of the sample. Of the 31 respondents qualifying in other countries, eleven had qualified in Europe, while the others were qualifiers from all over the world, with just under half coming from white Commonwealth countries or South Africa.

Table 2.3   Country of undergraduate medical education and medical school of UK qualifiers

column percentages

	Total nos	%	1981	Male 1985	1988	1981	Female 1985	1988
Aberdeen	76	6	8	5	3	10	6	4
Birmingham	55	4	4	9	4	5	4	1
Bristol	48	4	3	5	2	4	5	3
Cambridge	49	4	3	6	5	3	3	4
Dundee	40	3	5	1	2	5	4	2
Edinburgh	51	4	4	3	3	6	4	4
Glasgow	52	4	3	3	5	5	3	6
Leeds	50	4	3	3	3	4	6	5
Leicester	13	1	0	1	1	0	1	4
Liverpool	47	4	4	4	2	5	4	3
London	293	23	16	24	27	23	22	25
Manchester	88	7	8	7	3	8	8	7
Newcastle	56	4	4	2	5	3	6	7
Nottingham	19	0	0	1	3	*	1	4
Oxford	26	2	3	1	2	2	4	1
Sheffield	42	3	1	5	3	3	5	2
Southampton	19	2	0	0	2	*	1	5
Wales	45	4	3	4	3	5	3	3
Queen's Belfast	26	2	1	3	2	*	2	3
All UK qualifiers	1095	87	77	85	82	91	89	93
Ireland	44	3.5	5	4	7	1	2	2
Indian sub-continent	76	6	13	9	6	5	3	2
All other countries	31	2.5	4	2	2	1	4	2
n.a.	17	1	1	1	3	2	1	*
Base: all respondents	1263	1263	204	195	179	221	218	246

The highest proportion of qualifiers from medical schools outside the UK was found among the 1981 male sample, of whom 13 per cent had qualified in the Indian sub-continent.

The pattern of medical schools attended by the UK qualifiers was much as would be expected. Over a quarter were London qualifiers, and 21 per cent were from Scottish universities. Of the 75 qualifiers from Oxford and Cambridge, 46 (61 per cent) had also attended a London medical school. It was not possible to discern a real pattern among the different years or between the sexes. The 1981 men and the 1988 women Oxford and Cambridge qualifiers were more likely than the others to have been to a London medical school.

The distribution among London medical schools of the London qualifiers was also along expected lines, with fairly equal numbers from each school. The only notable features were the 6 per cent of the total sample of 1981 women who had been at the Royal Free and the 7 per cent of the total sample of 1988 men who had been at Charing Cross. Otherwise each London medical school accounted for 1, 2 or 3 per cent of each cohort of both men and women.

Year of qualification as a doctor

If a doctor were to pursue a completely straightforward career path, going straight into a pre-registration house job at qualification, and entering GP vocational training immediately after full registration as a doctor with the General Medical Council, it might be expected that four years would elapse from qualification to gaining the vocational training certificate. This would, of course, be the minimum possible time, given that the pre-registration period is one year, and three years have to be spent in completing the GP vocational training full-time.

It might therefore be expected that the peak year of qualification for the 1981 cohort would have been 1977, for the 1985 cohort 1981, and for the 1988 cohort 1984.

Table 2.4   Year of qualification as a doctor

column percentages

	1981			1985			1988	
	M	F		M	F		M	F
1974 and			1978 and			1981 and		
before	35	32	before	31	24	before	25	22
1975	9	13	1979	14	11	1982	17	19
1976	17	23	1980	20	27	1983	23	31
1977	36	24	1981	33	38	1984	35	38
1978-9	3	8	1982-3	2	0	1985	*	*
Base: all								
respondents	204	221		195	218		179	246

As Table 2.4 shows, the expected pattern was broadly established, but the 'peak' year was by no means a real peak, and, even if the preceding two years were added to the expected year, it certainly did not appear that most doctors gaining vocational training certificates had single-mindedly pursued a career in general practice once they had qualified.

The table indicates that around one third of men from all years had pursued a 'fast-lane' career in general practice, in that they had gained their VTC four years after qualifying. The women were rather different. Although under a quarter of the 1981 women had followed this path, nearly 40 per cent of the 1985 and 1988 women had done so.

If we look at those who had qualified four, five and six years before gaining the VTC, we see an interesting trend. They represented some 60 per cent of both men and women in the 1981 cohort. In the 1985 cohort, they represented 67 per cent of the men, but 76 per cent of the women, and in the 1988 cohort, they represented 75 per cent of the men and 78 per cent of the women. The indications are that doctors in general, who subsequently become GPs, are deciding at an earlier stage in their careers that they are going into general practice and that the women are deciding this at an earlier stage than the men. This finding would tend to confirm the trend noted in other studies and the official statistics of an increased interest in general practice during the 1980s among doctors as a whole, and among women in particular. It is especially interesting to note that such a high proportion of the two later cohorts of women moved so quickly after qualification to gain their vocational training certificate.

The trend among all three cohorts was away from delaying vocational training. Around one third of both men and women in the 1981 cohort had qualified seven years or more before they gained the certificate. Nearly one third of the 1985 men had done so, compared with under a quarter of the 1985 women, and by 1988, the proportions had dropped to a quarter of the men and just over a fifth of the women.

There are a number of reasons for this. The 1981 cohort undoubtedly included a number of doctors who were seeking the vocational training certificate as a qualification which had not been available before, so that the numbers include doctors who were 'catching up'. Some of them had qualified many years before. This makes it rather difficult to make a real comparison with the other two cohorts. However, there were some indications that the 1981 cohort included a rather higher proportion than the other cohorts of doctors who had come to general practice as an alternative to their first or second choice specialties.

The trend in the later cohorts appears to have been for doctors to make up their minds at an earlier stage that they wished to enter general practice. Nevertheless, there can be no doubt that a substantial proportion of doctors gaining their certificates have made serious attempts at other careers in medicine before considering general practice.

Looking at country of qualification, it was not perhaps surprising to find that doctors from the Indian sub-continent were likely to have qualified some years before the UK qualifiers. However, as many as 89 per cent of all the doctors qualifying in the Indian sub-continent had qualified in 1974 or before, compared with 11 per cent of the UK qualifiers. This can only partly be explained by the fact that nearly half of them had gained their VTC in 1981. As we shall see, they tended to be older when they gained their certificates, and they were more likely to have pursued other specialties before entering general practice.

Full registration as doctors in the UK

Before doctors can practise in the UK they have to be registered with the General Medical Council. British graduates automatically gain full registration when they have completed their pre-registration house jobs. The situation is rather more complicated for overseas qualifiers, who may well have to do more medical training to comply with the requirements of the GMC. We were interested, for the purposes of this study, in the year in which the doctors achieved full registration as doctors in the UK.

Table 2.5   Year of full registration as a doctor in UK

column percentages

	1981			1985			1988	
	M	F		M	F		M	F
1975 and			1979 and			1982 and		
before	24	29	before	27	22	before	20	20
1976	11	14	1980	15	10	1983	14	9
1977	20	22	1981	21	25	1984	22	30
1978	36	26	1982	35	41	1985	40	39
1979-81	8	9	1983-4	3	2	1986	0	1
						n.a.	4	0
Base: all								
respondents	*204*	*221*		*195*	*218*		*179*	*246*

If doctors had entered GP vocational training as soon as they achieved full registration as doctor, they could have gained their VTC three years after registration. Table 2.5 presents a picture similar to that found in Table 2.4. The potential 'peak' years for registration of 1978, 1982 and 1985 are indeed the peak years for the three cohorts. Rather higher proportions of the two later cohorts 'peak' in the expected year for registration than for qualification. This may be for a number of reasons, one of which is that not all doctors automatically register in the year following qualification. Looking at the two years before the peak year, it can be seen that increasing proportions of men and women in each successive cohort had achieved full registration in the period of three to five years before they gained their vocational training certificate. Of the 1988 cohort, only one fifth had registered seven years or more before.

Again, the doctors from the Indian sub-continent were rather different from the others, with three-quarters of them having achieved full UK registration by 1979, compared with one third of the British qualifiers. This cannot be accounted for only by their greater representation in the 1981 cohort. For example, looking specifically at the 1985 and 1988 cohorts, only a handful of the doctors qualifying in the Indian sub-continent had registered in 1982 and 1985 – the relevant 'peak' years for those cohorts. The proportions were considerably higher for the UK qualifiers, and it does appear that doctors from the Indian sub-continent tend to

Table 2.6   Average age at full registration as a doctor in the UK by country of qualification

		Country of qualification				
	Total	UK	Ireland	Indian sub-continent	All other countries	n.a.
Average age at full registration in years	25.4	24.9	26.4	30.5	30.0	25.1
Base: all respondents	*1263*	*1095*	*44*	*76*	*31*	*17*

decide on a career in general practice not only at a rather later stage in their overall medical careers but also rather later in their careers in the UK than British qualifiers.

This finding is reinforced by looking at the average age of the doctors at full registration. As Table 2.6 shows, the British qualifiers achieved full registration at a mean age of 24.9 years, with very little difference between the male and female qualifiers. The Irish qualifiers were aged 26.4 years on average, while the mean age of qualifiers from the Indian sub-continent was 30.5 years and of qualifiers from other countries 30.0 years. Over half the qualifiers from the Indian sub-continent were aged 30 or over at full registration compared with 2 per cent of UK qualifiers. There was surprisingly little difference in average age at registration between the sexes among the qualifiers from the various countries.

Looking at the three cohorts of qualifiers as a whole, the average age at registration fell slightly from 1981 to 1988 among both men and women – from 26.2 among the 1981 men to 25.7 among the 1988 men and from 25.1 among the 1981 women to 24.7 among the 1988 women. One of the reasons may be the rather higher proportion of non-UK qualifiers among the 1981 men, but there may be indications of a trend towards getting on with medical careers and deciding early on a specialty among young doctors who fear they may be left behind in the competitive career stakes.

Age at gaining vocational training certificate

Tables 2.7 and 2.8 show the average age at which the doctors gained their vocational training certificates. There is only a narrow distribution around the mean age of 30.1 years for the doctors as a whole. The women tended to be rather younger than the men in all three cohorts, but this could be expected, given their rather younger average age at qualification and registration.

The difference in average age at gaining the VTC between the UK qualifiers and those from the Indian sub-continent and other countries could also have been expected for the same reasons. There was little difference between the sexes according to the country of qualification. However, it is interesting to note that the average age of Indian sub-continent qualifiers when they gained their VTC was 37.8, and, indeed, one third of these qualifiers were over the age of 40 when they gained their certificate.

Table 2.7   Average age at which doctors gained vocational training certificate

	Total	Male 1981	1985	1988	Female 1981	1985	1988
Average age at gaining VTC in years	30.1	30.7	30.7	30.0	30.1	29.9	29.2
Base: all respondents	*1263*	*204*	*195*	*179*	*221*	*218*	*246*

Table 2.8   Average age at which doctors gained vocational training certificate by country of qualification

		Country of qualification		Indian	All other	
	Total	UK	Ireland	sub-continent	countries	n.a.
Average age at VTC in years	30.1	29.4	30.7	37.8	35.5	29.4
Base: all respondents	*1263*	*1095*	*44*	*76*	*31*	*17*

Personal characteristics of doctors
Age at completing questionnaire
As might have been expected, the doctors in each cohort tended to be concentrated in particular age-bands. Given an average age of around 30 at gaining the vocational training certificate, we would have expected the 1981 cohort to have been around 39, the 1985 cohort to have been around 35 and the 1988 cohort to be around 31 when they completed the questionnaire in 1990. This was indeed the case. However, Table 2.9 shows that the distribution around the mean was rather greater than that found among UK medical qualifiers in general (Allen, 1988a), and indicates the greater range of ages among those gaining VTCs than among those qualifying as doctors.

The average age of the responding doctors as a whole was 35.1 years, but among qualifiers from the Indian sub-continent it was 44.0 years, compared with 34.3 among UK qualifiers. Even allowing for the fact that nearly half the qualifiers from the Indian sub-continent gained their vocational training certificates in 1981, there was no doubt that these doctors tended to be quite a bit older than the UK-qualified respondents.

Marriage
There were clear differences between the men and women doctors in terms of marital status. 87 per cent of the men were married, compared with 76 per cent

Table 2.9   Age of doctors at completion of questionnaire

column percentages

	Total	Male 1981	Male 1985	Male 1988	Female 1981	Female 1985	Female 1988
26-30	20	0	0	50	0	1	64
31-35	39	14	72	37	15	72	26
36-40	28	59	16	7	59	18	5
41-45	8	15	4	5	14	5	4
46-50	4	9	4	1	7	2	0
51 and over	2	3	3	0	4	1	0
Average age	*35.1*	*39.3*	*35.3*	*31.6*	*39.1*	*34.5*	*31.0*
Base: all respondents	1263	204	195	179	221	218	246

of the women, while 7 per cent of the men were single, compared with 15 per cent of the women. This pattern was demonstrated in each of the cohorts, with the differences more marked among the 1981 and 1988 cohorts, as Table 2.10 shows. Among the 1988 cohort, 81 per cent of the men were currently married compared with 69 per cent of the women. It is notable that nearly one third of these 1988 women doctors were not married. As Table 2.9 showed, nearly two-thirds were in their late twenties, and their average age was 31.

Table 2.10   Marital status of doctors

column percentages

	Total	Male 1981	Male 1985	Male 1988	Female 1981	Female 1985	Female 1988
Single	11	3	8	11	11	13	20
Married	81	93	87	81	81	78	69
Living as married	4	1	3	6	4	5	7
Divorced	2	*	1	2	3	3	3
Separated	1	2	2	1	1	*	1
n.a.	*	0	1	0	0	*	0
Base: all respondents	*1263*	*204*	*195*	*179*	*221*	*218*	*246*

Overall, 2 per cent of the doctors said they were divorced or separated at the time, representing 1 per cent of the men and 3 per cent of the women. However, such figures do not show those who had embarked on a second or subsequent marriage, and our tables may well conceal divorce among those who were living as married. We therefore asked doctors whether they had *ever* been divorced. Table 2.11 indicates that this increased the proportions considerably, with 3 per

Table 2.11   Whether doctors had ever been divorced

column percentages

	Total	Male 1981	1985	1988	Female 1981	1985	1988
Yes	5	4	2	4	5	7	4
No	95	96	98	96	95	93	96
Base: all respondents	*1263*	*204*	*195*	*179*	*221*	*218*	*246*

cent of the men and 6 per cent of the women saying they had been divorced at some time.

There is said to be an increasingly high incidence of divorce among young doctors. This study did not indicate a particularly high level of divorce among those doctors who had gained their vocational training certificates in the 1980s, the vast majority of whom were working as GPs. It is a matter of some interest whether GPs are less or more likely to have experienced divorce than other doctors. There was certainly some evidence in *Doctors and their Careers* that the lifestyle and hours of junior hospital doctors were not thought to be conducive to stable marriage, and a number of doctors in that study gave this reason for changing specialty from hospital medicine to general practice. The evidence from the present research may indicate that general practice is indeed more conducive than hospital specialties to stable marriage. However, it should not be forgotten that a fairly high proportion of the women doctors had not got married at all, and the marital profile of these doctors needs to be compared with those in other studies and to be followed over time.

We were interested to know whom the doctors had married. Successive studies (Ward,1981; Elston; 1980, Stephen; 1987, Allen, 1988a) have shown that women doctors tend to marry other doctors. This finding was repeated among the women doctors in this study, as Table 2.12 shows. The pattern among these young women doctors was remarkably similar to that found in *Doctors and their Careers* where 47 per cent of married women doctors from three cohorts of UK qualifiers (1966, 1976 and 1981) were married to other doctors, compared with 50 per cent of married women doctors in the present study.

Table 2.12 shows that the proportion of married women gaining their VTC in 1988 who were married to other doctors was much higher at 58 per cent than the proportion in the earlier cohorts. This pattern repeated that found among the 1981 qualifiers in *Doctors and their Careers* compared with the 1966 and 1976 cohorts. One reason is, of course, that relatively fewer of the younger women doctors were married. The pattern may well change as more of this cohort get married. The social and working environment of young doctors in the years immediately post-qualification tends to include a lot of other doctors.

Nearly 30 per cent of the married women were married to GPs – a much higher proportion than that found among married women doctors as a whole. This was true of the 1988 cohort of women as well, and was in sharp contrast to

Table 2.12   Social class/occupation of husbands of women doctors

column percentages

	Total	Females 1981	1985	1988
Professional I	76	76	76	73
Managerial II	20	21	17	22
Skilled non-manual III N	*	0	1	1
Skilled manual III M	1	0	2	2
Semi-skilled IV & unskilled V	0	0	0	0
Other (1)	3	3	6	2
Working in medicine (doctors)	50	47	45	58
Working outside medicine	49	51	53	42
Not working	1	1	2	*
GP	27	28	23	30
Hospital doctor	15	15	14	17
Other doctor	8	5	9	10
Dentist	3	3	5	2
Nurse/paramedic	*	1	1	1
Base: all married women doctors for whom husband's occupation given	*511*	*177*	*167*	*167*

(1)   students, armed forces, househusband, retired, unemployed

the youngest cohort of women in *Doctors and their Careers* who, if they were married, were much more likely to be married to hospital doctors than to GPs.

The social class composition of the husbands of women doctors is, of course, striking, with nearly 100 per cent of them working in occupations in social classes I and II.

One of the most interesting aspects of the occupations of the wives of the men doctors was the high proportion of working wives among all three cohorts. Over 70 per cent of the wives of the 1981 and 1988 married men doctors were working, as were over 60 per cent of the wives of the 1985 married men. These proportions were all higher than those found among the UK qualifiers of roughly comparable ages (Allen, 1988a). It is particularly interesting that the tradition of the GP's wife being available to answer the telephone or to act as a paid or unpaid helper in the practice appears to be becoming increasingly eroded, as increasing proportions of GPs' wives have their own careers.

Around one fifth of the wives of doctors in all three cohorts were working in medicine. We did not ask doctors to record whether their spouses were medically qualified if they were not working, but some told us, as Table 2.13 shows. If the wives were working in medicine, they were more likely to be GPs

Table 2.13   Social class/occupation of wives of men doctors

column percentages

	Total	Males 1981	1985	1988
Professional I	23	21	22	28
Managerial II	33	32	33	34
Skilled non-manual III N	6	6	3	8
Skilled manual III M	1	2	0	0
Semi-skilled IV & unskilled V	0	0	0	0
Housewife	32	29	39	28
Other(1)	2	2	0	2
n.a.	3	7	3	0
Working in medicine (doctors)	18	17	18	21
Working outside medicine	45	46	40	50
Not working	32	30	37	28
Medically qualified but not working	1	0	2	2
n.a.	4	7	3	0
GP	9	7	9	12
Hospital doctor	3	4	2	4
Other doctor	6	7	8	5
Dentist	1	1	1	1
Nurse/HV/MW	20	19	20	23
Paramedic	3	2	4	4
Base: all married men doctors	*503*	*189*	*169*	*145*

(1)   Students, unemployed etc

or to be working in public health than to be working as hospital doctors, which is perhaps not surprising, given that most of their husbands were GPs.

The difference between male and female married doctors which comes up in most studies is the proportion of men doctors who are married to nurses, and this study was no exception, with around one fifth of the wives of doctors from each cohort working as nurses. Again, we did not have a record of the proportion of those who were not working at present but had been nurses in the past.

The pattern found among the women doctors was repeated among the men doctors. The working wives of doctors tended to be found in professional or managerial occupations. There was every indication that they were interested in maintaining their careers, since a high proportion (64 per cent) of the wives of doctors with children were working. Given the ages of the doctors concerned, it was equally clear that many of these had *young* children, and there are interesting implications for dual career families. It has always been apparent that women doctors with children have continued to work in large numbers. The indications from this research were that wives of men doctors were also following this pattern. Many of them were undoubtedly working part-time; nevertheless, the pattern of professional dual career families looked firmly established among these doctors, both male and female.

Children

There were marked differences between the three cohorts of doctors in terms of whether they had any children, and striking differences between the men and women doctors, as Table 2.14 shows.

Table 2.14   Whether doctors had children

(i) by year of VTC and sex

	Total	1981	1985	1988	Male	Female
Yes	68	84	72	47	76	61
No	32	16	28	53	24	39
Base: all respondents	*1263*	*425*	*413*	*425*	*578*	*685*

(ii) by sex and year of VTC

	Total	Male			Female		
		1981	1985	1988	1981	1985	1988
Yes	68	90	78	56	79	67	40
No	32	10	22	44	21	33	60
Base: all respondents	*1263*	*204*	*195*	*179*	*221*	*218*	*246*

76 per cent of the men but only 61 per cent of the women had children. The proportions in each cohort followed a similar pattern, with 90 per cent of the 1981 men having children, compared with under 80 per cent of the women from that year, 78 per cent of the 1985 men compared with just over two-thirds of the women, and 56 per cent of the 1988 men compared with 40 per cent of the women.

Although the proportions of men with children were consistently higher than the proportions of women in each cohort, the fact remains that the proportions of women doctors with children were still relatively high, given that most of the women were working.

The pattern found was similar to that found among all women qualifiers in *Doctors and their Careers* with the important exception of the youngest cohort of women in the two samples. Among the 1981 women qualifiers interviewed in 1986, only 14 per cent had children. Among the women responding in the present research, 40 per cent of the 1988 cohort had children. They were rather older on average than the 1981 qualifiers, but two-thirds of them were in their late twenties, the same age as the 1981 qualifiers had been.

There are strong indications that the fact that these women had chosen general practice as a specialty was linked to the considerably higher proportion of them who had children. The shorter period of postgraduate training and the greater opportunities for part-time working could well facilitate the decision to have children for women in general practice compared with those in hospital medicine. Nevertheless, there were clearly some hard decisions coming up for a substantial proportion of the women GPs in this study on whether and when to have children. The importance of the availability of part-time or less than full-time working in making these decisions cannot be underestimated.

Table 2.15   Number of children of doctors with children

column percentages

	Total	Male 1981	Male 1985	Male 1988	Female 1981	Female 1985	Female 1988
One	24	11	14	42	10	23	68
Two	47	48	54	48	46	53	24
Three	25	33	27	10	36	21	6
Four	4	6	6	1	7	3	0
Five plus	*	1	0	0	1	0	1
Mean no of children	2.1	2.1	2.2	1.7	2.4	2.0	1.4
Base: all doctors with children	*857*	*184*	*153*	*101*	*175*	*146*	*98*
Mean no of children of all doctors	1.4	2.1	1.8	1.0	1.9	1.4	0.6
Base: all respondents	*1263*	*204*	*195*	*179*	*221*	*218*	*246*

Doctors have traditionally had rather bigger families than average, and both men and women who had children had rather above average sized families, as Table 2.15 shows. It is, of course, probable that final family size will be bigger among the two later cohorts.

We asked the doctors how old they were when their first child was born. Table 2.16 shows that the majority of doctors, both male and female, were between 26 and 30 at the birth of their first child. There were interesting similarities between the men and women in each cohort. The rather younger

Table 2.16   Age of doctors when their first child was born

column percentages

	Total	Male 1981	1985	1988	Female 1981	1985	1988
Under 20	*	0	0	1	1	0	0
20-25	8	8	8	16	7	5	5
26-30	63	48	67	62	63	65	80
31-35	24	33	20	18	23	27	13
35-40	6	9	5	4	7	4	2
Over 40	1	2	1	0	0	0	0
Average age when first child born	29.3	30.2	29.2	28.3	29.3	29.3	28.8
Base: all doctors with children	*857*	*184*	*153*	*101*	*175*	*146*	*98*

average age among the 1988 cohort probably reflects the fact that a relatively higher proportion of them were childless. The average age of 29 for the women indicates a definite postponement in having a baby among women GPs. Given that 60 per cent of the 1988 women had not even embarked on motherhood, it is likely that the average age at first birth could go up quite markedly at least for this cohort, if not the others.

Qualifications

We were particularly interested in the academic and medical qualifications held by the doctors. It has been accepted in recent years that higher professional qualifications are becoming increasingly important, particularly if doctors wish to reach consultant status in hospital medicine, and this trend has also been noted in general practice.

All the doctors in our sample held a primary medical qualification. The vast majority had a medical degree, mainly in the UK, although a small number had primary medical qualifications from overseas. Only 1 per cent held conjoint only (MRCS/LRCP), although 6 per cent held it in addition to a medical degree. These doctors were concentrated in the 1981 cohort, and few of the later cohorts had taken it.

Just over 10 per cent had a BSc or BMedSci. It was usually not possible to deduce whether the BSc degrees were intercalated or not since we did not ask this specific question. The BA degrees were mainly held by Oxford and Cambridge graduates. A handful of doctors had masters degrees or doctorates.

A variety of diplomas were held by the doctors, but by far the most common was the DRCOG, held by 49 per cent of the men and 57 per cent of the women. This diploma was clearly thought highly desirable by GPs, since a much higher proportion of the doctors surveyed in this study held it than those interviewed in

Table 2.17   Qualification

column percentages

	Total	Male 1981	1985	1988	Female 1981	1985	1988
Primary qualifications							
Degree or conjoint	100	100	100	100	100	100	100
BDS	*	*	0	1	0	*	0
BSc/BMed.Sci.	13	12	16	12	11	14	14
BA	4	5	4	3	3	5	4
Doctorates							
PhD/DPhil	*	0	1	1	*	0	*
DM/MD	1	1	2	0	1	*	*
Masters							
MS/Ch	*	0	1	0	0	0	0
MSc	2	1	1	1	3	1	0
Ma/MPhil	4	4	7	6	1	5	4
Diplomas							
DRCOG	53	50	50	49	53	60	57
DCH	18	12	16	21	18	18	22
DPH	*	1	0	0	*	0	0
DPM	*	0	1	0	*	0	0
DO	1	*	1	3	*	*	0
DA	2	1	3	3	3	1	2
DMRT	*	*	0	0	0	0	0
DCP	*	*	0	0	0	0	0
DLO	*	2	0	1	0	0	0
DIH	*	2	1	0	0	0	0
Dip.ven/other med.dips	5	4	5	6	2	3	7
Certificates							
FP certificate	23	9	18	20	31	28	30
Memberships/Fellowships							
MRCGP	53	52	61	65	38	51	52
MRCP	6	6	8	8	5	7	4
FRCS	1	2	3	1	0	*	*
FFA.RCS	*	0	0	1	1	0	0
MRCOG	1	0	2	0	2	1	0
MRCPsych	1	1	1	0	2	1	*
MCPH/PCCM/MFCM	1	*	2	0	2	0	0
MFOM		1	0	0	0	0	0
AFOM	1	3	0	1	0	0	0
Elected fellowships							
FRCP	*	*	0	0	0	0	0
FRCGP	*	*	0	0	0	0	0
Other el. fellows	1	1	2	0	*	0	*
Overseas qualifications	3	5	4	2	3	3	2
Other non-med. degrees	1	1	1	1	*	1	2
Base: all respondents	*1263*	*204*	*195*	*179*	*221*	*218*	*246*

Doctors and their Careers. It was less popular among the overseas qualifiers in this study than among UK qualifiers, and less than 10 per cent of the doctors qualifying outside the UK or Ireland held it.

The DCH was held by 18 per cent of doctors, (16 per cent of men and 20 per cent of women). There was a slight increase in the proportions of doctors holding this diploma over the years. Again it was less popular among overseas-qualified doctors, but nearly half the Irish qualifiers held it.

Only small numbers of doctors held other postgraduate diplomas, which were usually held, it appeared, because of a professional interest in the specialty concerned.

The Family Planning Certificate was held by 16 per cent of the men and 30 per cent of the women. The proportion of women from the three cohorts was similar, but there was a definite increase in interest from the men, with the proportion rising from 9 per cent of the 1981 men to 20 per cent of the 1988 men. Again, overseas qualifiers were less likely to have gained this certificate than UK qualifiers.

The most common higher professional qualification held was, not surprisingly, the MRCGP. 59 per cent of the men and 47 per cent of the women had passed the MRCGP. As Table 2.17 shows, there was a considerable increase in interest among the latter two cohorts of both men and women, with the proportion of men with MRCGP rising from just over half the 1981 cohort to nearly two-thirds of the 1988 cohort, and the proportion of women rising from under 40 per cent of the 1981 cohort to over half the 1988 cohort. It was striking that over three-quarters of the Irish male qualifiers held the MRCGP, although less than one third of the Irish female qualifiers held it. On the other hand, less than 10 per cent of doctors of both sexes qualifying in the Indian sub-continent held the MRCGP, and around one fifth of doctors qualifying in other countries.

Table 2.18 indicates that most of those holding MRCGP in the later two cohorts had passed their membership in the year in which they had received their vocational training certificate. This was particularly notable among the 1988 men of whom nearly 80 per cent had passed their membership and gained their VTC in the same year. For the 1981 cohort, the picture was of course affected by the fact that 1981 was the first year in which VTCs were awarded. It was interesting that a quarter of the men and over one third of the women from that cohort who held the MRCGP had passed it in 1980 or before.

Membership or fellowship of other colleges or faculties was limited. Six per cent of doctors held the MRCP, with rather more men than women having passed it. One per cent of doctors held the FRCS, but it was noteworthy that it was held by as many as 9 per cent of the male qualifiers from the Indian sub-continent and 20 per cent of male qualifiers from other countries, underlining the evidence that general practice was not the first specialty choice of a substantial minority of overseas qualified doctors.

Few doctors held other memberships or fellowships. They had usually changed from a hospital specialty to general practice, although some had moved in the opposite direction, or had gained a higher qualification in public health or

Table 2.18   Year passed MRCGP

column percentages

	Total	Male 1981	Male 1985	Male 1988	Female 1981	Female 1985	Female 1988
1980 & before	10	26	1	0	35	4	2
1981	15	54	0	0	46	1	0
1982-84	9	11	15	1	13	17	1
1985	23	1	69	0	0	63	1
1986-87	12	7	11	11	3	13	21
1988	27	0	3	78	1	1	66
1989	4	0	2	10	1	1	9
Base: all those with MRCGP	*664*	*107*	*118*	*116*	*83*	*112*	*128*

occupational medicine to give them a further string to their bows while working in general practice.

Only a handful of doctors were elected fellows of one of the colleges or faculties.

Present employment status

One of the main aims of this study was to establish the pattern of work among the doctors who had gained their GP vocational training certificate. There were a number of factors which were of particular importance in assessing the future organisation of general practice.

First, it was important to establish what proportion of those who had gained their vocational training certificate were working in medicine and what proportion were working in general practice. There had been suggestions that doctors might be leaving medicine or leaving general practice. The material provided in this study could throw light on this.

Secondly, it was crucial to establish the extent of part-time or less than full-time working in general practice, as well as to examine the factors affecting part-time working. At the time of the study the new GP contract was in the process of being introduced. The material gathered relates mainly to the employment of doctors under the old contract, when the definition of 'part-time' was rather more fluid. Nevertheless, we collected details on hours of work, and there was little doubt in the minds of doctors about whether they were working full-time or part-time.

We used the same general categories for our analysis as those used in *Doctors and their Careers*, and illustrated in Table 2.19. The marked difference between the men and the women was shown in the extent to which women in all three cohorts were working less than full-time in comparison with the men. Overall, 93 per cent of the men were working full-time in clinical medicine compared

Table 2.19   Present employment status of all doctors

column percentages

	Total	Male 1981	Male 1985	Male 1988	Female 1981	Female 1985	Female 1988
Working FT in clinical medicine	66	95	93	92	39	37	51
Working less than FT in clinical medicine	26	2	2	3	50	49	40
Working outside clinical medicine but in medically related occupation	2	2	3	1	1	3	2
Working outside medicine	*	*	1	0	*	0	0
Working both inside and outside medicine	1	*	1	0	*	0	0
Not working (at present)	3	*	1	3	6	5	2
Maternity leave	2	0	0	0	2	6	4
(Overseas)	(4)	(4)	(5)	(4)	(5)	(6)	(3)
Base: all respondents	*1263*	*204*	*195*	*179*	*221*	*218*	*246*

with 43 per cent of the women. Only 2 per cent of the men were working less than full-time in clinical medicine, compared with 46 per cent of the women.

Table 2.19 shows that the 1981 and 1985 women were less likely than the 1988 women to be working full-time in clinical medicine – undoubtedly a reflection of the fact that they were more likely to have had children. Nevertheless, nearly 40 per cent of the 1981 and 1985 women were working full-time in clinical medicine, and so were over half of the 1988 women.

It is also noteworthy, but not surprising in the light of previous studies, that only a small proportion of doctors were not working at all, and that this was almost as true for women as it was for men. Only 4 per cent of women overall (28) were not working at the time of the survey, and 4 per cent (26) were on maternity leave, mostly with the intention of returning as soon as possible. This compares with 1 per cent of the men (7) who were not working at the time of the survey.

It has been well established that women doctors maintain a high level of participation in medical work of some kind (Elston, 1980; Ward, 1981; Day, 1982; Allen, 1988a), with recent surveys indicating that over 90 per cent of women doctors are working in medicine. However, this study was looking at women doctors in their thirties, a time at which there is a 'dip' in the proportion of women in the labour market in general. It might have been thought that we would find a rather lower participation rate among these women doctors than among women doctors as a whole, particularly since, as we have seen, nearly four-fifths of the 1981 cohort of women and over two-thirds of the 1985 women had children. But Table 2.19 shows that only 6 per cent of the 1981 women and 5 per cent of the 1985 women were not working at all. The evidence appears to be overwhelming that women GPs of this generation are very unlikely to give up work while they have small children.

Less than 5 per cent of the doctors in our survey were working outside clinical medicine in any capacity, and it seems clear that these vocationally trained doctors were not leaving clinical medicine in any numbers. Even if they left clinical medicine, only a tiny proportion left medicine altogether, with less than one per cent of the sample working outside medicine. Two per cent of the sample were working outside clinical medicine but in a medically related occupation. (These included those working in government departments, health authorities, pharmaceuticals and so on.) One per cent had jobs both inside and outside medicine. Further analysis of these doctors and their reasons for working outside clinical medicine is given in Chapter 5.

Table 2.19 also shows the proportion of doctors in each cohort who were working abroad at the time that they responded to the survey. They are all included in the other categories, but we thought it interesting to indicate the proportion of doctors living abroad. The majority of them were working, and their responses were among the most detailed we received.

Table 2.20 summarises the employment status of the doctors. It presents the material in a more detailed form than that presented in Table 2.19. It can be seen

Table 2.20 Summary table of employment status of all doctors

nos & col percentages

	Total Nos	Total %	Male 1981	Male 1985	Male 1988	Female 1981	Female 1985	Female 1988
Total working	1202	95	100	99	97	91	90	95
in GP	1059	84	91	91	87	74	78	85
not in GP	143	11	8	9	10	18	12	10
Total working but not in GP								
in medicine	134	11	6	8	10	17	12	10
not in medicine	9	1	2	1	0	*	0	*
Total not working	61	5	*	1	3	9	10	5
maternity leave	26	2	0	0	0	2	6	4
not working	24	2	0	0	1	5	4	1
unemployed	10	1	*	1	2	1	1	*
student	1	*	0	0	0	0	0	*
Base: all respondents	*1263*	*1263*	*204*	*195*	*179*	*221*	*218*	*246*

that nearly 100 per cent of each cohort of men were working, compared with 91 per cent of the 1981 women, 90 per cent of the 1985 women and 95 per cent of the 1988 women. There was no difference among the men according to country of qualification, but *all* the women who qualified in the Indian sub-continent or in other countries outside the British Isles were working, compared with 92 per cent of the UK women qualifiers. (It should be noted that we did not include the women on maternity leave as 'working' for the purpose of this analysis. If they are added to those who were working, it can be seen that 93 per cent of the 1981 women, 96 per cent of the 1985 women and 99 per cent of the 1988 women were 'active' in the workforce, with only a tiny number of these working outside medicine.)

Looking at the sample as a whole, 90 per cent of the men and 79 per cent of the women were working in general practice. The proportion of men in general practice was similar for each cohort, but, among the women, as might have been expected, a higher proportion of the 1988 women (85 per cent) were working in general practice than we found among the other two cohorts. Nevertheless, it can be seen from this table that three-quarters of the women who gained their vocational training certificates in 1981 and nearly four-fifths of their 1985 counterparts were working in general practice at the time of the survey. However, nearly 20 per cent of the 1981 women were working in medicine, but outside general practice.

The UK male qualifiers were rather more likely to be working in general practice (90 per cent) than the male qualifiers from the Indian sub-continent (85 per cent). Among the women, all the women doctors qualifying outside the British Isles were working in medicine at the time of the survey. All the women doctors qualifying in countries other than the British Isles and Indian sub-continent were working in general practice. Over three-quarters of the women qualifiers from the Indian sub-continent were in general practice, while the remainder were in other medical jobs. The UK women qualifiers were different, in that 79 per cent were working in general practice, 13 per cent in other medical jobs, while the rest were not working for some reason or were on maternity leave.

Analysing the figures in a rather different way, by looking at the proportion of those working in general practice as a proportion of those working at all, we found that 91 per cent of the working men and as many as 86 per cent of the working women were in general practice. In other words, if women were working, they were almost as likely as the men to have been working in general practice. The picture is slightly distorted because we did not include those on maternity leave in our 'working' category. However, the majority of the women on maternity leave were in general practice and intended to return to working in general practice on completion of their maternity leave.

Table 2.20 gives rather more information on the doctors who were not in general practice. 12 per cent of the whole sample (143 doctors) were working but not in general practice. The vast majority of these doctors (134) were working in medicine (45 men and 89 women), while 9 of them were working outside medicine (7 men and 2 women – all UK qualifiers).

Of the 61 doctors who were not working at the time of the survey, 26 (2 per cent of the total) were on maternity leave, but, as noted above, intended to return to work, mainly in general practice, 24 (2 per cent) were not working, usually because they had domestic responsibilities, and 10 (1 per cent) said they were unemployed (5 men and 5 women). One doctor (a woman) was a full-time student.

Present job/grade/status of the doctors

We thought it important to show in one table exactly what all the doctors were doing at the time of the survey, and Table 2.21 presents a snapshot of the present job/grade/status of all respondents.

General practice

A major difference between the men and women lay in the proportions who were working as GP principals: 89 per cent of the men and 60 per cent of the women from the 1981 cohort, 90 per cent of the men and 63 per cent of the women from 1985, and 76 per cent of the men and 59 per cent of the women from 1988.

We separated the jobs in general practice into full-time and part-time working, since one of the objects of the study was to establish a picture of the pattern of work in general practice. Looking at the men and women as a whole, we found that 83 per cent of the men and 32 per cent of the women were full-time GP principals. It can be seen that 87 per cent of the 1981 and 1985 men were full-time GP principals, compared with 73 per cent of the 1988 men. Among the women, 30 per cent of both the 1981 and 1985 cohorts were full-time GP principals, compared with 35 per cent of the 1988 cohort.

Although the difference between the 1988 men and the other cohorts of men was small, it was interesting to note that a slightly lower proportion of the 1988 men were working in general practice at all, and that 7 per cent of the total were working as GP locums, either full-time or part-time. There were indications, both in this table and within the responses, that some younger men were finding it difficult to get work as full-time GP principals. There was no difference among them according to country of qualification.

It was perhaps not surprising that a rather higher proportion of the 1988 women were working as full-time GP principals than we found among the other cohorts. The main difference among the women related to whether they had children or not. 49 per cent of the women without children in the sample as a whole were working as full-time GP principals, compared with 21 per cent of those with children.

For the purposes of this survey we separated the categories of part-time GP principal and 20-hour a week GP principal. These categories have been replaced in the new GP contractual arrangements, but at the time of the survey they were

Table 2.21   Present job/grade/status of all doctors (main/first job)

nos & col percentages

| | Total | | | Male | | | Female | |
	Nos	%	1981	1985	1988	1981	1985	1988
FT GP principal	694	55	87	87	73	30	30	35
FT GP assist.	5	*	0	0	2	0	*	0
FT GP locum	20	2	0	1	4	0	0	4
20 hr. GP princ.	99	8	1	1	1	16	15	11
PT GP principal	110	9	1	2	2	14	18	13
PT GP asst.	38	3	0	0	1	5	4	7
PT GP locum	40	3	*	1	3	4	3	7
GP retainer scheme	41	3	0	0	0	5	6	7
Private GP	6	*	1	1	0	0	*	*
GP Armed services	6	*	*	0	2	*	0	*
Total GP	1059	84	91	91	87	74	78	85
Consultant	13	1	3	1	0	2	*	0
Senior registrar	12	1	0	0	1	1	2	1
Registrar	12	1	0	2	1	1	1	1
SHO	13	1	0	0	3	1	0	2
Clin. Asst.	14	1	0	1	2	3	1	1
Staff grade/Ass. Spec	2	*	1	0	0	0	0	0
Lect/other acad.	5	*	0	2	0	*	1	0
DMO/DPH	2	*	0	0	0	1	0	0
SCM/Cons. PH	2	*	0	1	0	*	0	0
SCMO	5	*	0	0	0	2	0	0
CMO	28	2	0	1	0	4	5	3
MO - occ. health	3	*	0	1	1	0	0	*
MO - other	5	*	*	0	1	0	1	0
Medical - overseas	13	1	0	2	1	1	1	2
Other medical	5	*	1	0	1	0	0	*
Total other medicine	134	11	6	8	10	17	12	10
Total working outside medicine	9	1	2	1	0	*	0	*
Maternity leave	26	2	0	0	0	2	6	4
Not working	24	2	0	0	1	5	4	1
Unemployed	10	1	*	1	2	1	1	*
Student	1	*	0	0	0	0	0	*
Total not working	61	5	*	1	3	9	10	5
Base: all respondents	*1263*	*1263*	*204*	*195*	*179*	*221*	*218*	*246*

still in force. They give a picture of the pattern of working at the time, and have important implications for the pattern for the future.

In the sample as a whole, 14 per cent of the women and 1 per cent of the men were working as 20-hour a week GP principals and 14 per cent of the women and 1 per cent of the men were working as part-time GP principals. (All doctors in the latter category were assumed to be working fewer than 20 hours a week, although it must be recognised that there were enormous differences in the ways in which GPs calculated their hours of work.)

Table 2.21 shows that, adding these two categories together, around one third of the 1981 and 1985 women were working less than full-time as GP principals, compared with just under a quarter of the 1988 women. One third of the women with children and one fifth of the women without children were working less than full-time as GP principals.

2 per cent of the doctors were working as full-time GP locums. These posts were held by 4 per cent of the 1988 men and 4 per cent of the 1988 women. 3 per cent of the doctors were working as part-time GP locums. These posts were more likely to be held by women than men – 5 per cent of the women respondents and only 1 per cent of the men. Again, the 1988 women were rather more likely than others to be in such locum posts.

Only five doctors, four of whom were men, were working as full-time GP assistants. However, 5 per cent of the doctors, all but one of whom were women, were part-time GP assistants.

Six per cent of the women doctors working in general practice were on the Doctors' retainer scheme. They were fairly equally divided among the three cohorts, and all of them had children.

A small number of doctors of both sexes were private GPs or were working as GPs in the armed services.

Other medical posts

We have seen that 134 doctors (11 per cent) were working in medicine but not in general practice. Table 2.21 gives their present grade or status. Rather over half of them were in hospital medicine, just over a quarter were in public health or community medicine, while around 10 per cent were in medical posts overseas and around 10 per cent were in occupational health or other medical jobs.

1 per cent of the total were consultants, and 3 per cent were in training grades in hospital medicine. There was little difference between the men and women, except that ten of the twelve senior registrars were women. Most of the clinical assistants were also women.

The doctors working in hospital medicine were in a wide variety of specialties, although one quarter of them were in a psychiatric specialty.

Among the doctors working in public health, the majority were clinical medical officers (CMOs), and not surprisingly all but two of these were women.

The doctors working overseas in medicine but not in general practice were in a variety of posts, including work as medical missionaries.

Posts outside medicine
The nine doctors working outside medicine (as their first or main job) were in a variety of jobs. Two were in medico-legal work, two were missionaries with no direct medical responsibility, two were general managers in pharmaceutical firms, one was a director of a hospital overseas, one was in medical defence services and one was a professional artist.

Not working
The status of those who were not working at the time of the survey has been analysed in the discussion of Table 2.20 above.

Full-time and part-time working
The issue of full-time and part-time working was fundamental to this study, so we asked the doctors a number of questions to establish exactly what they were doing. We were aware that there were a number of ways in which 'full-time' could be interpreted, and that there were even more ways in which 'part-time' could be interpreted. We were therefore seeking as clear a picture as possible, although we knew that it would be difficult to elicit in a postal questionnaire.

Of the 1202 doctors who were working at the time of the survey, 99 per cent of the men and 48 per cent of the women said they were working full-time. This represented 45 per cent of the 1981 women, 44 per cent of the 1985 women and 55 per cent of the 1988 women. The remainder said they were working part-time.

We wanted to establish how the doctors' work was made up, since we were aware from previous studies that women working less than full-time often had quite complicated working patterns, in which they put together a number of jobs.

Table 2.22 shows that it was not only women who had complicated working combinations, but that they were much more likely than men to have a combination of posts which added to a less than full-time commitment.

Looking first at the differences between men and women as a whole, we found that 56 per cent of men and 33 per cent of women had one full-time post with no part-time work. On the other hand, 40 per cent of the men, but only 12 per cent of the women had one full-time post with one or more part-time posts. At the other end of the working spectrum, we found that less than one per cent of the men had one part-time post only, compared with 32 per cent of the women.

In the middle category, we found that 3 per cent of the men and 5 per cent of the women had more than one part-time post adding to a *full-time* commitment, while 1 per cent of the men and 19 per cent of the women had more than one part-time post adding to a *part-time* commitment.

There were some differences among the various cohorts. Table 2.22 indicates that around 60 per cent of the 1985 and 1988 men had one full-time post with no other work, compared with less than 50 per cent of the 1981 men, while 50 per cent of the 1981 men had a full-time post with one or more part-time posts, compared with only around one third of the men in the other two cohorts. Few men recorded other combinations of full-time and part-time work.

Table 2.22 Composition of work of all doctors by full-time and part-time posts

column percentages

	Total	Male 1981	1985	1988	Female 1981	1985	1988
One FT post with no PT work	44	48	60	61	32	28	39
One FT post with one or more PT posts	25	50	35	33	11	13	11
More than one PT post which add to a FT commitment	4	1	5	3	2	4	7
More than one PT post which add to a PT commitment	10	1	-	2	20	19	16
One PT post	17	-	1	1	35	36	27
Base: all in work at present	*1202*	*203*	*194*	*174*	*202*	*196*	*233*

On the other hand, women had much more complicated combinations of work, with interesting differences among the cohorts. Table 2.22 shows that the proportion of women with one full-time post and no other work ranged from one third of the 1981 cohort to just over a quarter of the 1985 cohort to 39 per cent of the 1988 cohort. The proportion of women with a full-time post combined with one or more part-time posts was fairly equal at around 12 per cent in all three cohorts.

The proportion of women with only one part-time post ranged from over one third of the 1981 and 1985 cohorts to just over a quarter of the 1988 cohort. The proportion of women with more than one part-time post adding to a full-time commitment rose from 2 per cent of the 1981 cohort to 7 per cent of the 1988 cohort, while the proportion with more than one part-time post adding to a *part-time* commitment ranged from one fifth of the 1981 women to 16 per cent of the 1988 women.

We collected details of the various combinations of work put together by the doctors. The analysis of these combinations was complicated. We have therefore simplified it by concentrating mainly on the posts held by doctors working in general practice, who not only constituted the vast majority of the doctors surveyed, but also were the main focus of our investigation. We shall return to a an examination of this in Chapter 5.

The detailed description in this chapter of the characteristics, qualifications and working status of the respondents to this survey is essential as background for the rest of the report and understanding the complicated profile of doctors in general practice. We turn now to their vocational training.

3 Vocational training in general practice

The doctors responding to this survey all had vocational training certificates issued by the Joint Committee on Postgraduate Training for General Practice, but we were aware that the composition of their vocational training was likely to be varied. As noted in Chapter 1, regulations are laid down which stipulate that for a certificate of prescribed experience, the doctor should have completed the equivalent of twelve months full-time as a trainee in general practice and two years in hospital medicine, with a minimum of two six-month posts in certain prescribed specialties. Doctors may also be issued with a certificate of equivalent experience.

Intention of entering general practice at end of vocational training
We were interested to establish how dedicated the doctors were to entering general practice when they completed their vocational training. We thought it best to ask them what had been their intentions at the *end* of their vocational training, since it had become clear in our preliminary enquiries that a question about their intentions at the *beginning* of their vocational training would have quickly run into the difficulties many doctors experience in defining when their vocational training actually began.

The concept of 'vocational' training implies a certain intention, if not dedication. However, in reality, it appeared that many doctors did not start posts which ended up as part of their vocational training with the intention either of entering general practice or of using these posts as part of their GP vocational training. The idea that vocational training in general practice is a neat and tidy training package, with most people following a certain pattern, was very quickly dispelled when we came to analyse our data, as the material presented later in this chapter will illustrate.

Overall 93 per cent of the men and 88 per cent of the women said that they had intended to enter general practice when they completed their vocational training. The pattern was clearly established for the men, as Table 3.1 shows, with 93 per cent of each cohort of men expressing this intention. However, the women were rather different, with 82 per cent of the 1981 women saying they had intended to enter general practice at the end of their vocational training, compared with over 90 per cent of the younger generations of women.

Table 3.1   Whether doctors intended to enter general practice at completion of
vocational training

column percentages

	Total	Male			Female		
		1981	1985	1988	1981	1985	1988
Yes	90	93	93	93	82	90	91
No	8	6	7	6	13	9	8
NA	1	*	1	1	5	*	1
Base: all respondents	*1263*	*204*	*195*	*179*	*221*	*218*	*246*

It was noteworthy that virtually all the overseas-qualified doctors had intended to enter general practice at the completion of their vocational training. It seems likely that this was related to the fact that they tended to be older than the UK and Irish qualifiers and had often had experience in another specialty first.

We looked at the present job of the doctors and compared it with their stated intention at the end of their vocational training. Of those at present working in general practice in any capacity, 94 per cent of the total (96 per cent of the men and 93 per cent of the women) had intended to enter general practice when they completed their vocational training. For the other doctors, the pattern was, not surprisingly, rather different. Of the 134 doctors working in medicine but outside general practice, 63 per cent of both men and women had intended to enter general practice at the completion of their vocational training. Of the nine doctors working outside medicine, eight had intended to enter general practice.

Looking at the intentions at the completion of vocational training of those who were not working, 85 per cent of those on maternity leave, 75 per cent of those who were not working for other reasons, and 73 per cent of the unemployed doctors had intended to enter general practice.

When we examined more closely the doctors at present working outside general practice, we found that over one third of the consultants and over half the doctors in hospital training grades had decided against general practice at the end of their vocational training, usually because they had more interest in another specialty. Similarly, over two-thirds of those at present working in medicine abroad had decided against general practice, mainly because they wanted to work abroad, although some added that they wished to change specialty as well.

However, nearly 90 per cent of those currently working as clinical assistants and 80 per cent of those currently working as SCMOs or CMOs had intended to enter general practice when they finished their vocational training. The majority of these were women, and it seems probable from scrutinising their responses that the community health and clinical assistant posts they held were usually a second-best to the general practice posts they wished to have.

It was interesting that eight of the nine doctors working outside medicine had intended to enter general practice on the completion of their vocational training. It usually seemed that other factors had intervened to make them change course, rather than that they had become disillusioned with general practice at an early stage.

Reasons for not wishing to enter general practice at end of vocational training

If doctors had gone through vocational training, why had they decided against general practice at the end of it? There were three main reasons: a wish to change to another specialty on a permanent basis, personal or domestic commitments and the wish to work abroad. These reasons accounted for over two-thirds of the doctors who said they had not intended to enter general practice after completing vocational training, whether they were now working in general practice or not.

The reasons were rather different for men and women. One third of the men who had not intended to enter general practice said they wanted to change to another specialty on a permanent basis, having completed their vocational training, an intention shared by one sixth of the women. On the other hand, over 40 per cent of the women who had changed their intention cited personal or domestic commitments. This was mentioned by over half the 1981 and 1988 women, and was clearly an important factor in their decision. The wish to work abroad was rather more evenly shared by men and women, and expressed by one-sixth of the men and one-fifth of the women.

In some cases the question of changing specialty was not new, since some of the doctors had clearly always intended to pursue another specialty, for example paediatrics, but had completed GP vocational training as a useful adjunct. Others had become interested in certain specialties as they had done Senior House Officer (SHO) jobs in those specialties as part of their vocational training, while others had become interested in aspects of medicine to which they had not been exposed before. In some cases, a combination of factors had helped change their intention, as a 1988 woman indicated: 'I was interested in palliative medicine. Also for medical reasons I have had to stop driving, which seemed to bar me from full-time general practice...'

It appeared that not all these doctors were lost to general practice for ever. Indeed, as we have seen, some of them were working in general practice at the time of the survey. However, particularly among those who cited personal or domestic commitments, there was a view that general practice was not a realistic option at the time they completed their vocational training. A 1988 woman summarised the experience of a number of her counterparts: 'I had just had my first baby and I did not feel ready to make the time commitment and cope with the number of hours and so on. I was also not hopeful of a practice wanting a young partner who had just started a family...'

It also seemed that not all of those who had intended to go abroad at the end of their vocational training were lost to general practice in this country on a permanent basis, since many said they wanted to widen their experience by working in a developing country. Even among those who wanted to work as medical missionaries, the possibility of returning to work in the UK was not discounted and most of them were intending to use the 'family practice' skills acquired in their GP vocational training in their work abroad.

A variety of other reasons were given by doctors who had not intended to enter general practice at the completion of vocational training, including the wish to gain more experience in another specialty on a temporary basis, to return to another specialty, to study for another qualification or to do research. A small number of doctors said they had not enjoyed their GP trainee year and had either been put off permanently or wanted to consider the long-term options, while others had not been sure what they wanted to do at the end of their vocational training.

Type of vocational training

There are essentially three options which can be pursued by doctors wishing to enter general practice. They can enter an organised vocational training scheme, they can put together their own vocational training, or they can put together a package which is partly organised by themselves and partly part of an organised scheme.

Table 3.2   How GP vocational training was organised

column percentages

	Total	Male			Female		
		1981	1985	1988	1981	1985	1988
All on organised VTS	36	43	39	37	27	33	39
Part organised/part self-organised VT	17	16	14	15	16	19	21
All self-organised	43	38	44	42	49	45	40
Other*	4	3	3	6	8	3	1
Base: all respondents	*1263*	*204*	*195*	*179*	*221*	*218*	*246*

*   includes those exempt from vocational training etc

As Table 3.2 shows, just over one third of all doctors in the survey had all their vocational training on an organised scheme, 17 per cent had part of their vocational training on an organised scheme and had organised the rest themselves, while just over 40 per cent had organised the whole thing themselves. A small proportion, mostly from the 1981 cohort, said they had never had any vocational training and that they were either exempt because of their previous experience or that they had had 'equivalent experience'.

The men in general were more likely to have been on an organised scheme than the women – 40 per cent compared with 33 per cent. However, as the table shows, there were some differences between the cohorts as well as the sexes.

Essentially, there was a slight trend for the younger men to have become less likely and the women to have become more likely to be on an organised scheme. This led to a convergence in the 1988 cohort, among whom 37 per cent of the men and 39 per cent of the women had been on a fully organised vocational training scheme.

There were several reasons for some of the apparent differences among the cohorts. The 1981 women, as noted before, included a number of doctors who had qualified many years before and had been working as GPs for some time. Although this was also true of the 1981 men, it appeared that the women had put together their vocational training in a more ad hoc way. The historical nature of this is probably underlined by the fact that later cohorts of women became increasingly more likely to have been on an organised scheme, at least for part of their training.

There was a marked difference between the overseas qualifiers and the UK and Irish qualifiers. Around three quarters of those qualifying outside the British Isles had put together their own packages of vocational training, compared with around 40 per cent of the UK and Irish qualifiers. Less than 10 per cent of the male qualifiers from the Indian sub-continent had been on a fully organised scheme, compared with 45 per cent of the male UK qualifiers.

Number of applications made for vocational training schemes

General practice has become relatively more popular as a specialty choice over the past few years, and this was reflected in an increase in applications for organised vocational training schemes, certainly up to 1990. We asked the doctors how many applications they had made for vocational training schemes or rotations, and Table 3.3 demonstrates the evidence that later cohorts were making more applications on average than the 1981 cohort.

Overall, 30 per cent of the doctors had made no applications for vocational training schemes: 27 per cent of the men and 34 per cent of the women. The 1981 women were again rather different from the others, with 42 per cent of them making no applications for vocational training schemes, compared with only 28 per cent of the 1981 men. Looking at the other cohorts, it can be seen from Table 3.3 that one third of the 1985 women and around a quarter of the 1985 and 1988 men and 1988 women had made no applications.

Around a quarter of the doctors as a whole had made one application, but again the range was wide – from nearly 40 per cent of the 1981 men and women to 15 per cent of the 1988 women.

The table shows a trend towards a greater number of applications for organised schemes being made by the later cohorts. Those who made zero, one or two applications account for 90 per cent of the 1981 women and 80 per cent of the 1981 men. But there was a fairly steady decline in this proportion to 73 per cent of the 1985 women and 54 per cent of the 1985 men, and just over 50 per cent of both men and women in the 1988 cohort.

At the other end of the scale, there was additional evidence that vocational training schemes were becoming more competitive. Only 2 per cent of the 1981

Table 3.3   Number of applications made for vocational training schemes or rotations

column percentages

	Total	Male 1981	Male 1985	Male 1988	Female 1981	Female 1985	Female 1988
None	30	28	27	24	42	33	26
1	26	39	18	18	38	28	15
2	11	13	9	11	10	12	13
3	8	6	8	12	3	8	10
4	5	4	3	3	4	5	8
5	4	1	7	7	*	5	5
6 - 9	6	2	9	8	1	3	8
10	4	3	6	5	1	3	5
11 - 15	1	-	3	2	-	1	2
16 - 20	2	2	5	4	*	1	3
20 plus	3	1	5	5	-	1	4
Median no. of applications (incl. 0 applications)	0.7	0.5	1.5	1.7	0.2	0.6	1.7
Median no. of applications (excl. 0 applications)	1.7	1.0	3.3	2.7	1.0	1.5	2.9
Base: all respondents	*1263*	*204*	*195*	*179*	*221*	*218*	*246*

women and 8 per cent of the 1981 men made six or more applications, compared with 22 per cent of the 1988 women and 24 per cent of the 1988 men. The figure for the 1985 men was even higher, with 28 per cent of them making six or more applications.

It should be noted that around 10 per cent of both the 1985 and 1988 men made 16 or more applications, and that 5 per cent of both of these male cohorts made 20 or more applications.

There was a difference in general between the UK male qualifiers and the men who qualified in the Indian sub-continent. Only 5 per cent of the UK male qualifiers made 20 or more applications for organised schemes, compared with 24 per cent of the male Indian sub-continent qualifiers. These men certainly seemed to find it more difficult to get on an organised vocational training scheme than their UK-qualified counterparts, and perhaps it was not surprising that such a relatively low proportion of them had been on a fully organised scheme compared with the UK qualifiers, as noted above. The differences among the women were not so marked, and in any case the numbers were much smaller.

Although Table 3.3 shows that the majority of doctors made three or fewer applications for vocational training schemes, there was a very long 'tail' to the distribution, particularly among the 1985 men and the 1988 doctors of both sexes. This meant that the mean number of applications was not really a suitable comparative measure. For example, the mean number of applications made by the 1988 men, including those who made no applications, was 5.5, which did not really represent the picture of two-thirds of these doctors having made three or fewer applications.

We concluded that the median would be a more meaningful measure of the average number of applications made, and we calculated it in two ways: by including and excluding those who made no applications. Table 3.3 shows the steady increase over the years in the average number of applications made, and also shows the general tendency for the men to make more applications than the women. The long 'tail' among the 1985 men can also be seen from the relatively high median number of applications made by those who had made any applications.

We were interested to see whether doctors who organised their own vocational training were actually those who did not apply for vocational training schemes or were people who had made numerous applications for schemes but had failed to get on them for one reason or another. We also wanted to find out whether doctors who had all their vocational training on a scheme were more or less likely to have made numerous applications than others. Table 3.4 suggests that the situation was far from simple.

We found that nearly 60 per cent of those who had organised their own vocational training had made *no* applications for schemes, compared with only 2 per cent of those on organised schemes and 11 per cent who had had part of their vocational training on an organised scheme.

At the other end of the scale, we found that as many as 10 per cent of those who had had a completely self-organised scheme had made 10 or more applications, compared with 15 per cent of those who had had a completely organised scheme. It looks as though there was a group of doctors who had wanted to get on an organised scheme but had found it impossible to do so.

Looking only at doctors who had made any applications for schemes, we found that the median number of applications made by doctors who had a completely self-organised scheme was marginally higher than among those who had been on a fully-organised scheme (a median of 2.2 applications compared with 1.9). In other words, if doctors organising their own schemes had applied for vocational training schemes at all, they had made more applications on average than those who had been on organised schemes. This was particularly true of the men, where the median was 3.5 applications among those on a self-organised scheme compared with 1.9 among those on a fully organised scheme.

There was additional evidence that male doctors from the Indian sub-continent had found it rather more difficult to get on a vocational training scheme than UK or Irish male qualifiers. We found that the median number of applications made by male qualifiers from the Indian sub-continent was 3.8 (including those who made no applications) compared with 0.8 among the UK qualified men. Looking only at those who had made applications, the median figure among the Indian sub-continent male qualifiers was 4.9 compared with a

Table 3.4   Number of applications made for vocational training schemes or rotations by type of vocational training

column percentages

	Total	All VT on organised VTS	Part org. VTS/ part self-organised	All self-organised	Other(a)
None	30	2	11	59	64
1	26	34	41	14	19
2	11	16	18	5	9
3	8	14	6	4	0
4	5	8	6	2	2
5	4	5	4	3	4
6-9	6	6	5	4	2
10	4	6	2	3	0
11-15	1	2	2	1	0
16-20	2	4	1	3	0
20+	3	3	3	3	0
Median no. of applications (incl. 0 applications)	0.7	1.9	1.0	*	*
Median no. of applications (excl. 0 applications)	1.7	1.9	1.2	2.2	*
Base: all respondents	*1263*	*457*	*216*	*543*	*47*

(a)   includes doctors exempt from VT, Armed Forces training schemes, equivalent experience etc.

figure of 1.8 for their UK-qualified counterparts. There was no difference among the women according to country of qualification.

Regions in which vocational training carried out

Since the need to be geographically mobile is well-established as a potential constraint on the careers of doctors, particularly women doctors (Allen, 1988a), we were interested to see whether doctors had moved around much during their vocational training.

Table 3.5 shows the number of regions in which the doctors had carried out their vocational training. It can be seen that 82 per cent of all doctors had done all their vocational training in one region only. The men from each cohort were marginally more likely to have stayed in one region than the women. The 1988 women were less likely than the 1981 women to have done all their vocational training in one region, and indeed nearly a quarter of the 1988 women had done their vocational training in two or more regions.

Table 3.5 **Number of regions in which doctors had had vocational training**

column percentages

	Total	Male			Female		
		1981	1985	1988	1981	1985	1988
One region only	82	86	86	84	82	79	76
2 regions	13	11	11	9	13	15	18
3 regions	4	2	3	6	2	5	4
4 regions	1	*	-	1	1	*	2
Base: all respondents	*1263*	*204*	*195*	*179*	*221*	*218*	*246*

The UK and Irish qualifiers, both men and women, were rather more likely than the overseas qualifiers to have had vocational training posts in more than one region.

All the regions were well-represented, and, with one exception, no one region was notable for attracting more doctors than others in this sample. However, it should be noted that 24 per cent of the 1981 women had done at least part of their vocational training in Scotland, compared with 17 per cent of the men from that year. The comparable proportions of 1985 and 1988 women who had done at least part of their training in Scotland were 14 per cent for each year. There were some indications, found also in *Doctors and their Careers*, that a rather higher proportion of older women doctors had qualified and trained in Scotland than we found among the younger cohorts. We have also seen that a substantial minority of the 1981 cohort of women in this study had qualified some years before 1977, when it might have been expected they would cluster. It may be that Scottish women GPs were more interested than others in acquiring the vocational training certificate in 1981 when it was first available, even if they were exempt from it, or it is possible that the finding may simply reflect a relatively high proportion of Scottish women among women doctors of that generation.

Geographical mobility and organisation of vocational training
We were interested to see whether the question of being tied to a particular geographical area had affected the doctors' decisions about what kind of vocational training 'package' they had, for example, a completely organised scheme, a completely self-organised package or some of each. We knew that the frequent geographical moves which doctors in training often have to make were not universally popular among either men or women, and we wanted to look at the extent to which this had actually affected their decisions on the organisation of their vocational training. We were also aware that women were more likely to be restricted by geographical ties than men were (Allen 1988a).

Nearly 50 per cent of the women, compared with just under one third of the men, said the question of geographical ties had affected their decision on the type of vocational training they would go for. Table 3.6 indicates that the question

Table 3.6   Whether the question of being tied to a particular area affected the
              doctors' decision about the organisation of their vocational training

column percentages

| | Total | Male | | | Female | | |
		1981	1985	1988	1981	1985	1988
Yes	40	28	35	33	42	45	50
No	59	72	64	66	55	54	49
NA	1	0	1	1	3	1	1
Base: all respondents	*1263*	*204*	*195*	*179*	*221*	*218*	*246*

became marginally more important for both men and women in the later cohorts.
It was interesting that only one fifth of the doctors who qualified in the Indian
sub-continent said that the question of geographical ties affected their decision
about the type of vocational training to seek.

The doctors did not always interpret the question in the strict sense in which
it was intended, since some did not restrict their comments about geographical
ties simply to the question of the organisation of their vocational training.
However, it was clear that the two main factors affecting the doctors in their
choice of vocational training 'packages' were a desire for geographical stability
and the constraints of being tied to an area because of a spouse's or partner's job.

Among the doctors who had been influenced by geographical ties, 44 per
cent of the women said they had been tied to an area by their spouse's job,
compared with 18 per cent of the men. On the other hand, 40 per cent of the men
who had been influenced by geographical ties said they wanted geographical
stability for personal or domestic reasons, compared with 28 per cent of the
women.

The question of being tied to an area by a spouse's or partner's job is
undoubtedly a constraint on the careers of women doctors, particularly if they
are married to other doctors, and this is explored in more detail later in this report.
It appears from the evidence on the organisation of vocational training schemes
that this constraint starts at an early stage in the careers of these young doctors,
which is not particularly surprising, since most of the GP vocational training
takes place among doctors in their late twenties, a time when many of them are
newly married or thinking of getting married. It is also a time when doctors in
hospital training are moving around, and, if one partner in a marriage is moving
all the time, it is difficult for the other partner to follow suit if they are tied to a
particular area by being on a vocational training scheme. These factors
undoubtedly influenced the choice of a substantial proportion of doctors,
particularly women doctors, among whom the plaint of a 1988 respondent was
reflected many times - 'I wanted to work somewhere reasonably near my
husband...'

The difficulty of planning ahead was underlined by a 1985 woman, who had
organised all her vocational training herself, in spite of having made three

applications for vocational training schemes: 'My husband got a job in Yorkshire. As an "outsider" from London, there seemed little chance of getting a place on an organised VTS there. Also, by the time he got his job in hospital medicine, the vocational trainees were long since appointed...'

The desire for some geographical stability was expressed in a heartfelt fashion by both men and women, although as we have seen, it was relatively more likely to have been mentioned by the men. The wish to live somewhere for longer than six months and to buy a house was repeated time and again, and doctors often mentioned that the 'nomadic life' of young doctors in training was not for them.

Some of the doctors had started on an organised scheme and had then had to move to a self-organised package or try and get on another scheme because of their spouse's job moves. This was mentioned by 10 per cent of the women, but only by a couple of men.

Nearly 20 per cent of the men, but only 10 per cent of the women, who had been influenced by geographical ties said that a preference for a particular area had affected the type of vocational training 'package' they had gone for. Similarly, men were more likely than women to say that they had chosen a particular type of 'package' because they had wanted to train in an area where they wanted to practise as a GP principal. On the other hand, some doctors, both men and women, said that they did not want to be tied to a particular area and had therefore put together a package which allowed them to train in more than one region.

A few doctors said that they had had no choice because there was no organised vocational training scheme in their area, while others had only wanted an organised scheme and had been prepared to go anywhere to get on one.

Composition of vocational training

The expected pattern of vocational training laid down by the JCPTGP is 12 months in a GP trainee post and 24 months in SHO posts. We asked the doctors to record how their GP vocational training was made up, by length of time in GP trainee posts and in SHO posts. We specified the seven most likely specialties in the questionnaire, but left space for the doctors to record other specialties. We also asked respondents to specify whether the different posts were held full-time, part-time or both.

We had thought that there would be some deviation from the expected pattern of vocational training, but we had not imagined that the respondents would display such a wide variation in the composition of their vocational training. In the event, the expected pattern of 12 months GP trainee posts and 24 months in SHO posts was found among only 50 per cent of the respondents.

Table 3.7 shows that the length of vocational training described by the doctors covered a very wide spectrum. In fact, the spectrum was so wide that we doubted whether some of the jobs were actually part of the doctors' vocational training, but, if the respondents recorded them, we had no way of distinguishing which jobs were recognised by the JCPTGP as part of the vocational training and

Table 3.7 Composition of GP vocational training by length of time in GP trainee and SHO posts

column percentages

	Total	Male 1981	Male 1985	Male 1988	Female 1981	Female 1985	Female 1988
No voc.training	1	2	1	0	3	0	0
GP= <12 months/ SHO= 0 - any length	1	0	1	1	2	2	1
GP=12 SHO=0	3	6	3	1	9	1	*
GP=12 SHO=<12	2	2	4	1	6	*	1
GP=12 SHO=12-23	6	5	8	5	13	5	2
GP=12 SHO=24	50	49	47	48	39	59	54
GP=12 SHO=25-29	5	3	4	2	7	5	7
GP=12 SHO=30	9	8	8	11	7	8	12
GP=12 SHO=31-35	3	3	4	2	3	4	3
GP=12 SHO=36	5	5	6	7	3	3	6
GP=12 SHO=37-110	9	10	13	18	3	6	9
GP= >12 SHO= anything	5	5	4	4	6	7	5
Base: all respondents	*1263*	*204*	*195*	*179*	*221*	*218*	*246*

which were not. In the end, we simply had to analyse all SHO jobs entered by the doctors in answer to the question of how their vocational training was made up. If a doctor recorded registrar posts, which some of them did, we recorded these separately, either as part of 'equivalent experience' or as additional jobs to their SHO posts. They are not covered in Table 3.7.

A tiny proportion of doctors – 1 per cent – insisted that they had had no GP vocational training at all. As the table shows, they were mainly concentrated among the 1981 men and women. A further 1 per cent said they had had less than 12 months as a GP trainee, with half saying they had had no SHO posts and half saying they had spent some time in SHO posts.

Three per cent of doctors, again mainly concentrated among the 1981 cohort, said that they had spent 12 months as a GP trainee but had had no SHO posts, while 2 per cent said they had spent 12 months as a GP trainee and less than 12 months as an SHO.

A further 6 per cent had spent 12 months as a GP trainee and between 12 and 23 months as an SHO. Over 10 per cent of the 1981 women came into this category, as Table 3.7 shows.

In all, therefore, 13 per cent of respondents said that their vocational training had taken less than the minimum time now stipulated of 12 months as a GP trainee and 24 months as an SHO. However, there was a marked difference between the 1981 women and all other groups, with one third of these 1981 women saying their vocational training had taken less than the present minimum time.

This difference was reflected in the proportions from each cohort who had completed their vocational training in the expected time of 12 months GP trainee and 24 months SHO. The proportion of men hovered around an average of 48 per cent, but the proportion of 1981 women was 39 per cent compared with 59 per cent of the 1985 women and 54 per cent of the 1988 women.

Table 3.7 shows that 32 per cent of respondents had 12 months GP trainee posts plus more than two years of SHO posts: 5 per cent had had 25-29 months of SHO posts, 9 per cent 30 months, 3 per cent 31-35 months and 5 per cent 36 months. As many as 9 per cent said they had had more than three years of SHO posts in their vocational training. There was quite a marked difference in this group between the men and the women: 13 per cent of the men and 6 per cent of the women. On the whole the younger cohorts of both sexes cited longer periods of SHO posts as part of their vocational training than the 1981 cohorts.

Finally, 5 per cent of the respondents said that they had spent longer than 12 months in GP trainee posts. Among the men this was often accounted for by doctors who had been in the armed services and had usually done 18 months as GP trainees, and among the women it was largely accounted for by part-time working in GP trainee posts. In addition, there were some men and a tiny number of women who had done more than twelve months as a GP trainee for unspecified reasons.

There was a difference between the UK qualifiers and those qualifying in other countries, most especially in the Indian sub-continent. Whereas 54 per cent of men and women UK qualifiers had spent 12 months as a GP trainee and 24 months in SHO posts, this was true of only 11 per cent of the men qualifiers from the Indian sub-continent and 9 per cent of the women. It was also true of only one third of the Irish qualifiers and around one in six of those who had qualified in other countries.

One of the main reasons for the difference was that 40 per cent of the men qualifying in the Indian sub-continent had done 12 months as a GP trainee and three years or more in SHO jobs. This reinforced the evidence that a number of the Indian sub-continent male qualifiers had come to general practice as a second choice, having tried to make a career in hospital medicine first.

On the other hand, one third of both men and women qualifying in the Indian sub-continent had done less than 24 months in SHO posts, compared with just over 10 per cent of the UK qualifiers. This was clearly due to the fact that some of the Indian sub-continent qualifiers were rather older than average, had been working for some years in this country and had gained their vocational training certificate at the first possible opportunity in 1981 without going through the more formal vocational training required after that date.

Full-time or part-time GP training

We did a further broad analysis of whether respondents had had any *part-time* vocational training in a GP trainee post or an SHO post. We found that 43 doctors (3 men and 40 women), representing 3 per cent of respondents (1 per cent of the men and 6 per cent of the women) said that they had spent some or all of their GP trainee posts working part-time. (More details are given in Table 3.8).

We found that 31 doctors (10 men and 21 women), representing 2 per cent of the respondents (2 per cent of men and 3 per cent of women), said that they had spent any part of their SHO vocational training posts working part-time. These doctors were found fairly equally distributed among the cohorts. They did not account for more than 2 per cent of those in any one specialty mentioned. The greatest numbers of doctors saying they had done any part-time SHO training were found in obstetrics and gynaecology, with 12 doctors (1 per cent of those mentioning the specialty), psychiatry, with 8 doctors (2 per cent of those mentioning the specialty), and paediatrics, again with 8 doctors (1 per cent of those mentioning the specialty).

It should be noted that there was some doubt about whether all the doctors who reported any part-time training as SHOs during vocational training fully understood the question. For example, it is highly unlikely that any SHO posts in surgery were part-time, but a tiny number of doctors said they had had some part-time training as SHOs in this specialty.

When we asked doctors specifically whether they had had any part-time postgraduate training in medicine in the next question, we found, as we discuss in Chapter 4, that 19 doctors said they had had part-time training as SHOs as part of their vocational training and 9 said they had had part-time training as SHOs other than as part of their vocational training, a total of 28 doctors. It is probable that these doctors were reporting correctly, and it is possible that, among those reporting any part-time SHO training in answer to our question on the composition of vocational training posts, there might have been some misunderstanding or misinterpretation. However, it should also be noted that many doctors were clearly quoting jobs in answer to the present question which were additional to their actual SHO vocational training posts. The numbers are not great, but the reader's attention should be drawn to the slight discrepancy.

In any case, whether the slightly higher or lower numbers are taken as completely correct, the fact remains that part-time training in general practice, whether in GP trainee posts or in SHO posts, was very limited among the doctors responding to this survey.

GP trainee posts

Table 3.8 shows the breakdown by cohort of the length of time spent in GP trainee posts and shows the proportion working full time, part time and both full and part time in these posts. The table excludes the 14 doctors who said they had spent no time in GP trainee posts. We have seen that only three of the men had worked part time but 7 per cent of the 1981 and 1985 women and just over 4 per cent of the 1988 women had done so, at least for some of their GP trainee post. All these women had children.

Table 3.8   Length of time spent in GP trainee posts in months and by full-time and part-time working

column percentages

	Total 1981	Male 1985	1988	Female 1981	1985	1988
No. of months						
less than 12 months	*	0	1	1	*	2	*
12 months	94	94	96	95	92	91	94
13 plus months	5	6	3	4	7	7	5
Full-time or part-time						
Full time	97	99	99	100	93	93	96
Part time	1	1	1	-	2	4	*
Full and part time	2	-	1	-	5	3	4
Base: all respondents who had had a GP trainee post	*1249*	*199*	*194*	*179*	*214*	*217*	*246*

How were the GP trainee posts made up? Again, as Table 3.9 shows, there was a wide variation. Overall, 57 per cent of the respondents had had one 12-month post. There were differences between the cohorts, but no real pattern emerged, except that the 1988 women were less likely than any other group to have followed this course, with 50 per cent of them having had one twelve month post. It was interesting to note that 80 per cent of the qualifiers from the Indian sub-continents had had just one twelve-month post.

Around a quarter of the doctors had had two six-month posts – a pattern far less frequently found among the 1981 women than among the 1988 women. 5 per cent of doctors had had one nine-month and one three-month post, and this pattern was found among all cohorts.

Other combinations were complicated, and we broke them down into one post of more than six months with one other post, one post of more than six months with two other posts, and any other combination of more than two posts. The younger doctors tended to fall into these categories more frequently than the other cohorts.

5 per cent of doctors had spent more than 12 months in their GP trainee posts and 1 per cent said that they had spent less than 12 months.

Essentially, this analysis showed how varied the organisation of the GP trainee year was, let alone the organisation of any other part of the vocational training.

Table 3.9   How doctors' GP trainee year was made up

column percentages

	Total	Male 1981	Male 1985	Male 1988	Female 1981	Female 1985	Female 1988
One 12-month post	57	56	61	57	61	56	50
Two 6-month posts	24	28	22	26	17	24	29
One 9-month & one 3-month post	5	3	6	3	5	5	5
One post of 6+ months & one other post	6	4	5	8	3	4	9
One post of 6+ months & two other posts	1	0	2	1	2	2	1
Other combinations of more than two posts	1	0	1	0	1	*	0
More than 12 months	5	5	3	4	6	6	4
Less than 12 months	1	0	1	2	1	1	1
GP pre compulsory VT	*	1	0	0	0	1	0
n.a.	1	1	2	0	4	0	1
Base: all respondents	*1263*	*204*	*195*	*179*	*221*	*218*	*246*

SHO posts in vocational training

What specialties did the doctors cover in their SHO posts which went to make up their GP vocational training?

Not surprisingly, the most frequently mentioned specialty was obstetrics and gynaecology, in which 85 per cent of both men and women had had an SHO post. Table 3.10 shows that the later the cohort the more likely it was for the doctors to have had a post in this specialty, and, indeed, 93 per cent of the 1988 men and women had had such posts.

The two specialties mentioned next most frequently were paediatrics, mentioned by 66 per cent of both male and female doctors, and Accident and Emergency (A and E), mentioned by 61 per cent (63 per cent of the men and 59 per cent of the women). Again, later cohorts were a little more likely to have done paediatrics, and were certainly more likely to have done A and E, illustrated by the fact that 70 per cent of the 1988 women had done it compared with 47 per cent of the 1981 women.

SHO posts in general medicine had been held by 44 per cent of the doctors (49 per cent of the men, 41 per cent of the women), with a relatively low proportion of the 1981 women having done it. Psychiatry was mentioned by 39 per cent of the doctors (42 per cent of the men and 37 per cent of the women).

Table 3.10   **Proportions of doctors reporting different specialties as part of their vocational training**

column percentages

	Total	Male 1981	Male 1985	Male 1988	Female 1981	Female 1985	Female 1988
O & G	85	80	86	92	74	87	93
Paediatrics	66	61	71	65	60	67	70
A & E	61	57	65	68	47	61	70
General medicine	44	48	50	50	31	49	42
Psychiatry	39	35	44	46	35	35	41
Geriatric med.	36	27	42	46	23	32	48
Other med. spec.	12	13	11	9	12	12	12
Surgery	7	10	9	11	5	5	5
Mixed specs.	7	7	8	7	7	8	8
ENT	6	8	7	8	5	5	7
Anaesthetics	5	3	4	6	5	3	7
Dermatology	3	3	3	2	2	3	4
Orthopaedics	3	4	4	4	1	4	2
Radiology	2	1	-	-	1	-	-
Radiotherapy	1	*	1	2	-	3	1
Other	2	1	1	2	2	2	2
Base: all respondents	*1263*	*204*	*195*	*179*	*221*	*218*	*246*

The next most frequently mentioned specialty was geriatric medicine, with 36 per cent of both male and female doctors. This subject was much more popular among later cohorts, with nearly half the 1988 doctors mentioning it compared with around a quarter of the 1981 doctors. Other medical specialties were mentioned by 12 per cent of both sexes.

The place of surgery was interesting in that 10 per cent of the men and 5 per cent of the women said they had done SHO jobs in this specialty, but the proportion of male qualifiers from the Indian sub-continent mentioning surgery was 28 per cent, compared with 7 per cent of UK male qualifiers. Again, there were indications of some Indian doctors having tried without success to make a career in a hospital specialty.

Mixed specialties were held by 7 per cent of the doctors. These tended to be six-month jobs made up of three specialties. If jobs were held for three months they were usually coded under the specialty in question. Other specialties, which accounted for 6 per cent or fewer of doctors, were ENT, anaesthetics, dermatology, orthopaedics, radiology and radiotherapy.

Length of time in SHO vocational training jobs

There were marked variations in the length of time that doctors had held SHO posts in the different specialties. Posts in two specialties, dermatology and ENT, had been held for between five and six months on average. There were seven specialties in which the average length of time of SHO posts was between six and seven months: A and E (in which the average was exactly six months), geriatric medicine, psychiatry, other medical specialties, mixed specialties, obstetrics and gynaecology and orthopaedics. Paediatric and radiotherapy posts had been held for just over seven months on average. General medicine posts had been held for 8.4 months on average, surgery for an average of 9.1 months, but anaesthetics was quite different from all the other specialties, in that SHO posts had been held for an average of 12.2 months.

There were few major differences between the sexes or cohorts in the length of time SHO posts had been held in different specialties. However, it was notable that women from all cohorts were more likely to have held anaesthetics posts for longer than the men – an average of 14 months compared with 9.7 months for the men. In surgery, it was the other way round, with men having held surgery posts for an average of 10 months, compared with 7.4 months for the women. There was also evidence of 1985 men holding surgery posts for longer – an average of 12.6 months.

These average lengths of time in SHO posts was reflected in the differences found among the proportions of doctors who had spent six months exactly in the various specialties. This ranged from 86 per cent of those doing obstetrics and gynaecology to 14 per cent of those doing anaesthetics. Over 70 per cent of those who had had SHO posts in paediatrics, A and E and psychiatry had spent exactly six months in their posts, while between 60 and 70 per cent of those doing geriatrics, mixed specialties and radiotherapy had done so. The proportion was between 50 and 60 per cent of those doing orthopaedics, general medicine, other medical specialties and radiology. In surgery it was 48 per cent, dermatology 46 per cent and ENT only 28 per cent. As we have seen only 14 per cent of those doing anaesthetics had spent exactly six months in an SHO post.

It appeared that, as far as anaesthetics and surgery were concerned, there was an important minority of doctors in this sample, who had set out on their careers in the hope of becoming anaesthetists or surgeons, but, for one reason or another, had not succeeded in their chosen specialty. This was undoubtedly true of other doctors in other specialties, but it was particularly marked among the potential anaesthetists and surgeons, some of whom had continued into registrar posts, which are not analysed in this table.

Equivalent experience and other posts mentioned

We knew that some of the doctors responding to the survey were likely to have had 'equivalent experience' which would have qualified them for a vocational training certificate, or that they might have had other experience before 1981 which would have exempted them from the vocational training pattern laid down by the regulations after that date.

We asked the doctors, therefore, for details of equivalent experience training posts if relevant. We assumed that doctors with vocational training certificates would be aware of the meaning of 'equivalent experience' as understood by the JCPTGP in this context. We were wrong in our assumption, and the ensuing discussion attempts to disentangle the information supplied in response to this question.

Twenty-two per cent of doctors gave us some information about what they understood to be 'equivalent experience'. These doctors have all been included in the preceding analysis of vocational training packages, since we wished to have a full profile of the composition of training by which the doctors met the vocational training requirements of the JCPTGP.

We then scrutinised the answers given to the question on equivalent experience in an attempt to distinguish the 'real' equivalent experience doctors from the others. We found that 8 per cent of the doctors claimed that they had met pre-vocational training requirements. This accounted for 11 per cent of the 1981 men and as many as 34 per cent of the 1981 women, and is borne out by the vocational training packages described by them and analysed in Table 3.7. Only 1 or 2 per cent of doctors from other cohorts claimed to be in this category.

Looking at what appeared to be a proper interpretation of 'equivalent experience' at present, we found that

- 3 per cent of doctors (4 per cent of men and 2 per cent of women) said that they had had equivalent experience as registrar and/or SHO instead of the prescribed SHO posts;
- 2 per cent of doctors (4 per cent of men and 1 per cent of women) said that they had had equivalent experience in the armed services;
- 2 per cent (2 per cent of men and 3 per cent of women) said that they had had equivalent experience abroad;
- 1 per cent of both men and women said that they had had equivalent experience in SHO posts for a longer period than required instead of the prescribed SHO posts;
- 1 per cent of women said that they had had community health experience which had been allowed as equivalent experience under the regulations.

These doctors – those with pre-vocational training experience and those who appeared to have real 'equivalent experience' – accounted for 17 per cent of the total respondents. It should be noted that many who had had equivalent experience in other specialties had often set out with the intention of making a career in those specialties and had turned to general practice as a second choice.

In addition, 5 per cent gave us what we interpreted to be additional information about their careers. We record this here, but should add the proviso that other doctors may well have had similar experience but did not record it for us under the heading of 'equivalent experience'. Indeed, as we saw in our analysis of the vocational training packages, we were given a great deal of information about 'additional' SHO posts by the 31 per cent of respondents who reported more than 24 months in such posts as what they considered to be part of their vocational training (see Table 3.7). It should perhaps be added that the proportion with additional SHO posts could have been greater than 31 per cent, since we assume that some doctors interpreted the question correctly and only gave us the SHO posts which made up their vocational training, rather than giving us details of every SHO post they had held before gaining their vocational training certificate.

We consider it to be of interest, however, to take a brief look at the additional information given in answer to the question on equivalent experience, because it did throw light on some of the careers of doctors who gained their vocational training certificates having sometimes had many years of experience in another specialty or pursuing other lines of medical activity. They had, in fact, put together a package which met the vocational training requirements, so that they did not need to meet the 'equivalent experience' criteria, but, for one reason or another, they recorded information for us in answer to this question.

We found that almost 3 per cent of doctors (3 per cent of men and 2 per cent of women) recorded hospital experience as a registrar as well as enough prescribed SHO posts for the vocational training package, a further 1 per cent recorded hospital experience as an SHO as well as enough prescribed SHO posts, and 1 per cent recorded recognised experience abroad as well as enough prescribed SHO posts. We have already noted that a substantial minority had done more SHO posts than was strictly necessary for their vocational training certificate. But we were interested in the fact that almost 3 per cent had done registrar posts as well, in addition to the 3 per cent who had recorded these as part of their genuine 'equivalent experience', thus reinforcing the evidence found throughout this report of doctors entering general practice having had an initial preference for a hospital specialty.

4   Part-time training

One of the aims of this report was to look at the extent to which the doctors had worked part-time in medicine, and, more especially, in general practice. Part-time postgraduate training was of particular interest, since postgraduate training in medicine usually takes place during a doctor's mid to late twenties and early thirties – a time when many women might want to have a career break or work part-time because of commitments to babies or children.

Not only did we want to know to what extent the doctors had had part-time postgraduate training, we also wanted to explore whether they would have wanted any part-time training, and whether there were constraints affecting their decision. In addition, we wished to examine the question of whether these doctors, all of whom had completed vocational training in general practice, might have wanted to stay in hospital medicine if part-time postgraduate training had been more readily available in their preferred specialty.

Extent of part-time postgraduate training in medicine

The vast majority of doctors had had no part-time postgraduate training in medicine. 98 per cent of the men and 91 per cent of the women had done all their postgraduate training full-time.

Table 4.1   Whether doctors had ever had any part-time postgraduate training in medicine

| | | | | | | column percentages |
| | Total | | Male | | | Female |
		1981	1985	1988	1981	1985	1988
Yes	6	3	2	2	13	10	5
No	94	97	98	98	87	90	95
Base: all respondents	1263	204	195	179	221	218	246

Table 4.1 shows that the proportions of men from each cohort who had had any part-time training remained constant at 2 or 3 per cent, but among the women we can see a gradual decrease in the proportion having any part-time training from 13 per cent of the 1981 cohort to 10 per cent of the 1985 cohort to only 5

per cent of the 1988 cohort. Having children clearly made a difference to the women. 15 per cent of the women with children had had part-time training, compared with less than 1 per cent of those without children.

Table 4.2   Grades in which doctors trained part-time

numbers

	Total	Male 1981	Male 1985	Male 1988	Female 1981	Female 1985	Female 1988
SHO (not part of GPVT)	9	2	-	-	1	3	3
SHO (part of GPVT)	19	1	2	1	9	4	2
Registrar	20	2	1	1	9	5	2
Senior registrar	3	-	-	-	3	-	-
GP trainee	41	3	2	1	11	14	10
Base: all ever trained part-time	*76*	*7*	*3*	*3*	*29*	*22*	*12*

*   numbers add to more than total because some doctors trained part-time in more than one grade

It was not perhaps surprising that the most common grade in which the doctors had trained part-time was as a GP trainee. Table 4.2 shows that more than half of those who had trained part-time (41 doctors) had done so during their GP trainee period, while one quarter (19 doctors) had done so as SHOs as part of their GP vocational training. Only 9 doctors had done part-time training as SHOs other than as part of their vocational training.

We noted in Chapter 3 that 43 doctors said that they had trained part-time, at least for part of the time, as GP trainees. The slight discrepancy is insignificant. However, we drew attention in Chapter 3 to the rather greater number of doctors than we found here who said they had worked part-time as SHOs during their training (31 altogether). We assumed that this was due to a misinterpretation on the part of a small number of doctors of the meaning of part-time training, and concluded that the figures for part-time SHO training quoted in this chapter are more likely to be accurate. It is also likely that some of the slight difference is due to different interpretations of which SHO posts actually constituted the doctors' vocational training. Whatever the explanation, it can be seen that only a small number of doctors had any part-time training as SHOs, whether during vocational training or not.

It was interesting that as many as a quarter of those who had trained part-time had done so as registrars (20 doctors). Most of these were women and it looked as though some of them had got as far as part-time training in a registrar grade in a hospital specialty, but had felt unable, for one reason or another, to continue, even with the part-time training. It can be seen that less than a handful in the entire sample (3 doctors) had trained part-time at senior registrar level.

The doctors had not usually spent long training part-time, which was to be expected since the majority of them had done so as part of their GP vocational training, which is only three years full-time. Even so, it appeared that they spent as little time as possible in part-time training posts. Just over one quarter of them had spent six months or less in part-time training, a further quarter had spent between 7 and 12 months, a further quarter between 13 and 24 months and just under a quarter had spent over two years in part-time training posts.

Reasons for part-time training

The main reason given for seeking part-time training was to fit in with domestic or family commitments. This reason was given by 90 per cent of the women. Two other reasons were given by more than a handful of doctors: to gain experience in an additional specialty while working in their present job and to allow more time to study for a higher qualification. Over half the men who had had part-time training had done it for additional experience, while a third of the men had done it while studying for a higher qualification.

The women who had had part-time training often saw no alternative if they were to save their marriage, or their sanity, or both, like this 1981 woman: 'When both myself and my husband were working full-time we scarcely saw each other or the children. Family life deteriorated and stress levels rose accordingly...'

Some put forward practical reasons, like this 1988 woman - 'To enable me to spend time with my baby and in particular to enable me to continue to breast-feed him...' The stress on the lives of some of these young women had clearly led to a change in specialty, as this 1988 woman explained: 'The post was obstetrics and gynaecology. I felt unable to cope with a full-time post's on-call hours and manage to look after my son and fit in with my husband's unsocial hours...'

If the domestic commitments were combined with the wish to gain a higher qualification, the burden was often too much, as another 1988 woman explained in giving her reasons for seeking part-time training: 'I was married, wanted to get the MRCPsych and found I didn't have enough time to study...'

Effects of part-time training

Less than one fifth of those who had had part-time training thought that it had had an adverse effect on their careers, although the 1981 women were rather more likely to think so than women from the later cohorts. There was no real consensus about the adverse effects, but the two main ones were thought to be a slowing down of career progress and difficulty in ensuring that their part-time training was recognised or taken seriously by other doctors. It was also thought that part-time training prolonged the period of postgraduate training and that suitable part-time training jobs were hard to find. Sometimes the adverse effects were combined, as this 1988 woman explained: 'You're not taken seriously. Your peer GPs and seniors feel you are less committed. You end up doing more than part-time. Jobs are very scarce and there is very little choice. It required a tremendous effort on my part to obtain the posts...'

Consideration of part-time postgraduate training by those who had not had it

We found that 4 per cent of the men (20 doctors) and 14 per cent of the women (84 doctors) who had *not* had postgraduate training had considered it at some point in their careers, with an even distribution among the three cohorts for each sex. Nearly one fifth of the women with children who had not had part-time training had considered it at some time.

Rather over one third of the doctors had considered it as SHOs as part of their GP vocational training and a similar proportion had considered it as GP trainees. Around a quarter had considered it as SHOs, but not during vocational training, while nearly one third had considered it as registrars. Nearly one fifth of the women had considered it at senior registrar level.

Around half of those who had considered part-time training would have wanted to have had such a post for between 12 and 24 months. Ten per cent of the women but over a third of the men would have wanted it for less than six months. Around a quarter of the women would have wanted it for more than two years.

The main reason the doctors had considered it was again to fit in with domestic or family commitments – a reason given by four-fifths of the women and over one third of the men. Two other reasons were given by more than a tiny number of doctors: to develop more specialised techniques in another specialty or to develop their interest in another specialty, while working in their present jobs. These reasons were given more often by men. A handful of doctors had considered part-time training because they had found full-time training too stressful, or to give them more time to study or to pursue interests outside medicine.

We asked the doctors why they had not proceeded to a part-time post having considered it. More than half of them, both men and women, said that there had been no available part-time training posts. Around 10 per cent said that it would have taken too long to train part-time, a further 10 per cent said their circumstances had changed and they had no longer needed part-time training, and another 10 per cent said they had changed to a less demanding job or specialty instead of pursuing the idea of part-time training. A number of doctors had been deterred by the thought that it would be difficult to have their part-time training taken seriously, while others had found that the part-time training was not acceptable to committees for higher training or other regulatory bodies. Others had been turned down because their domestic commitments had not been recognised as grounds for eligibility. A handful of doctors had been put off part-time training for financial reasons, while some of the young women said they had deferred having children so that they could complete their training full-time.

There was no doubt that some of the women respondents had been lost to hospital medicine because they had been unable to train part-time. One 1988 woman had wanted to train part-time as a registrar and senior registrar in surgery, for a total of 48 months in all. She had wanted to continue her surgical career, but had three young children and had been constrained by the geographical limitations of her husband's job as a GP. She was now a full-time GP principal, and gave the main reasons for abandoning her idea of part-time training: 'The joint committee for higher surgical training was very unhelpful. The interview ended with, "You should go home and look after your children..."'

Another woman GP principal had wanted part-time training as an SHO during her vocational training: 'At the time I was doing a busy one in two and found it hard work combining that with running a house and so on. I would have appreciated more spare time... I was advised that a "house-husband" was not enough of a "domestic commitment" to qualify. It was better for me to continue full-time and to complete the training quicker...'

Some women found the decision to continue with full-time training very hard, like this 1988 woman who had considered part-time training - '...in order to have a child. Later I considered going part-time or taking time out during my very busy O and G job. I would have ideally taken time out. As it was I found a job with less hours than the one in two paediatrics job I was due to do...Part-time training was not available at the beginning, so I had a termination of pregnancy. I had just started the vocational training scheme which would not have accommodated taking time out or training part-time. I did not think if I left it I would be able to find part-time posts elsewhere, and I did not think I could cope with a small child and a full-time SHO post...'

Opportunities for part-time training in general practice

We were interested to know whether the doctors thought there should be more opportunities for part-time training in general practice. The women were more in favour of it than the men, but nevertheless, overall, 93 per cent of the women and 74 per cent of the men thought there should be more part-time training opportunities in general practice.

Table 4.3 shows a consistency in the views of both men and women in the three cohorts, with around three-quarters of the men and over 90 per cent of the women from each of the cohorts thinking there should be more part-time training opportunities in general practice. There was, however, a difference between the UK-trained doctors and those who qualified in the Indian sub-continent, which was particularly marked among the men. Nearly 80 per cent of the UK qualified men thought there should be more part-time training opportunities, compared with only 60 per cent of the men qualifiers from the Indian sub-continent.

The main reason given by both men and women for increasing part-time training opportunities was to enable doctors to combine training with family or domestic commitments. This reason was cited by over 80 per cent of the women and nearly two-thirds of the men who thought there should be more opportunities.

Table 4.3   Whether doctors thought there should be more opportunities for
part-time training in general practice

column percentages

	Total	Male 1981	Male 1985	Male 1988	Female 1981	Female 1985	Female 1988
Yes	84	75	72	77	90	95	93
No	13	21	21	21	8	4	6
Don't know/NA	3	4	7	3	2	1	1
Base: all respondents	*1263*	*204*	*195*	*179*	*221*	*218*	*246*

It was thought that the present emphasis on full-time training in general practice was unfair to many doctors, both men and women, who wanted to have families, as this 1985 woman explained: 'Becoming a parent is a positive and maturational experience which makes better, caring and more understanding family doctors...'

Another 1985 woman reflected the views of many who thought that more part-time training opportunities would allow more flexibility in a postgraduate training system which was thought to be unnecessarily rigid: 'The training is long – five years medical school and a minimum of three years thereafter. Doctors are human too. They want families or they become ill, and there is little room for anything "unconventional" at present... Family life could do with more support...'

The need for more flexibility was the second most important reason cited for increasing part-time opportunities, and was, in fact, considered relatively more important by the men than by the women. Nearly one fifth of the men who wanted more part-time training opportunities in general practice said that a more flexible system should be designed to suit the needs of individual doctors.

It was not only for domestic reasons that some doctors thought there should be more part-time training opportunities. Both men and women expressed the view there was more to life than work, as this 1988 woman pointed out: 'Medicine is more than a full-time occupation at any level. The demands of life outside the job need to be met. This is especially true for people with young families, but can be equally true for many others...'

Over 10 per cent of the men thought that more part-time postgraduate training would enable doctors to develop other interests or acquire new skills in medicine. Many of these doctors interpreted the question as going beyond the strict sense in which it was put. What they had in mind was the extension of part-time training in another specialty or subject while continuing to work in their first specialty, which was general practice in most cases in this survey. This interpretation was also found among doctors in *Doctors and their Careers*, and is clearly of importance. The actual postgraduate training might not be undertaken with a view to obtaining a consultant post, but was clearly more than just undertaking a few courses.

This kind of part-time training was seen as particularly important by some doctors who thought general practice was demanding more skills, like this 1981 man: 'With the present emphasis on specialisation within general practice, for example paediatric surveillance, more qualifications are expected, eg DCCH. I am sure time should be allowed (ie locums paid for) to principals to attempt these extra skills. I am sure I would be finding my self-imposed task of getting the AFOM much easier if I could do it in the daytime, instead of pretending I'm not falling asleep over my books at night...'

Some doctors thought that part-time training could lead to a greater choice of careers among doctors who did not necessarily want to enter general practice at the end of vocational training. Again, the question of acquiring a wider range of useful skills was seen as desirable, and this view permeated the replies of many doctors, both men and women, to this question.

There was a fear among both men and women, however, that doctors who trained part-time might be discriminated against, and this fear appeared to be fuelled by worries about the effects of the new GP contract on the prospects of people who had had 'unconventional' careers.

The question of the stress caused by the demands of working full-time in medicine, which underlay many responses throughout this survey, surfaced in response to this question. A 1985 man, whose wife was a doctor, pointed out: 'Some of the on-call is so stressful that one way to reduce mortality and morbidity would be to extend the time of training...'

However, one fifth of the men and six per cent of the women who had not trained part-time thought there should not be increased opportunities for part-time postgraduate training in general practice. The main reasons given by the men were that general practice required a full-time commitment and that part-time training was an inadequate preparation for work in general practice. A 1981 man summarised the views of many of those who disagreed with part-time training: 'A career choice, in my opinion, should be a *total* commitment. General practice is complex and demanding...'

Over 10 per cent of the doctors who disagreed with increasing opportunities for part-time training thought that it would take too long, while 10 per cent thought there were enough opportunities already. Some of these doctors saw full-time training as preferable in that it got the training over and done with, but thought that part-time posts were required at a later stage. This view was expressed by most of the women who disagreed with increasing part-time training opportunities, like this 1988 woman - 'Training is not the problem. It is the availability of suitable posts afterwards...'

Availability of part-time training in hospital medicine

There can be no doubt that the length of the training period in hospital medicine is off-putting for both men and women doctors, and may encourage many to consider general practice, even if it was not their first specialty choice. There is also evidence that women have found it difficult to get the part-time training posts in hospital specialties which would have enabled them to stay in hospital medicine (Allen, 1988a).

We wished to establish the extent to which doctors who had gained their vocational training certificates during the 1980s would have stayed in hospital medicine if part-time training had been more readily available. We were particularly interested in seeing which specialties had been most affected by these doctors opting out of hospital medicine because part-time training opportunities were not readily available.

There was a remarkable consistency in the replies, with 25 per cent of the women in each cohort saying that they would have wished to make a career in hospital medicine if part-time training had been more readily available (a total of 171 women). The proportion of men was very much lower, with 7 per cent of the 1981 men and 2 per cent of both the 1985 and 1988 men saying a hospital specialty would have been their choice if part-time training had been more available (a total of 22 men). It is quite possible that more men would have preferred hospital medicine if other factors had been different, but our question was quite specifically about part-time training opportunities.

It was notable that 50 per cent of the 22 women qualifying in the Indian sub-continent would have wanted to pursue a hospital specialty if part-time training had been more readily available. The numbers were small, of course, but there was evidence throughout their responses that these women were not in general practice as a first choice.

In which specialty would the doctors have liked to pursue a career? The most commonly mentioned were paediatrics (36 per cent of the women who would have wanted to pursue a career in hospital medicine if part-time training had been more readily available), obstetrics and gynaecology (24 per cent of the women), and general medicine or one of the medical specialties (23 per cent of the women). Nearly half of the men mentioned general medicine or one of the medical specialties. The 1981 women were more likely to have opted for paediatrics (43 per cent), while the later cohorts of women were more likely to mention general medicine or obstetrics and gynaecology.

Other specialties mentioned only by women were dermatology (6 per cent), psychiatry (6 per cent), geriatrics (4 per cent), radiotherapy and pathology. Anaesthetics and radiology were mentioned by 5 per cent of both men and women.

Surgery was mentioned by 4 per cent of the women, but by three of the men who would have continued with hospital medicine if part-time training had been more available, and Accident and Emergency was mentioned by two men and two women.

It is quite clear that a substantial minority of women entering general practice in the 1980s would have preferred to stay in hospital medicine, and the fact that a quarter of the women respondents in this survey of doctors gaining their vocational training certificates in these years would have wanted to make a career in hospital medicine if part-time training had been more readily available must surely give some cause for concern.

We did not ask the doctors to give reasons for their answers, but many of them volunteered their views on this subject. Some of them had, in fact, managed to return to hospital medicine having completed their GP vocational training, albeit in a different specialty from their first choice, like this 1985 woman: 'I was interested in a career in neonatal paediatrics, but after twelve months experience it was obvious that this was not compatible with anything resembling a normal life, with social life, time for interests and hobbies and family commitments. Now I'm a senior registrar in psychiatry for the elderly...'

The loss to paediatrics, and the enormous regret expressed by many of the women who had reluctantly given it up, came through time and again in answer to this question. It often appeared to have been given up after a great struggle to continue, as another 1985 women explained: 'Having achieved MRCP in paediatrics, the realities of what the next ten years entailed forced a move to general practice...'

5   In and out of general practice

In Chapter 2 we examined the employment status of all the respondents to the survey, and found that 90 per cent of the men and 79 per cent of the women were working in general practice. When we excluded those who were not working at the time, we found that 91 per cent of the working men and 86 per cent of the working women were in general practice. It is with these doctors that this chapter is mainly concerned, although we examine in some detail at the end of the chapter the plans and intentions of those who were not working in general practice.

Present job, grade and status of those in general practice
Table 2.21 showed the present job, grade and status of all doctors responding to the survey, giving the numbers in each category as proportions of the sample as a whole. For the purposes of this chapter, we reproduce the first part of

Table 5.1   **Job title of those working in general practice by sex and year of vocational training certificate**

column percentages

	Total	Male 1981	Male 1985	Male 1988	Female 1981	Female 1985	Female 1988
FT GP principal	66	95	95	84	41	38	41
FT GP assistant	*	-	-	3	-	1	-
FT GP locum	2	-	1	5	-	-	5
20 hour a week GP principal	9	1	1	1	21	20	13
PT GP principal	10	1	2	2	18	24	15
PT GP assistant	4	-	-	1	7	5	8
PT GP locum	4	1	1	3	5	4	8
GP retainer scheme	4	-	-	-	6	8	9
FT private GP	*	1	1	-	-	-	*
Armed services	1	1	-	2	1	-	*
Base: all working in general practice at present	*1059*	*186*	*177*	*156*	*163*	*169*	*208*

Table 5.2   Job title of those working in general practice by sex

column percentages

	Total	Male	Female
FT GP principal	66	92	40
FT GP assistant	*	1	*
FT GP locum	2	2	2
20 hour a week GP principal	9	1	18
PT GP principal	10	2	19
PT GP assistant	4	*	7
PT GP locum	4	2	6
GP retainer scheme	4	-	8
FT private GP	*	*	*
Armed services	1	1	*
Base: all working in general practice at present	*1059*	*519*	*540*

Table 2.21, but this time we show the numbers of doctors in each category as proportions of those working in general practice.

Tables 5.1 and 5.2 show that two-thirds of those working in general practice were full-time GP principals, that 10 per cent were part-time GP principals and that 9 per cent were 20 hour a week principals (see Chapter 1 for an explanation of their status). But these percentages mask marked differences between the sexes.

Table 5.2 shows that 92 per cent of the men in general practice were full-time principals, compared with 40 per cent of the women. 2 per cent of the men were part-time GP principals, compared with 19 per cent of the women, and 1 per cent of the men were 20-hour a week principals, compared with 18 per cent of the women. If these last two categories are added together, we can see that 37 per cent of the women and 3 per cent of the men in general practice were working as less than full-time principals.

Putting the full-time and less than full-time principals together, it can be seen that 95 per cent of the men and 77 per cent of the women working in general practice were, in fact, principals. The difference between the men and women was marked for each cohort:

- of the 1981 cohort working in general practice, 97 per cent of the men and 80 per cent of the women were GP principals;
- of the 1985 cohort working in general practice, 98 per cent of the men and 82 per cent of the women were GP principals;
- of the 1988 cohort working in general practice, 87 per cent of the men and 69 per cent of the women were GP principals.

But the main difference between men and women principals lay in the proportion of women principals who were working less than full-time. Table 5.1 breaks the figures down into the cohorts, and, as noted in Chapter 2, shows that the 1988 men were less likely to be full-time principals than the men from the earlier cohorts, while the proportion of women who were full-time principals was much the same for all three cohorts.

The proportion of less than full-time principals was higher among the 1981 and 1985 women than among the 1988 women. The proportion of full-time and part-time locums was higher among the 1988 men and women than among the other cohorts.

Very few of the GPs were working as full-time GP assistants: 7 per cent of the women and less than 1 per cent of the men. 8 per cent of the women were on the GP retainer scheme. A handful of doctors were working in private general practice or in the armed services.

Status of principals in general practice

There have been fears that women principals might find it more difficult than men to become full partners in practices. We therefore asked the doctors whether they were full or salaried partners in their practice. We were also interested to know what proportion of the GPs were single-handed.

Table 5.3   Status of those working as principals in general practice at present

column percentages

	Total	Male			Female		
		1981	1985	1988	1981	1985	1988
Full partner	87	89	87	93	85	88	90
Salaried partner	4	-	-	2	7	7	9
Single handed	7	10	13	8	7	3	-
Profit sharing 50% partner	*	-	-	-	-	1	-
Private practice	*	1	-	-	-	-	-
Other GP/GP abroad	1	-	1	-	2	1	1
N.A	1	1	1	1	1	1	1
Base: all GP principals	*903*	*181*	*173*	*135*	*132*	*138*	*144*

It can be seen from Table 5.3 that 87 per cent of the GP principals were full partners, representing virtually equal proportions of men and women. The table shows that marginally more principals were full partners in the 1988 cohort than in the other cohorts. The main differences between men and women lay in the proportion of women principals who were salaried partners: 7 per cent of the women compared with 1 per cent of the men overall. Men, on the other hand, were rather more likely to be single-handed principals: 10 per cent of the men compared with 3 per cent of the women.

Composition of work by full-time and part-time working

We drew attention in Chapter 2 to the issue of full-time and part-time working and the difficulty in interpreting what doctors meant by 'full-time' and 'part-time'. We noted that of the 1202 doctors who were working at the time of the survey, 99 per cent of the men and 48 per cent of the women said that they were working full-time. We found that of the 1059 doctors who were working in general practice, 98 per cent of the men and 47 per cent of the women regarded themselves as working full-time.

But, as Table 2.22 showed, the composition of the doctors' work was complicated. Table 5.4 shows the same categories, but compares the doctors working in general practice with the doctors not working in general practice. There are some interesting differences.

Table 5.4 Composition of work by full-time or part-time working by GP and other posts

column percentages

	Working in GP			Not working in GP		
	Total	Male	Female	Total	Male	Female
One FT post with no PT work	41	53	30	65	87	53
One FT post with one or more PT posts	27	43	13	8	12	5
More than one PT post which add to FT commitment	4	3	5	1	2	1
More than one PT post which add to PT commitment	11	1	20	7	1	11
One PT post	17	*	32	19	*	30
Total: all in work at present	*1059*	*519*	*540*	*143*	*52*	*91*

It can be seen that the doctors working in general practice were more likely than those in other specialties to have a full-time post combined with one or more part-time posts. This was particularly true of the men, but was also true of the women. (Of the 9 doctors working outside medicine, included in the 143 not working in general practice, 7 had one full-time job only, 1 had a full-time job and a part-time job, and 1 had one part-time job only.)

53 per cent of the men working in general practice had one full-time post and no part-time work, compared with 87 per cent of the men in other medical specialties or outside medicine. On the other hand, 43 per cent of the male GPs

had a full-time post combined with one or more part-time posts, compared with 12 per cent of the male doctors working outside general practice.

Less than one third of the women GPs had one full-time post only, compared with over half the women doctors working outside general practice. However, 13 per cent of the women GPs had a full-time post combined with one or more part-time posts, compared with only 5 per cent of the other women doctors.

Women GPs were rather more likely to have put together a package of part-time posts than the other women doctors, as Table 5.4 shows, although just under one third of both types of working women doctors had one part-time post only. Among the men, only tiny proportions had any part-time packages of work, whether they worked in general practice or in other medical specialties.

Looking at the differences between the men and women GPs, the expected pattern emerges, with 52 per cent of the women GPs having a post or posts which added to a part-time commitment, compared with 1 per cent of the men.

We looked in more detail at the composition of the work of the four main categories of posts in general practice: full-time GP principals, 20-hour a week principals, part-time GP principals and part-time GP assistants. We wanted to know how these doctors put together their packages of work and to see whether there were any differences between the men and the women.

Table 5.5 shows some interesting differences between men and women GPs who were working in the same category of jobs. Looking first at the full-time GP principals, we can see that 55 per cent of the men but 71 per cent of the women had one full-time post with no part-time work. On the other hand, 44 per cent of the men and only 29 per cent of the women had one or more part-time posts in addition to their full-time principal job.

The number of 20-hour a week male principals was too small for any comparisons to be drawn between men and women, but it was interesting to see how the 20-hour a week women principals put together their packages of work. The vast majority of them had described themselves as working part-time, but only 61 per cent of them had only one part-time post – their 20-hour a week principal post. 24 per cent of them had more than one part-time post, adding to a part-time commitment in their view, while 12 per cent had more than one part-time post adding to a full-time commitment.

The part-time GP principals were very similar to the 20-hour a week principals. Again, there were too few men to make any meaningful comparisons, but it was interesting that only 65 per cent of the women had only one part-time post. A further 28 per cent had more than one part-time post, adding to a part-time commitment, while 7 per cent had a package of part-time posts adding up to a full-time commitment.

Among the part-time GP assistants, all but one of whom were women, the pattern was rather different, with over 50 per cent of them having more than one part-time post adding to a part-time commitment, 38 per cent having just one part-time post, while the rest had put together complicated packages which, in their view added up to a full-time commitment.

Table 5.5 Composition of work by full-time or part-time working in selected posts

column percentages

	FT GP principals			20 hour principals			PT GP principals			PT GP assistants		
	Total	M	F	Total	M	F	Total	M	F	Total	M	F
One FT post with no PT work	60	55	71	2	0	2	0	0	0	3	0	3
One FT post with one or more PT posts	39	44	29	1	0	1	2	25	1	8	100	5
More than one PT post which add to a FT commitment	*	*	0	14	75	12	8	25	7	3	0	3
More than one PT post which add to a PT commitment	0	0	0	24	25	24	28	25	28	50	0	51
One PT post	0	0	0	59	0	61	62	25	65	37	0	38
Base: doctors in selected GP posts	694	477	217	99	4	95	110	8	102	38	1	37

Composition of practice

We collected information from those working in general practice about the composition of the practice in which they were working. We asked them to give us the numbers and sex of GP principals, GP assistants and GP trainees, together with details of whether the doctors concerned were working full-time or part-time in the practice. (We asked for details of 20-hour a week principals, but have included these in the analysis as part-time principals, as elsewhere in this study.) Doctors were asked to include themselves in the practice profile, and it must be remembered that our respondents included GP assistants and locums as well as GP principals.

Table 5.6 (i)   Number of principals in GP respondents' practice by sex of respondent (including single-handed practices)

			column percentages
Number of principals	Total	Male	Female
One	9	12	6
Two	15	15	15
Three	18	16	19
Four	19	19	19
5 - 7	34	33	35
8 - 10	5	4	5
More than 10	1	1	1
Base: all working in general practice giving practice details (incl. single-handed practices)	*1009*	*501*	*508*

Table 5.6 (ii)   Number of principals in GP respondents' practice by sex of respondent (excluding single-handed practices)

			column percentages
Number of principals	Total	Male	Female
Two	17	17	16
Three	19	19	20
Four	21	22	20
5 - 7	38	37	38
8 - 10	5	5	5
More than 10	1	1	1
Base: all working in general practice giving practice details (excl. single-handed practices)	*914*	*439*	*475*

Of the 1059 doctors working in general practice, 50 gave no practice details. 31 of these were GP locums (23 part-time and 8 full-time), most of whom, it appeared, were working intermittently or in more than one practice. Seven were GP principals (4 full-time and 3 part-time), 3 were part-time GP assistants, 6 were on the retainer scheme and 3 were 'other GPs' in private practice or the armed services.

Tables 5.6 to 5.9 therefore refer to the 1009 doctors (519 men and 540 women) who gave details of the composition of the practice in which they were working. The information collected was complex and the analysis complicated. We have restricted the tables in this report to a relatively simple analysis of the GP principals in the practices. It can be deduced from the number of tables which we have constructed simply to show the distribution of male and female full-time and part-time principals that a whole chapter could be written on general practice composition.

Table 5.6 (i) shows that just under 10 per cent of the GP respondents were working in single-handed principal practices, 15 per cent in practices with two principals, just under one fifth in practices with three and a similar proportion in practices with four principals. Just over one third of respondents were in practices with between 5 and 7 principals, while 6 per cent were in practices with eight or more principals. There were great similarities between the men and women respondents in the size of the practice in which they were working, apart from single-handed practices, where there was a higher proportion of men, reflecting the fact that men were more likely than women to be single-handed practitioners in any case.

Table 5.6 (ii) uses the same data, but excludes doctors working in single-handed practices in order to make it comparable with the material collated in Table 10 of *Your Choices for the Future* (Electoral Reform Ballot Services, 1992), which was based on responses from over 22,000 GPs. The proportions of doctors working in the various practice sizes (as measured by number of principals) were almost identical in the two surveys.

Tables 5.7 (i) and (ii) show the number of full-time and part-time principals respectively working in the respondents' practices. (All the remaining tables in this analysis include the single-handed practices.) Only 1 per cent of practices had no full-time principals, and consisted usually of job-sharing principals. The proportions of full-time principals in each size of practice were much as might be expected from the material presented in Tables 5.6 (i) and (ii). There appeared to be a very slight difference between the men and women in that a rather higher proportion of women than men were in practices with two or three full-time principals.

However, there was a difference between the men and the women in the number of part-time principals in the practices. Nearly two-thirds of the men, but only 42 per cent of the women were in practices with *no* part-time principals, while a quarter of the men and 40 per cent of the women were in practices with one part-time principal. This clearly reflects the fact that a relatively high proportion of women respondents were part-time or less than full-time principals

Table 5.7 (i) Number of full-time principals in GP respondents' practice by sex of respondent (including single-handed practices)

column percentages

Number of FT principals	Total	Male	Female
None	1	1	1
One	12	14	11
Two	20	18	22
Three	22	21	24
Four	20	20	19
5 - 7	22	23	20
8 - 10	3	3	3
More than 10	0	0	0
Base: all working in general practice giving practice details (incl. single-handed practices)	*1009*	*501*	*508*

Table 5.7 (ii) Number of part-time principals in GP respondents' practice by sex of respondent (including single-handed practices)

column percentages

Number of PT principals	Total	Male	Female
None	53	63	42
One	32	25	40
Two	12	10	15
Three	2	1	2
Four	*	*	1
5 - 7	*	*	*
8 - 10	0	0	0
More than 10	0	0	0
Base: all working in general practice giving practice details (incl. single-handed practices)	*1009*	*501*	*508*

themselves. It also indicates that a high proportion of male GPs had no current experience of working *with* part-time principals, a factor which has a bearing on much of the material gathered in this study.

We were, of course, interested in the extent to which the practices in which the GPs were working contained *women* principals, and, if so, whether they were full-time or part-time. Tables 5.8 (i), (ii) and (iii) show the distribution of women principals in the types of practices.

Table 5.8 (i) Number of women GP principals in GP respondents' practice by sex of respondent (including single-handed practices)

column percentages

Number of women principals	Total	Male	Female
None	26	45	8
One	45	39	52
Two	23	14	31
Three	4	2	6
Four	1	1	2
5 - 7	*	*	*
8 or more	*	0	*
Base: all working in general practice giving practice details (incl. single-handed practices)	*1009*	*501*	*508*

Table 5.8 (ii) Number of full-time women principals in GP respondents' practice by sex of respondent (including single-handed practices)

column percentages

Number of FT women principals	Total	Male	Female
None	54	67	40
One	37	26	47
Two	8	6	10
Three	1	*	1
Four	*	*	*
5 or more	*	*	*
Base: all working in general practice giving practice details (incl. single-handed practices)	*1009*	*501*	*508*

Table 5.8 (i) shows that a quarter of the GP respondents were working in practices with *no* women principals, but it is noteworthy that this represented 45 per cent of the men and only 8 per cent of the women. Again, the fact that nearly half the male GPs were working in practices with no women principals at all has important implications.

Over half the women but less than 40 per cent of the men were working in practices with one woman principal, and nearly one third of the women but only 14 per cent of the men were in practices with two women principals. Very few respondents of either sex were in practices with three or more women principals.

Table 5.8(iii) Number of part-time women principals in GP respondents' practice by sex of respondent (including single-handed practices)

column percentages

Number of PT women principals	Total	Male	Female
None	59	72	47
One	31	21	41
Two	9	7	10
Three	1	*	2
Four	*	*	*
5 or more	0	0	0
Base: all working in general practice giving practice details (incl. single-handed practices)	*1009*	*501*	*508*

As might have been expected, over two-thirds of the men were in practices where there were *no full-time* women principals, and, indeed 40 per cent of the women were also in such practices. As Table 5.8 (ii) shows, nearly half the women but only a quarter of the men were in practices with one full-time woman principal, 10 per cent of the women and 6 per cent of the men were in practices with two full-time women principals, but there were virtually no practices with more than two full-time women principals.

The proportion of men in practices with *no part-time* women principals was even higher, with 72 per cent of men working in such practices, compared with nearly half the women. As Table 5.8 (iii) shows, women were twice as likely as men to be working in practices with one part-time woman principal, but only slightly more likely to be working in practices with two or more part-time women principals.

Finally, we analysed our data on practices with no women principals to see how this was related to size of practice. This analysis was comparable to Table 11 in *Your Choices for the Future* and came up with very similar results. Table 5.9 shows that nearly 80 per cent of practices with single-handed principals had no women principals, that 43 per cent of those with two principals had none, and that the proportion of practices with no women principals fell steadily as the size of practice increased. Nevertheless, 10 per cent of practices with 5-7 principals had no women principals and nearly the same proportion of those with 8 or more principals had none.

This analysis of the practices in which the GP respondents were working, concentrating on the proportion of GP principals of different types gives only a brief glimpse at the complexities of practice composition. However, it underlines the fact that, even among these relatively young GPs, nearly half the men were working in practices with *no* women GP principals, either full-time or part-time, that two-thirds had no current experience of working with full-time women

Table 5.9   Proportion of practices with no women GP principals by size of practice

No. of principals in practice		Percentage of each size of practice with no women principals
One	(N = 95)	78 %
Two	(N = 151)	43 %
Three	(N = 178)	28 %
Four	(N = 190)	22 %
5 - 7	(N = 343)	10 %
8 - 10	(N = 47)	9 %
More than 10	(N = 12)	8 %

principals, and that nearly three-quarters were not working with part-time women principals. This background must be borne in mind throughout this report.

Work done by GPs other than in general practice

We saw in Table 5.4 that 53 per cent of the male GPs and 62 per cent of the female GPs said that they had only one post, either full-time or part-time. Almost all the men with only one post had one full-time post, but the women in this category were almost equally divided between those holding one full-time post and those holding one part-time post. Just over half the women held one part-time post only and just under half held one full-time post only.

However, this meant that nearly half of the male and nearly 40 per cent of the female GP respondents had more than one job. What were they doing? Did they have more than one job in general practice, or were they doing something else in addition to general practice? It appeared that the vast majority of those with more than one job did at least some work outside general practice.

We asked all those working in general practice whether they did any work in or out of medicine other than in general practice. Overall, 43 per cent of them (50 per cent of the men and 37 per cent of the women) said they did some additional work. Table 5.10 shows the proportions in each cohort. It can be seen that the 1981 men were more likely than those from later cohorts to have been engaged in additional work outside general practice, but that the proportions of women remained the same for each cohort.

It should be remembered that not all those working in general practice had their main job as GPs, but were hospital doctors or academics doing one or more sessions in general practice for a variety of reasons. However, it was noteworthy that 43 per cent of the full-time GP principals said they did additional work outside general practice, compared with 41 per cent of the 20-hour a week principals and 42 per cent of the part-time principals. Indeed, the proportions hovered around 40 per cent for all categories apart from part-time GP assistants and part-time GP locums, of whom 60 per cent of both grades said they did additional work outside general practice.

Table 5.10   Whether GPs do any work in or out of medicine other than in general practice

column percentages

	Total	Male 1981	Male 1985	Male 1988	Female 1981	Female 1985	Female 1988
		1981	1985	1988	1981	1985	1988
Yes	43	56	45	47	36	40	37
No	57	44	55	53	64	60	63
Base: all working in general practice at present	*1059*	*186*	*177*	*156*	*163*	*169*	*208*

The vast majority (78 per cent) of the GPs who did some work outside general practice held one additional post only, as Table 5.11 indicates. But there were differences between the men and women, particularly in the 1985 and 1988 cohorts, where 29 per cent of the men from both years held two or more additional posts, compared with 21 per cent of the 1985 women and 17 per cent of the 1988 women.

Table 5.11   Number of other jobs held by those working in general practice

column percentages

	Total	Male 1981	Male 1985	Male 1988	Female 1981	Female 1985	Female 1988
		1981	1985	1988	1981	1985	1988
One other job	78	79	71	71	83	79	83
Two other jobs	17	13	24	21	12	18	13
Three other jobs	6	8	5	8	5	3	4
Average no. of other other jobs held	1.3	1.3	1.3	1.4	1.2	1.2	1.2
Base: all working in general practice with other jobs	*459*	*105*	*79*	*73*	*59*	*67*	*76*

What kind of jobs were they doing? The vast majority held other jobs in medicine rather than outside it. Table 5.12 shows what kind of jobs the doctors held, according to how many additional jobs they held. The material is presented in this way to summarise the complexity of the packages of jobs held. It was not easy to compile a table which showed the exact contents of the various types of packages, although we shall return to this.

Looking at the first column, which shows the second job of the 356 doctors who held only one other job, it can be seen that just over 40 per cent were working as clinical assistants, just over 20 per cent as some kind of medical officer, often

Table 5.12 Grade of other jobs in medicine held by those working in general practice with one, two or three additional jobs

column percentages

	Those with 1 other job	Those with 2 other jobs	Those with 3 other jobs
Clinical assistant	41	56	62
Med. Off. (other)	22	36	65
SCMO/CMO	13	17	15
Med. Off. (occ. health)	11	10	27
(Senior) lecturer	3	5	0
SHO	3	1	15
GP trainer/tutor	1	4	12
Research fellow	1	5	4
Registrar	1	3	4
VT course organiser	1	4	0
Consultant	1	4	0
Base: all respondents in GP with one, two or three other jobs	*356*	*77*	*26*

doing work in connection with benefits paid by the Department of Social Security, 13 per cent were working in community health as a SCMO or CMO and just over 10 per cent were working in occupational health. The rest had jobs in hospital medicine or in another branch of general practice. (Although we specified other work *outside* general practice, some doctors gave us details of work they did as deputising doctors or other work in general practice not covered by the grades we specified in the questionnaire.) A small proportion had jobs outside medicine, but this was usually free-lance work of some kind.

It should be remembered that the question was asked of *all* doctors working in general practice, some of whom were mainly working in another field, for example in hospital medicine, which is why some of the jobs like 'consultant' might look a little unusual as an 'additional' job.

There was little doubt that clinical assistant posts were the most common additional jobs held by doctors working in general practice, as can be seen by the extent to which clinical assistant posts were recorded as the second, third and even fourth jobs of those doing other work. It was quite common for doctors to have a combination of two or even three clinical assistant posts in addition to their work in general practice.

It was noteworthy that medical officer posts were often held as third or even fourth posts by doctors with three or more jobs. The packages of additional work were often complicated, and some of the posts amounted only to one or two hours a week or even less.

Table 5.12 indicates the proportion of doctors with one, two or three additional posts who held a post in the grade or of the type mentioned. The bases for those holding two or three additional jobs are rather small, but it can be seen that the more additional jobs the doctors held, the more likely they were to hold a clinical assistant, medical officer or SHO post. The table shows the proportion of *people* who mentioned holding a post in the grade at all – and is not an addition of the jobs. Thus, each grade is only counted once. The table indicates, for example, that whereas 41 per cent of those holding one additional job held a clinical assistant post, 56 per cent of those holding two additional jobs held at least one clinical assistant post, while 62 per cent of those holding three additional jobs held at least one clinical assistant post.

Table 5.13 **Grade or type of other jobs held by those working in general practice with one additional job only**

	Total	Male			Female		
		1981	1985	1988	1981	1985	1988
Grade in medicine							
Clinical assistant	41	43	48	38	37	40	38
Med. officer/other	22	16	27	33	18	26	19
SCMO/CMO	13	1	2	4	22	21	30
Medical officer/ occ.health	11	24	13	12	4	6	3
(Senior) lecturer	3	5	4	2	2	4	2
SHO	3	1	2	6	2	0	5
GP trainer/tutor	1	0	0	2	2	4	0
Research fellow	1	1	2	0	0	0	0
Registrar	1	0	0	2	2	4	0
VT course organiser	1	2	2	0	0	0	0
Consultant	1	1	0	0	4	0	0
Type of other work							
Journalism	1	2	2	2	0	0	0
Management	1	2	0	0	0	0	0
Commercial	*	0	0	0	0	0	2
Proofreading	*	0	0	0	2	0	0
Counselling	*	0	0	0	2	0	0
FHSA audit team	*	0	0	2	0	0	0
Base: all working in general practice with one other job	*356*	*83*	*56*	*52*	*49*	*53*	*63*

column percentages

Looking at the difference between the sexes across all groups, it could be seen that men were rather more likely to hold clinical assistant posts and women much more likely to hold posts in community health. Medical officer work was held fairly equally by both sexes, while occupational health posts were more likely to be held by men.

We looked in more detail at the 356 doctors holding one additional job only, since they constituted the biggest group, and we wanted to look at any differences between the cohorts.

There were some minor differences among the cohorts, with clinical assistant posts most likely to be held by the 1985 men, and other medical officer work most likely to be held among the 1988 men. The pattern of SCMO/CMO posts being held by women and occupational health posts being held more frequently by men is found, although the 1981 men were more likely to have these posts than the younger men.

We were interested to know whether doctors working in general practice with other jobs were likely to work in particular specialties, but we found that they were working in a wide variety of specialties or branches of medicine, according to our analysis of those with one other job only.

The most common specialties were, not surprisingly, community health or public health, closely followed by occupational health. General medical specialties were the most common specialties in which doctors had clinical assistant posts, followed by obstetrics and gynaecology, geriatrics and A and E. Table 5.14 shows how broad a spectrum was covered in the additional posts held by doctors working in general practice with one other job. This pattern was repeated among those holding more than one other job. Work in private clinics or hospitals was not usually ascribed a specialty.

The grades and specialties in which doctors with more than one additional job were working were more difficult to present in a simple form. We therefore analysed the more common combinations of jobs.

We found that, of the 77 doctors holding two other jobs, 26 per cent held two clinical assistant jobs, 12 per cent held two medical officer (other) jobs and 4 per cent held two SCMO/CMO jobs. Other important combinations were clinical assistant and medical officer posts (10 per cent) and clinical assistant and other medical posts (12 per cent). These combinations together accounted for two-thirds of the doctors holding two additional posts. Other combinations were very varied.

Looking at the 26 doctors holding three other jobs, we found that 12 per cent held three clinical assistant posts, 19 per cent held two clinical assistant posts and another medical job, while 31 per cent held one clinical assistant post and other medical jobs. Thus nearly two-thirds of these doctors with three additional posts held a combination of posts including a clinical assistant post.

Essentially, the analysis, although complicated and difficult to present in a simple form, indicates how much doctors working in general practice were involved in clinical assistant work, often, it appeared, to give them additional interest outside general practice, and to keep up their expertise in a particular

Table 5.14 Specialty of other jobs in medicine of those working in GP with one additional job only

column percentages

Specialty	Total	Male 1981	1985	1988	Female 1981	1985	1988
General medicine	3	5	4	6	2	2	2
Other med. specs.	12	11	14	15	10	9	10
Geriatrics	6	5	4	12	6	8	5
Dermatology	2	1	4	0	2	2	2
Paediatrics	1	1	2	0	2	2	0
A & E	5	5	7	10	2	0	8
Surgery	1	1	4	0	0	0	0
O & G	7	4	9	0	6	13	11
Anaesthetics	2	2	5	2	2	2	0
Radiology/radiotherapy	1	1	0	0	0	0	2
Pathology	0	0	0	0	0	0	0
Psychiatry	3	2	4	2	4	0	6
General practice	6	7	5	8	6	8	3
Community medicine/ public health	16	5	5	6	24	25	33
Occ. med./hlth.	12	25	13	12	4	8	3
DSS/govt department	7	6	7	8	10	9	3
Hosp. management	1	0	0	0	0	0	3
Physical/mental handicap	2	5	2	2	0	0	2
Prison doctor/ police surgeon	2	4	2	6	0	2	0
Armed forces	1	1	2	2	0	2	2
Private clin/hosp	7	2	9	6	12	9	6
Base: all working in general practice with one other job	*356*	*83*	*56*	*52*	*49*	*53*	*63*

hospital specialty. They were also involved in more mundane work as medical officers, but this work usually took up less time than hospital or community health work. Work in community health was more often undertaken by women, and was usually in family planning clinics or in school health.

Time spent by doctors on additional work outside general practice

How much time did the doctors spend on their work outside general practice? Table 5.15 shows that 44 per cent spent between one and five hours a week, (almost identical proportions of men and women), a further 23 per cent spent

Table 5.15 Number of hours a week spent on other work by GPs who do work other than general practice

column percentages

	Total	Male 1981	1985	1988	Female 1981	1985	1988
Hours a week							
1 - 5	44	49	47	36	42	55	32
6 - 10	23	24	27	23	25	19	17
11 - 20	11	10	9	12	17	9	13
21 - 30	4	5	6	1	3	1	6
31 - 40	1	2	1	1	2	0	1
40 plus	1	0	0	3	0	0	3
Variable	11	4	5	21	2	10	26
n.a.	5	8	5	3	8	4	3
Median no. of hours worked (excl. 'variable' hours)	4	4	4	5	5	3	5
Base: all working in general practice who do other work	*459*	*105*	*79*	*73*	*59*	*67*	*76*

between six and ten hours a week (a quarter of the men and one fifth of the women), and 11 per cent spent between 11 and 20 hours a week (10 per cent of the men and 13 per cent of the women).

6 per cent of the doctors doing work outside general practice spent over 20 hours a week on this work, but most of these were actually engaged in some other work as their main job and were working in general practice as a secondary occupation.

11 per cent of doctors working in general practice said that they spent a variable amount of time on their other work. Some of these were doing odd sessions or occasional or irregular work. They were more frequently women, and, as Table 5.15 shows, they were more often found among the 1988 doctors of both sexes. It appeared that the doctors from the 1981 and 1985 cohorts doing other work had tended to settle on regular work of between one and ten hours a week: this accounted for three-quarters of the 1981 men and 1985 men and women and two thirds of the 1981 women. Rather fewer of the 1988 cohort had such jobs, but were more likely to work variable hours or sessions.

The median number of hours spent working in other jobs ranged from three for the 1985 women, four for the 1981 and 1985 men, to five for the 1981 women and 1988 men and women. (This median figure excluded the 'variable' category.) We calculated the average on the basis of the median, since the mean was distorted by the relatively small number of doctors working more or less full-time in jobs other than general practice.

Whether GPs with other jobs would like to increase their work outside general practice

Overall, 30 per cent of the men and 22 per cent of the women with other jobs wanted to *increase* the amount of work they did outside general practice. But, as Table 5.16 shows, there were differences between the cohorts, with over a third of the 1985 and 1988 men and over a quarter of the 1988 women wanting to increase their work outside general practice, compared with less than a quarter of the 1981 men and under a fifth of the 1981 and 1985 women. It was interesting that the full-time GP principals, who, as we have seen, accounted for two-thirds of those doing additional work outside general practice, were just as likely as others to wish to increase the amount of work they did outside general practice.

Table 5.16   Whether those working in general practice with other jobs would like to increase the amount of work done other than in general practice

	Total	Male			Female		
		1981	1985	1988	1981	1985	1988
Yes	27	23	35	36	19	19	28
No	73	77	65	64	81	80	72
Base: all working in general practice with other jobs	*459*	*105*	*79*	*73*	*59*	*67*	*76*

column percentages

Why did these doctors want to increase the amount of other work they did? As we have seen, there was little or no difference between the cohorts in the average number of hours spent by those who actually did any work outside general practice. The main reason given by the GPs was the desire to add variety to their work and to broaden their interests. Around 60 per cent of both men and women gave this as the main reason for wanting more work, but interestingly, the 1981 men and women and the 1988 men were much more likely to mention this than the other cohorts.

There was evidence throughout these responses of some GPs finding general practice rather restricted, not to say tedious. Their views were summarised by a 1981 male full-time GP principal: 'I find general practice totally boring and I miss the challenge of actually *doing* something. As soon as something interesting happens, the patient is taken away from me. *I* want to do the X-ray and put the plaster of paris on. I want to look after the patient in a cottage hospital. I want to assist the surgeon with the operation. Hence, I want to try to fill my unstimulated life with outside interests...'

Other younger doctors, like this 1988 woman, could see that they might become bored with general practice, or that they might want more stimulus in future: 'Full-time general practice is very demanding of time and commitment, and I feel there is a tendency to slip into bad habits after a period of time...'

Although most doctors who wanted more variety in their work answered this question in fairly general terms, some were much more specific. Over one in ten mentioned a particular desire to diversify into hospital medicine, while just under one in ten said that they wanted to diversify outside hospital medicine. An 1981 woman, working part-time in general practice, and putting together a complicated package of work, stated her aims in wanting to increase the amount of work she did outside general practice:

> Now my children are older, I feel I could undertake more work in specialties I am interested in, like family planning, cytology, obs. and gynae. I feel I would like all the work I do now, (which is for three different health authorities and is all sessional, with no holiday allowance apart from two hospital sessions), to come under the umbrella term of "Community Gynaecologist". I feel I am well experienced for this, but there is no such job in this area. I would be interested in doing further training if such a job existed...

Some of those who wanted to increase the amount of time they spent on hospital medicine often had a particular interest in a specialty in which they were currently working as a clinical assistant, while others, particularly those currently working as GP locums, were more interested in developing a career in hospital medicine. Nearly half of those currently working as part-time GP locums wanted to do more work outside general practice.

A small number of those working in general practice wanted to diversify outside medicine, like this 1988 woman: 'I would like to do some non-medical work to broaden my interest and experience and for personal satisfaction - and perhaps as a way out of medicine altogether...'

Others wanted to decrease the amount of work they did in general practice, while increasing their other work. Some wanted to do more hospital work so that they could improve their rapport and contact with hospital staff, while a handful wanted to diversify their career options in general.

However, the second most important reason, given by around one third of GPs who wanted to increase their other work, was financial. The men were more likely than the women to give this reason, and, indeed, it was mentioned by nearly half of the 1985 and 1988 men who wanted to increase their work outside general practice. Perhaps not surprisingly, both men and women with children were more likely to mention it than those without children.

Whether GPs with no outside work would like to do any additional work

Over half the men and more than 60 per cent of the women currently working in general practice did no outside work, but this did not mean that they did not want to do any.

As Table 5.17 shows, nearly one third of the 459 doctors in general practice with no outside work would have liked some, representing nearly 40 per cent of the men but only just over one fifth of the women. It can be seen that the younger men and women were more likely than the older ones to have wanted additional

Table 5.17   Whether those working in general practice but not at present doing other
work would like to do any

column percentages

	Total	Male 1981	Male 1985	Male 1988	Female 1981	Female 1985	Female 1988
Yes	29	31	41	40	13	24	29
No	70	68	57	60	86	76	69
n.a.	1	1	2	-	2	-	2
Base: all working in general practice who do no other work	*600*	*81*	*98*	*83*	*104*	*102*	*132*

work, illustrated by the fact that 40 per cent of the 1988 men and just under 30 per cent of the 1988 women without outside work would have liked some. Those without children were rather more likely to have wanted additional work than those with children, probably reflecting the age of those who wanted extra work. Only just over 10 per cent of the 1981 women who had no outside work wanted any, and it is likely from their comments that if the 1981 women had wanted other work, they had already got it.

Looking in more detail at the present jobs of these doctors currently without outside work, one third of those working as full-time GP principals, but only around 20 per cent of those working part-time in general practice, wanted additional work. However, over one third of those on the retainer scheme who did no additional work at present would have liked some, probably reflecting the common complaint that the retainer scheme does not offer enough sessions for women.

The most popular option, perhaps not surprisingly, considering what most GPs tended to do if they had additional jobs, was work as a clinical assistant. Again, this was sought more by the younger doctors than by the 1981 cohort. Nearly half the 1985 and 1988 men and well over half the 1985 and 1988 women who wanted work outside general practice said they would like to be clinical assistants, compared with around one fifth of the men and women in the 1981 cohort.

Over 10 per cent of the GPs without outside work wanted to work as SHOs, with fairly equal proportions of men and women but rather more younger doctors, while 3 per cent wanted to work as registrars. Otherwise, 16 per cent of the women, but very few men, wanted work in community health as SCMOs or CMOs, while 8 per cent of both sexes wanted some work in occupational health.

Over 10 per cent wanted some work outside medicine, with some kind of business or commercial enterprise the favourite for the men, while others wanted to work in medical journalism, academic medicine, or the cultural field.

In terms of medical specialty, the choice was as wide as that found among those actually working outside general practice, (see Table 5.14), but the distribution had some interesting differences. Although 20 per cent wanted to work in general medicine or one of the medical specialties, a similar proportion to those who already had jobs outside general practice, it was interesting to see that 10 per cent wanted to work in paediatrics, compared with 1 per cent who actually had found work in paediatrics. Other specialties appeared more attainable, with 10 per cent wanting to work in obstetrics and gynaecology and 10 per cent in A and E. 6 per cent wanted to work in dermatology, 5 per cent in surgery, 4 per cent in psychiatry, 2 per cent each in geriatrics, anaesthetics, radiotherapy and radiology. Community health attracted 10 per cent of the aspiring additional workers, compared with the 17 per cent of those with other jobs already, and occupational health attracted 9 per cent, compared with 13 per cent of those with other jobs.

5 per cent of those who wanted additional work – mainly men from the 1981 cohort – said that anything would do.

Nearly 90 per cent of those who wanted additional work said that they wanted only one job, and most of them wanted to spend between four and five hours a week on their outside work. However, there was an interesting exception, in that the 1981 women who wanted additional work wanted to spend much more time on average than the others – ten hours a week was the median time desired. There were indications that some of these women were looking for alternatives to general practice rather than additional work. In some cases, this appeared to be because they were tired of general practice, particularly if they had been working full-time, while, in other cases, it appeared that they had only gone into general practice because it was the easiest option to combine with bringing up small children, but now they were thinking of broadening their horizons. The main aim for some of them was to get out of medicine. A 1981 woman explained her reasons:

> The hours are too long in general practice. I have lost my enthusiasm and am burnt out. I have the opportunity of being a company director and a farmer, the first within one year and the second in five years. I wish to be normal again and have a normal life. I wish to see my children. I wish to cook them their meals, help them with their homework, bath them and tell them bed-time stories...

Another woman from the same year had similar feelings about general practice:

> I would like to spend more time at home doing normal family things I was always good at – dressmaking, painting, talking to the children, gardening. "Full-time" general practice is *much more* than "full-time" anything else. The reason I opted for full-time general practice is because, in this area at least, there are very few part-time partners who are happy with their lot, because they have inadequate pay pro rata, they

are not treated as partners in decision-making and they are expected to do family planning and smears and *not* full family medicine...

But the main reason the doctors who were currently not working outside general practice wanted additional work was to add variety and to broaden their interests, exactly the same reasons given by the GPs who had already taken on other work. The younger doctors were more likely to mention this than the older ones, and over two-thirds of the 1988 men and just under two-thirds of the 1988 women who wanted additional work said they were looking for more variety in their work. Nearly 40 per cent of the 1988 women said they wanted to diversify into hospital medicine, sometimes to enhance their work in general practice, like this woman - 'I would like to develop my interest in paediatrics. It would increase my job satisfaction, and my greater expertise would benefit the practice...' In other cases, there was evidence of a more deep-seated dissatisfaction with general practice, as this 1988 woman indicated - 'I have an interest in obs. and gynae. The hospital environment is attractive and a change from the solitary life of general practice...'

There were fears about the impact of the new GP contract which were making GPs look around for alternatives, some of them outside medicine, like this 1981 man: 'I would like to do anything except medicine. I feel that the NHS changes and the contract make general practice extremely unattractive. I could be earning as much, with less stress, outside medicine...'

There were certainly many indications of dissatisfaction with general practice, combined with fears of what the future would bring, which were making some doctors look around for potential alternatives which they could build up into a full-time career. Some of the 1981 men and women showed clear signs of disillusionment and some of the women, like those quoted above, were tired of the demands on their personal lives caused by the pressures of general practice and the on-call work. This factor, as we shall see, permeated many of their replies to other questions.

Doctors not working in general practice

In Chapter 2, we looked at the present status of all the respondents to the survey, summarising their present employment status in Table 2.20 and giving more detailed information in Table 2.21. In this section, we look in more detail at those who were not working in general practice at the time of the survey. There were 204 doctors in this category - 16 per cent of the total 1263 respondents. 143 of them working, but not in general practice, and the remaining 61 were not working at the time of the survey.

Table 5.18 shows the present status of the 204 doctors who were not currently working in general practice. Of these, 143 (representing 70 per cent of the total: 88 per cent of the men and 63 per cent of the women) were working, but not in general practice. Of the remainder, 26 doctors (18 per cent of the women) were on maternity leave, 24 doctors (3 per cent of the men and 15 per cent of the women) were not working at present for some other reason, 10 doctors (8 per

Table 5.18 Status of doctors not working in general practice at present

column percentages

	Total	Male			Female		
		1981	1985	1988	1981	1985	1988
Maternity leave	13	-	-	-	9	24	24
Not working	12	-	-	9	21	16	5
Unemployed	5	6	6	13	3	4	3
Other (full time student)	*	-	-	-	-	-	3
Working: not in GP	70	94	94	78	67	55	66
Base: all not working in general practice at present	*204*	*18*	*18*	*23*	*58*	*49*	*38*

cent of the men and 3 per cent of the women) described themselves as unemployed and one woman was a full-time student.

We gave details in Chapter 2 of the present jobs of those who were working but not in general practice. The vast majority (134) of the 143 doctors in this category were working in medicine, and only 9 had left medicine, although most of these were in medically-related occupations. Rather over half of those working in medicine were in hospital medicine, in a wide variety of specialties (although we noted that one quarter were in a psychiatric specialty), just over a quarter were in public health, while around 10 per cent were in medical posts overseas and around 10 per cent were in occupational health or other medical jobs.

Most of the doctors working outside general practice had only one job (see Table 5.4). In order to give a comparison with Tables 5.10 and 5.11, which showed whether and how many additional jobs were held by those working in general practice, we found that, of the 134 doctors who were working in medicine outside general practice, 122 had one job only, 11 had two and one doctor had three jobs altogether. Eight of the nine doctors not working in medicine had one job only.

We asked all these doctors, whether they were working or not, a series of questions about their present status, since we wanted to elicit their reasons for not working in general practice at present and to see whether this was a temporary or permanent phenomenon.

It can be seen from Table 5.19 that the most important reason for doctors not working in general practice was the non-availability of suitable GP posts. This was true for both men and women, and, perhaps surprisingly, was a more important reason for women than maternity leave or having young children. It was mentioned by 22 per cent of the women answering this question, compared with 17 per cent who mentioned maternity leave and 19 per cent who mentioned young children. Nearly one third of the men answering this question mentioned this as the main reason for not working in general practice at the moment, and

Table 5.19   Main reasons for doctors not working in general practice at present

column percentages

	Total	Male			Female		
		1981	1985	1988	1981	1985	1988
Non availability of suitable GP posts	25	17	22	48	21	22	24
Became interested in another specialty	16	17	22	17	19	14	11
Young children	14	-	-	-	29	18	5
Maternity leave	12	-	-	-	9	22	21
Present work more more interesting	12	44	17	9	10	4	8
Abroad/just returned from abroad	10	-	22	9	5	4	24
GP work not interesting	8	28	-	17	3	4	8
Moved around due to spouse's job	8	-	-	-	7	16	11
Not prepared to do on-call/hours	8	11	6	-	12	4	11
Probs with GP post	6	-	17	9	3	10	3
Financial reasons	3	6	11	9	-	2	3
Politics/paperwork new contract	3	6	-	-	5	4	3
Health reasons	2	-	6	-	3	-	5
Discrim. v. women re principal posts	1	-	-	-	2	2	3
Difficult to get GP post if single	*	-	6	-	-	-	-
Dislike sick people	*	6	-	-	-	-	-
Racial discrimination	*	6	-	-	-	-	-
Armed services	*	6	-	-	-	-	-
Base: all not working in general practice at present	*204*	*18*	*18*	*23*	*58*	*49*	*38*

indeed nearly half the 1988 men not working in general practice gave it as their reason. Although the base was very small, there were definite indications that the younger men were finding it more difficult than their older counterparts to get full-time partnerships in general practice.

There appeared to be some difference in what the men and the women were looking for in terms of 'suitable' jobs in general practice, with indications that men were looking for permanent full-time partnerships, while women were more likely to be looking for part-time principal posts. Qualifiers from the Indian sub-continent accounted for over one in ten of the men who were not working in general practice, and the overwhelming reason they gave was the difficulty they had experienced in finding suitable posts in general practice, which was very different from the reasons given by UK male qualifiers. One such Indian qualifier who had gained his vocational training certificate in 1981 gave his reasons for not working in general practice:

> After completing my training I applied for more than 500 posts. I got interviews from three to four places where the job was as a salaried partner, full of exploitation and no future. I waited for two years, while earning my bread and butter from the deputising service. I got a salaried partnership in Cardiff where I worked day and night as a donkey, and the reward was very little. I worked in another practice in the Midlands, where the same story was repeated. Therefore I decided to leave the country...

But not all the women were looking for part-time posts. There was evidence that women were also finding it difficult to find full-time principal jobs, as a 1988 woman explained: 'I can't get a full-time job with equal rights with the male partners. I was fed up with being asked about maternity leave at interviews...' She was 28 and single and was now a senior registrar. She did not intend to return to general practice...'unless anti-female attitudes change...'

Women on maternity leave generally gave this as their main reason for not working, although sometimes their stories were much more complicated. A 28-year-old woman on maternity leave was married to a surgical registrar and described her problems in finding suitable work which could fit in with having a baby and a geographically mobile husband in a competitive specialty. Her problems were by no means unique:

> My husband is pursuing a career in general surgery and is on short-term two-year contracts at present. It's difficult as we cannot therefore commit ourselves to one area for any significant length of time for me to be considered to join a partnership. We therefore decided to start our family early for me to "keep my hand in", either by doing the retainer scheme or locums or an assistant post, until he is a consultant and our children are older when I can give more time to my career. (That's the theory!)...

It was not uncommon for women doctors to give more than one reason for not working in general practice, and it was clear that being married to a hospital doctor was an inhibiting factor for women who wanted partnerships in general practice, whether full-time or part-time, as another 1988 woman, now working as a CMO, pointed out: 'My husband is a registrar in cardiology. This necessitates frequent moves around the country. Therefore when applying for practices, the first question they ask is when am I likely to move again, and the second is when am I going to have children. These were the only two questions asked at one particular interview for a job as a part-time principal...'

There was no doubt that some doctors had settled for another specialty in which they had become more interested, and that there was little chance of their returning to general practice. This positive decision to change direction was rather more evident among men than among women.

Around 10 per cent of the doctors working outside general practice were abroad or had just returned from abroad. Nearly a quarter of the 1988 women fell into this category.

Nearly 10 per cent of the women said that they were tired of the on-call duties and the hours involved in general practice, while 15 per cent of the men said they had found general practice uninteresting. Some of these had found other specialties more to their liking. It appeared that fears about the bureaucratic demands of the new contract had made some doctors decide to leave general practice, while others cited financial reasons, health reasons, a dislike of sick people, racial and sexual discrimination and other personal difficulties.

We were particularly interested in whether finding suitable *part-time* posts had affected the doctors' decision not to work in general practice. 32 per cent of the women and 10 per cent of the men said that it had. (This represented only 6 men so that no conclusions can be drawn from their experience.) Rather over one third of the 1981 and 1985 women not currently working in general practice had been affected by a lack of suitable part-time posts, compared with just over a quarter of the 1988 women, who were, as we have seen, less likely to have children.

The overwhelming reason given by the women who had found difficulty in finding suitable part-time work in general practice was that no suitable posts were available locally. Some of the doctors had tried the retainer scheme, but found it too restrictive or too boring, like this 1981 woman: 'I considered the retainer scheme, but having been refused by three local practices, I changed my mind because my motivation to do such trivial work in general practice, rather than the substantial long-term commitment I feel necessary for patient and job satisfaction, did not stand up to the humiliating process...'

The constant moves necessitated by hospital doctor husbands came up time and again in the questionnaires, not least in answer to this question where the difficulty in making contacts in new areas arose, as with a 1985 woman who had one child and was pregnant: 'I found it very difficult to organise either the retainer scheme or one or two sessions in a new area. No-one seemed to know how to find a position...'

The problems seemed to be compounded for overseas women qualifiers, as an Indian doctor, with a number of postgraduate qualifications, pointed out: 'I have made a reasonably above average number of applications, but the response has been disappointingly poor. It didn't take long for me to realise that a female, foreign and forty-plus doctor is not the best candidate around for most practices...'

Two women had had difficulties in getting their practices to allow part-time work after they had had babies, while other women were worried about taking on part-time work for fear of being exploited.

Returning to general practice

To what extent were those not working in general practice lost to it? There were certainly indications that the women were more likely to have left general practice for reasons which were more temporary than those expressed by the men.

Table 5.20   Whether doctors working outside general practice intended to return to it

column percentages

	Total	Male			Female		
		1981	1985	1988	1981	1985	1988
Yes	28	6	17	48	16	31	50
Possibly	29	17	33	13	29	35	34
No	28	67	33	30	33	20	11
Don't know	15	11	17	9	22	14	5
Base: all not working in general practice at present	*204*	*18*	*18*	*23*	*58*	*49*	*38*

Just under one third of the women and a quarter of the men were definitely intending to return to general practice, while a further third of the women and one fifth of the men considered that they might possibly return. Table 5.20 indicates that the proportion of definite returners was considerably higher among the 1988 cohorts of both sexes, probably because they were more likely to have been working outside general practice through being abroad or because they had not yet attained the partnership they were looking for. It should be noted that over 40 per cent of the men and a quarter of the women said that they did not intend to return to general practice, and that the relative proportions were higher for the 1981 cohorts of men and women. Over two-thirds of the 1981 men said they did not intend to leave their present specialty.

The extent to which women intended to return to general practice was clearly affected by their reasons for leaving. For example, 19 of the 26 women on maternity leave said that they definitely intended to return to general practice at the end of their maternity leave, and a further four of them said they intended to return as soon as they could find suitable part-time work. Overall, of the 90 women who said that they intended to return to work in general practice, nearly half said they would do so when they found suitable part-time work, one fifth said they would return after maternity leave, one in seven said they would return when their child or children started school, and the same proportion said they would do so when they returned home from abroad. Just under 10 per cent said they would return to general practice when they could find suitable full-time work. A handful said they would return if they decided to change specialty or before going abroad.

Among the 27 men who said that they intended to return to general practice, more than half said they would do so if they could find suitable full-time work, while just over one fifth said they would return if they could find suitable part-time work. One in six said they would return when they came back from overseas, and a handful mentioned returning if they changed specialty or if they decided to leave the armed services. Eight of the 27 were qualifiers from the Indian sub-continent, and all of them said they would return if they could find suitable work, either full-time or part-time, in general practice.

We asked the doctors who thought they would or might return to general practice in what capacity they intended to return. Two-thirds of the men said they wanted to return as full-time GP principals, compared with only 13 per cent of the women. 56 per cent of the women said they wished to return as a part-time GP principal or a 20-hour a week principal, which, in effect, was part-time under the new contract. A further 11 per cent wanted to return as a part-time GP assistant, and 7 per cent wanted to return on the retainer scheme. However, around 10 per cent of both sexes did not know in what capacity they wanted to return to general practice, and a handful said they would take anything that was available or would return as locums.

Part-time working in medicine is often undertaken by women who wish to return to full-time work when their children are older or their domestic commitments are fewer. We asked the 68 women and 6 men who said they intended to return to general practice in a part-time capacity whether they intended to return to full-time work in general practice at a later stage. It was perhaps surprising that only just over a quarter of the women said that they did.

But there were 58 doctors (25 men and 33 women) who definitely did not wish to return to general practice. Around half of them of both sexes said that this was because they preferred the specialty or job they were working in at present, while over 10 per cent intended to pursue a career in hospital medicine. A quarter of the women and one in six of the men said that they did not like general practice, while around a fifth of the women said they had been out of general practice for too long to find it easy to get back into. A handful of other reasons were given including racial discrimination, a feeling of being unsuited to medicine in general and an inability to find suitable work in general practice, mainly because of the new contract.

There was little doubt that the question of 'suitable' jobs dominated the minds of many women doctors, including those who did not know whether they would return to general practice. Well over half of these doctors who were unsure of whether they would return or not said that it would depend on the number of hours required or the amount of time they would have to spend on-call or the availability of part-time posts. Others were holding their options open and said it would depend on how much they enjoyed their present jobs in another field or specialty. Well over a third of the women who were not certain about whether they would return to general practice said that much depended on their domestic circumstances and their husbands' jobs, and these factors, as we shall see, were of overwhelming importance in the career decisions of women doctors.

6 Part-time working in general practice

One of the main aims of this study was to establish the extent to which the doctors gaining their GP vocational training certificates were working or had ever worked full-time or part-time in general practice. We were asked to distinguish in particular between part-time working as principals and as assistants in general practice.

Since we wished to make the questionnaire as simple as possible, we asked a general question asking doctors whether they had *ever* worked part-time or less than full-time in general practice *either in the past or at present*. We asked respondents to include 20 hour a week principal posts as part-time for the purpose of this analysis. In addition, although we wished to concentrate on part-time principals and assistants, we knew that we would pick up some other types of part-time working. In general, we were able to slot the answers of those who had worked as part-time locums or on the retainer scheme into the categories of part-time principal and assistant respectively.

Table 6.1   Whether doctors had ever worked part-time in general practice, either in the past or at present

| | | | | | | *column percentages* |
| | Total | Male | | | Female | | |
		1981	1985	1988	1981	1985	1988
Yes	40	8	7	12	69	68	60
No	60	92	93	88	31	32	40
Base: all respondents	*1263*	*204*	*195*	*179*	*221*	*218*	*246*

Table 6.1 shows clearly that part-time working in general practice is largely a female occupation. We found that 500 doctors (40 per cent of the total) said that they had worked part-time in general practice, of whom 448 were women, representing 90 per cent of those who had ever worked part-time.

The first part of this chapter is mainly concerned with the doctors who had ever held a part-time principal or part-time assistant post in general practice. Overall, 65 per cent of the women respondents and 9 per cent of the men said that they had ever held such a post. The 1988 women were rather less likely to have held a part-time post in general practice than the 1981 or 1985 women; nevertheless, as many as 60 per cent of these recently qualified women GPs had done so. The 1988 men were a little more likely to have worked part-time in general practice than the earlier male cohorts, mainly because more of them had done part-time GP locum work than the older men.

We wanted to distinguish between those who were currently working part-time in general practice, those who had worked part-time in the past but were no longer doing so, and those who had *ever* worked part-time, ie a combination of the past and present part-time workers. We also wanted to distinguish between those who were working or had worked as part-time principals only, those who were working or had worked as part-time assistants only, and those who had done both.

Table 6.2   Type of part-time GP post held in past or at present by doctors

							column percentages
	Total		Male			Female	
		1981	1985	1988	1981	1985	1988
(i) Currently:							
PT GP principal (inc 20 hr a wk)	17	2	2	2	30	34	24
PT GP assistant	3	-	-	1	5	4	6
Total	20	2	2	3	35	38	30
(ii) In past but not now:							
PT GP princ. only (inc 20 hr a wk)	7	2	2	4	15	8	9
PT GP asst. only	9	3	2	4	13	17	15
PT both posts	4	*	2	1	5	6	6
Total	20	6	5	9	34	30	30
(iii) Ever had a PT post (inc. current and past):							
PT GP princ. only (inc 20 hr a wk)	24	4	4	7	45	41	33
PT GP asst. only	12	3	2	4	19	21	21
PT both posts	4	*	2	1	5	6	6
Total	40	8	7	12	69	68	60
Base: all respondents	*1263*	*204*	*195*	*179*	*221*	*218*	*246*

In Table 6.2, it can be seen that the doctors who had ever worked part-time divided almost exactly into those who were currently working part-time and those who had worked part-time only in the past. 20 per cent of the total respondents were currently working part-time in general practice, and 20 per cent had done so only in the past. There were differences between the sexes: 34 per cent of the women doctors were currently working part-time, compared with 2 per cent of the men, and 31 per cent of the women and 7 per cent of the men had worked part-time in the past.

Table 6.2 (i) confirms the findings of Table 2.22, which showed that the proportion of 1988 women currently working part-time in general practice was slightly less than those of the earlier two cohorts of women. The overwhelming majority of women currently working part-time in general practice were working as part-time principals rather than as part-time assistants.

Table 6.2 (ii) shows that among those who had worked part-time in the past only, the picture was rather different. Rather more women had worked as part-time assistants only than as part-time principals only, and around 6 per cent of women respondents had worked in both capacities.

Table 6.1 gave the broad breakdown of those who had *ever* worked part-time in general practice. Table 6.2 (iii) gives a more detailed analysis. It can be seen that 45 per cent of the 1981 women had held a part-time principal post only, compared with 41 per cent of the 1985 women and 33 per cent of the 1988 women. Around one fifth of the women respondents from each cohort had held a part-time assistant post only, while around 6 per cent had held both types of post. The material is presented in this way so that it can clearly be seen what proportions of doctors held which types of post, and so that the categories can be counted and added up separately to give the total number of doctors involved.

Table 6.3   **Whether doctors had ever held part-time GP principal or part-time GP assistant posts**

						column percentages
	Total		Male			Female
		1981	1985	1988	1981	1985	1988
Ever held PT GP princ. post	27	5	6	7	50	47	39
Ever held PT GP asst. post	16	4	3	5	24	27	27
Of which:							
Ever held both	4	*	2	1	5	6	6
Base: all respondents	*1263*	*204*	*195*	*179*	*221*	*218*	*246*

However, the material is presented in a rather different way in Table 6.3, so that an overall assessment can be made of the proportion of doctors who had ever held a part-time GP principal post (at all) and the proportion who had ever held a part-time GP assistant post (at all). It can be seen that around 50 per cent of the 1981 and 1985 women had ever had a part-time GP principal post, compared with just under 40 per cent of the 1988 women. Around a quarter of women in all three cohorts had ever had a part-time GP assistant post. (The table shows the proportion of those who had held *both* types of post within these proportions.)

The comparable proportions for men were in single figures, confirming that part-time working in general practice is largely confined to women.

The main reasons for this are not hard to find. 52 per cent of the women with children had ever had a part-time principal post and 33 per cent of them had had a part-time assistant post, compared with 35 per cent and 14 per cent respectively of the women without children. (7 per cent of women with children and 4 per cent of women without children had ever had both types of part-time post.)

Table 6.4   **Whether women working in general practice at present had ever held part-time GP principal or part-time GP assistant posts**

column percentages

	All in GP now	FT GP princ	FT GP locum	20 hr princ	PT GP princ	PT GP asst	PT GP locum
Ever held PT GP principal post	51	22	36	100	100	19	44
Ever held PT GP assistant post	25	10	36	8	10	100	53
Of which:							
Ever held both	6	*	9	8	9	16	13
Base: all women working in GP at present	*540*	*217*	*11*	*95*	*102*	*37*	*32*

But what are the implications of this? Does part-time working help to keep women in general practice? Table 6.4 shows the proportions of women working in general practice and Table 6.5 shows those working outside general practice or not working at present who had ever worked part-time as GP principals or assistants. Table 6.4 indicates that rather more than half the women working in general practice at present had ever had a part-time principal post, while Table 6.5 shows that this was true of only just over a fifth of those outside general practice. Indeed, only just over 10 per cent of the women working in medicine outside general practice had ever worked part-time as a GP principal. The women on maternity leave were very similar to those working in general practice, but, of course, since most of them intended to return almost immediately to general practice, this was not particularly surprising.

Just over one fifth of the full-time women principals had ever held part-time principal posts. It is probable that the availability of such part-time posts had helped to keep these women in general practice, and indeed had enabled them to return to full-time principal posts.

However, it is difficult to deduce much about the effect of part-time GP assistant posts from these tables. They had been held disproportionately by women who were currently working as full-time or part-time GP locums and by those who were still working as part-time assistants. And, although the bases

Table 6.5   Whether women *not* working in general practice at present had ever held part-time GP principal or part-time GP assistant posts

Column percentages

	All not in GP	In medicine not GP	Non-medical jobs	Maternity leave	Not working	Un-employed
Ever held PT GP principal post	22	11	50	54	27	17
Ever held PT GP assistant post	29	25	0	38	36	33
Of which ever held both	4	2	50	12	5	0
Base: all women outside GP at present	*145*	*89*	*2*	*26*	*22*	*6*

were small, they had been held disproportionately by women outside general practice, including those who were on maternity leave or not working for some other reason.

It is clear from these tables that both full-time and part-time GP women principals were less likely to have ever held a part-time GP assistant post than other women. What is not clear from the tables is *why* this was so. It is possible that the women principals had never had to have a GP assistant post for domestic reasons. It is possible that they might take such posts in future. It is also possible that holding a part-time assistant post is unlikely to be looked on as a positive achievement by those seeking partners, and that women who wanted to work as GP principals, whether full-time or part-time, had avoided part-time assistant jobs if they could.

But in order to examine the attitudes of doctors to part-time GP assistant posts as well as to part-time GP principal posts, we first had to explore further the experience of the doctors who had worked part-time in general practice.

Reasons for seeking part-time posts in general practice

We asked all the doctors who had ever worked part-time why they had sought a part-time principal or part-time assistant post, or indeed, both types of post. The reasons given for seeking part-time principal and assistant posts were remarkably similar, with the overwhelming reason given being a wish for a job to fit in with family or domestic commitments. Over 70 per cent of the women who had ever had a part-time principal post and two-thirds of those who had ever had a part-time assistant post cited this reason, compared with 9 per cent of the men who had worked as part-time principals and none of the men who had worked as part-time GP assistants.

Some of the women responded sharply to this question, like this 1981 woman: 'Because I am a female human being and it falls to me to have babies. Because I wish to combine work and family. Unfortunately my husband is unable to conceive and carry a pregnancy to term. Do the government realise this?'

Some women indicated why they had only considered part-time work as principals, like this 1988 woman: 'It was natural progress up the career ladder to become a principal. I was unable to find totally suitable childcare outside school hours. My husband has a demanding out-of-hours schedule...'

Why then did women become part-time GP assistants? In many cases it appeared that it was the only possible option, as this 1988 woman explained: 'My husband and I wanted to job-share, but opportunities were non-existent. Job-sharing is not recognised in our area. My husband took a single-handed practice and made me his assistant...'

There were clear differences between the women with and without children. Nearly 90 per cent of the women with children who took part-time principal posts said that it was to fit in with domestic commitments compared with one third of those without children. The comparable proportions for women taking part-time assistant posts were nearly 80 per cent of those with children and 16 per cent of those without.

What were the other reasons for taking part-time posts in general practice? Around one third of the men and nearly a quarter of the women without children said they had taken a part-time principal post because they had been unable to get a full-time principal post. A 1988 woman explained why she had taken a 20-hour a week post: 'One was available in a practice with a "near retirement" senior partner, and it was better than doing locums. There were no "full-time" vacancy practices who replied to my 25 applications...'

Sometimes the factors were rather more complicated, as this 1988 woman reported: 'I was planning a family and wanting time to do other things – hobbies – even looking for a different career in the future. There was a lack of fair pay in a full-time post until parity was reached, by which time I would have hoped to become part-time anyway to look after children...'

The new contract was clearly beginning to bite at the time of the survey, and a 1988 woman felt adversely affected: 'A part-time partnership was offered to me before the details of the White Paper were finalised. It has now been put "on hold" by the practice due to financial concerns – and by myself. I am unwilling to work 26 hours over five days with a small baby at home...'

Similar proportions of men and women gave the lack of full-time posts in general practice as a reason for taking part-time assistant posts: nearly 40 per cent of the men and 30 per cent of the women without children who had worked as part-time assistants said they had had to take such a post because they could not get a full-time post in general practice. They were by no means confining their sights to GP assistant posts.

Over a quarter of the men working part-time either as principals or assistants said they had done so as locums while trying to get another job. Less than 10 per cent of the women came into this category, but they tended to be 1988 women or without children.

Men were more likely than women to say that they had sought a part-time principal or assistant post so that they could combine general practice with another specialty. Around one sixth of the men in both categories mentioned this. Some of these doctors were working in academic general practice, and others were in a hospital specialty, while yet others were working mainly in occupational health but did some general practice to keep in touch. Women often combined some general practice with community health, but were clearly looking to the future and a return to more work in general practice.

Among both men and women who had taken part-time principal posts, there were those who said they had wanted more time for other interests, both inside and outside medicine. There was a constant undercurrent in these questionnaires of doctors commenting plaintively on the quality of their lives, which they thought had been adversely affected by the demands of medicine as a career.

Hours or sessions spent in part-time general practice posts

We wanted to get some measure of the amount of time doctors spent in part-time posts in general practice. Tables 6.6 and 6.7 give details of the time spent per week by the doctors in part-time GP principal and assistant posts. We asked them to indicate the time they spent *either* in hours *or* sessions. For the purposes of these tables, we did not distinguish between those who were currently working part-time and those who had worked part-time in the past, since there was no discernible difference. We give the figures for men as well as women, to maintain continuity in the presentation of the tables, although, of course, the bases for the men are very small.

Table 6.6 shows that the doctors who were working or had worked as part-time principals spent an average of 24 hours *or* 5.7 sessions a week in these posts. The averages were consistent for all three cohorts of women. It was particularly interesting that so few doctors – only 5 per cent of those who had ever worked as part-time GP principals – said they worked fewer than 20 hours or 5 sessions a week. It can be seen that the majority said they worked more than 21 hours or more than 6 sessions a week, although the most common practice as a part-time principal was 20 hours or 5 sessions. However, around 10 per cent said they worked more than 30 hours a week in their part-time principal posts.

There were some indications that those currently working as part-time GP principals spent or had spent longer hours in their posts than those currently working as 20-hour a week principals – an average of 25.8 hours or 6 sessions compared with 22.9 hours or 5.4 sessions.

The relatively high proportion of men who said that they worked variable hours was mainly due to the fact that most of the men who had worked as part-time principals had done so as locums.

Table 6.6   **Hours or sessions a week spent by doctors in part-time GP principal posts**

column percentages

	Total	Male 1981	1985	1988	Female 1981	1985	1988
Hours							
1 - 19	2	0	0	0	4	2	3
20	24	20	55	15	26	23	19
21 - 24	12	10	0	0	14	17	8
25 - 29	14	10	0	8	12	17	15
30 plus	9	0	9	0	13	9	4
Variable	5	20	36	31	2	3	5
Mean no of hours (excl.variable)	*24*	*22.5*	*21.4*	*21.7*	*24.2*	*24.4*	*23.6*
OR							
Sessions							
1 - 4	3	10	0	10	3	1	3
5	13	0	0	23	9	11	20
6	9	20	0	0	6	11	11
7 - 9	9	10	0	8	7	6	10
10 plus	1	0	0	8	1	0	0
Variable	*	0	0	0	3	0	1
Mean no of sessions (excl.variable)	*5.7*	*5.8*	*0*	*5.8*	*5.9*	*5.7*	*5.7*
Base: all who have ever had PT GP principal post	*344*	*10*	*11*	*13*	*110*	*104*	*96*

Table 6.7 underlines the difference between those working as part-time GP principals and those working as part-time GP assistants. Whereas only 3 per cent of doctors who had worked part-time as principals worked between 1 and 4 sessions a week, this was true of 51 per cent of those who had worked as part-time assistants. The mean number of hours worked as a part-time assistant was 14.6 and the mean number of sessions was 3, which was just over half the number of hours and sessions worked by the part-time principals.

Although the most common time spent working by part-time GP assistants was a couple of sessions a week, this was largely accounted for by women on the GP retainer scheme. Those currently on the scheme accounted for over a quarter of those who had ever worked as part-time GP assistants (39 doctors), and it was interesting to compare their hours and sessions with other GPs. For example, women currently on the retainer scheme averaged 8 hours or 1.6

Table 6.7   **Hours or sessions spent by doctors in part-time GP assistant posts**

column percentages

	Total	Male 1981	Male 1985	Male 1988	Female 1981	Female 1985	Female 1988
Hours							
1 - 9	11	0	0	33	9	15	7
10 - 19	5	13	0	0	6	6	2
20	7	25	0	0	9	7	3
21 - 29	3	0	17	0	0	0	5
30 plus	3	0	0	11	2	2	3
Variable	5	13	33	22	0	3	3
Mean no of hours (excl. variable)	*14.6*	*17.3*	*24.0*	*11.0*	*14.3*	*12.9*	*17.1*
OR							
Sessions							
1 - 4	51	25	33	0	59	43	63
5	9	13	17	11	2	15	7
6	3	13	0	11	0	3	2
7 - 9	5	0	0	11	8	4	4
Variable	4	0	0	0	6	2	4
Mean no of sessions (excl. variable)	*3.0*	*4.3*	*3.0*	*6.3*	*2.6*	*3.1*	*2.8*
Base: all who have ever had PT GP assistant post	*198*	*8*	*6*	*9*	*54*	*60*	*61*

sessions a week as GP assistants, compared with those who were currently working as full-time principals (35 doctors), who had averaged 19 hours or 4.7 sessions in their part-time GP assistant posts. Even those who were currently working as part-time GP assistants (36) averaged 11.3 hours or 3.2 sessions a week.

Range of general practice work covered in part-time posts

The extent to which those working part-time in general practice covered the full range of general practice work and the extent to which they did a restricted range of work, for example, child development, well-woman, family planning, was of interest to the Department of Health, who also wanted more information about the preferences of doctors working part-time as far as the range of work was concerned.

There were differences between the range of work covered by those working as part-time principals and those working as part-time assistants. Of the 344 doctors who had ever held a part-time GP principal post, 98 per cent had covered the full range of work, while of the 198 doctors who had ever held a part-time GP assistant post, 85 per cent had covered the full range of work.

When those who had worked as part-time principals were asked what they personally preferred in a part-time principal post, 96 per cent expressed a preference for the full range of work. Among those who had worked as part-time assistants, 87 per cent said that they preferred the full range of work, with 89 per cent of the women expressing this preference.

There was really no doubt in the minds of the vast majority of doctors, whether they had worked part-time as principals or as assistants, that the full range of work was eminently preferable to a restricted range. More than half of them said that the full range offered more variety, interest and enjoyment, as this 1988 woman said: 'I am trained to do the full range of work and would find a restricted range frustrating and demoralising...'

It was certainly true that most doctors thought that a restricted range would become very boring - 'I enjoy using all my skills as a doctor, and get fed up with women's bottoms alone...' was the comment of a 1985 man – and 'variety is the spice of life...' was the view of an 1988 woman. Nearly a third of the doctors thought that the full range of work helped to maintain their skills and breadth of experience, a view expressed more by the younger women than the 1981 women - 'Certainly with only two sessions you need to keep your hand in with everything...'

It was also thought important for doctors to keep up-to-date with developments in all aspects of GP work, and over 10 per cent said that they thought the full range was essential since they wished to contribute as much as possible to the practice and to provide complete care to the patients - 'Part-time should not imply part service nor part commitment...'

The limited number of doctors who did not want the full range of general practice work in their part-time posts usually said they wanted less commitment or responsibility than the full range entailed, while a handful of doctors wanted to specialise in a particular type of work. A couple of doctors – both men – said they had no preferences, but took whatever was available.

Effects of working part-time on the careers of doctors

The question of whether part-time or less than full-time working has an adverse effect on the careers of doctors in general, and of women doctors in particular, is of considerable importance at a time when 50 per cent of medical qualifiers are women. If the majority of women doctors are going to work part-time at least at some time in their careers, and this part-time working has an adverse effect on their career prospects, there is clearly a considerable danger not only that women are not being offered equal opportunities with men but also that the best use is not being made of the available medical manpower.

How did the doctors who had worked part-time or less than full-time see the situation? Overall, 26 per cent of the 500 doctors who had worked part-time thought that this part-time working had had an adverse effect on their careers: 13 per cent of the men and 27 per cent of the women. Among the women, the proportions ranged from 31 per cent of the 1981 cohort to 26 per cent of the 1985 cohort and 24 per cent of the 1988 cohort. 30 per cent of women with children who had worked part-time thought it had had an adverse effect, compared with only 21 per cent of those without children.

There was some difference between those who had worked part-time as a GP principal and those who had worked part-time as a GP assistant. One quarter of the women who had had a part-time principal post thought it had had an adverse effect, compared with one third of those who had had part-time assistant posts. There was little difference between the cohorts among those who had had part-time principal posts, but among those who had had part-time assistant posts, over 40 per cent of the 1981 women thought their careers had suffered because of the part-time working compared with one third of the 1985 women and just over one fifth of the 1988 women.

It did not make any difference whether the women were currently working in these posts or had done so in the past. It was the type of post which was thought to have affected the career prospects rather than the distance from it.

The main reason for concern about the adverse effects of part-time working was that it was said to give doctors less status in the practice. Over a third of the women who thought their careers had been adversely affected were worried about this aspect, a view strongly expressed by a number of them, including this 1988 woman: 'As a full-time principal one tends to have more of a say in the planning of the practice and more respect from staff and patients – ie you're a REAL doctor...'

Women often mentioned that they were treated less well than their full-time counterparts, and referred to being treated as 'an inferior being' and of having less chance of getting the 'political jobs, for example on the LMC...' Some women appeared to have had partnerships which were less than harmonious: 'Women are considered to be a useful appendage if they're part-time. I do not do nights on-call and because of this I am called a variety of rude names by my male partners who consider that I have an easy time...'

The perceived loss of status was also thought to have financial implications, and one in six of the doctors mentioned this as a factor which had led to some acrimonious situations, as this 1985 woman explained: 'I was not treated as a full-time partner so far as the finance of the practice was concerned. They misused me and that is why I separated and established on my own from a zero list...'

Over 10 per cent thought that part-time working impeded the chance of getting full-time work, particularly full-time partnerships: 'Perhaps it won't look impressive on my CV when I'm applying for future posts. Less esteem and credibility are given to part-timers by some people!' A similar proportion of doctors thought that part-time working meant that their careers had progressed more slowly, and others thought their careers had developed in a more piecemeal way because of their part-time working.

A different light was cast on the problem by the doctors who said that the non-availability of both full-time and part-time posts had limited their choice of career. They thought they had been forced into part-time working of a kind which had adversely affected their careers. This was particularly true of those who had been on the retainer scheme or had worked as part-time assistants.

Nearly 10 per cent of those who had worked part-time said that they had lost confidence in their abilities as a result of it, a view eloquently expressed by a 1985 woman:

> My self-confidence has been significantly eroded by part-time work on the retainer scheme. I would prefer 20-25 hours per week, and feel I could give something worthwhile to general practice and still maintain my "mother" role at home. It has been frustrating that my ideal job has been unavailable. The time has not been enough to maintain my skills and thus my confidence in my abilities has suffered...

Other doctors commented that they had found the whole process disillusioning, while other thought it had impeded their chances of working in hospital medicine.

There was no doubt that among those who thought their career prospects had been adversely affected by part-time working there were some angry and disappointed women, and it must be remembered that the majority of those responding to this survey were in their twenties or thirties. If over a quarter of the women GPs who had worked part-time thought their careers had suffered as a result, the role models they were offering young women leaving medical school were not very encouraging. After all, many women go into general practice because it is thought to be the easiest specialty in which to work less than full-time. It appeared that the results did not always live up to expectations.

Advice to doctors contemplating part-time working in general practice

We asked all those who had ever worked part-time what advice they would give to those contemplating working part-time as a GP principal, a GP assistant and on the GP retainer scheme. It was at this point in the questionnaire that the respondents began to come into their own with a plethora of advice.

The two main pieces of advice to doctors contemplating working part-time as a GP principal were each given by one fifth of the respondents: the need to ensure clear-cut partnership agreements or contracts and the need to beware of exploitation and unfair treatment. Some very wary women part-time GP principals were discovered in this survey.

They ranged from one 1988 woman - 'Research your practice timetable and future partners' attitudes thoroughly, particularly regarding holiday and finishing time. Obtain a watertight partnership agreement before starting work...' - to another - 'Do not become a salaried partner. Have a practice centre with a share of the profits proportional to your share of the work. Otherwise you may feel used...'

The question of exploitation was often combined with advice that the doctors should expect to have to work longer hours than they were paid for and should beware of being deprived of the full range of GP work. This 1981 woman had words of advice on a number of topics: '1. Choose your practice carefully. Don't just take the first offer – wait for the right practice. 2. Ensure flexibility of your contract. In years to come you may want to increase your commitment. 3. Do the full range of work. Don't be a token lady to organise the family planning or the smears. 4. Have a good back-up system for home, husband and kids. Disasters will happen and the practice "must go on"...'

However, over 10 per cent of the women said that their advice would be to 'go for it', although often adding little provisos of caution. The 1981 women were more likely than the others to advise that the women should make sure they took full part in partnership decisions. The new contract was thought to be holding out some dismal prospects for women, as this 1981 woman commented: 'One is lucky if one's male partners will allow you to work part-time. Many male GPs now - under the new contract – will not contemplate their female partners doing less than 26 hours a week over five days because of the proposed drop in the basic practice allowance and thus reduced income into the practice. Women will have to become assistants if they wish to work part-time. The result will be low morale. A few women doctors I know are considering resignation...'

Some women doctors counselled caution at every turn, like this pregnant 1988 woman: 'Make sure you are paid adequately for the work you do. Many part-timers receive one-third of the pay for three-quarters of the work. Full-time male partners tend to exploit part-time female partners by giving them little say or power in practice decisions, making them work awkward hours, expecting them to do all the work that involves women patients, especially those with gynaecological or emotional problems. In one practice in which I worked, all the women with a problem "below the waist and above the knee" were sent by male colleagues to the "well woman clinic", which soon became the "ill woman clinic" with no appointments left for well women...'

It was perhaps surprising that only 2 per cent of the respondents advised those contemplating part-time GP principal work to have reliable child-care help at home. These were all 1981 women with children. It appeared that adequate child-care facilities were regarded as so obvious that they did not need to be mentioned. Certainly, most respondents appeared to be much more interested in giving advice on watertight contracts and lack of exploitation by partners than in making sure that everything was looked after on the home front. Even those who mentioned childcare usually added it to other advice, like this 1981 woman:

> Remember the many hours of on-call weekly and check that childcare is available. Work out the costs of all childcare. Remember practice meetings – meeting with accountants, lawyers, health board etc. – tend to take place outside normal part-time hours but within full-time hours, and negotiate a fair recompense...

The advice given to prospective part-time GP assistants was rather less comprehensive, but the two main pieces of advice were again to beware of exploitation and to ensure a clear-cut contract or agreement. A 1988 doctor gave this advice: 'Be very firm about hours and on-call from the start and don't be blackmailed into doing all the extra sessions, holiday cover and sick cover...'

Whereas virtually no-one advised against part-time working as a principal, nearly 10 per cent of respondents advised against it as an assistant, with many of them advising the doctor to get a part-time principal post instead. The lack of status in the practice, the potential restriction of skills, the potential financial exploitation were all mentioned again. There was clear evidence that part-time GP assistant posts were not regarded as being as attractive as part-time GP principal posts, and few doctors had good words to say for them.

The GP retainer scheme has received a mixed press. Women doctors interviewed in *Doctors and their Careers* who had been on it were less than enthusiastic about it, but the Department of Health Working Party's report *Women Doctors and their Careers* (Department of Health, 1991) recommended the retention of the scheme. It has been criticised for being too restrictive in terms of the sessions allowed, poorly publicised, difficult to understand, and providing too little money.

All these views were heard from respondents in this survey who had worked part-time, although less than half of them had any advice to give. Around 10 per cent of respondents thought it was a useful way of keeping in touch with general practice skills. However, many of these and others thought that the scheme as it operated at the moment had a number of drawbacks, like this 1985 woman of 35: 'I am at present on the retainer scheme doing two sessions a week which helps me keep in touch with general practice and is more enjoyable. But financially, if you have to pay a child minder while working, there is little gain. In addition, to complete your seven educational sessions a year is important, but may be difficult. Study leave should be allowed, and certainly financial help towards the cost of these sessions...'

The question of the financial rewards in the retainer scheme exercised a number of respondents who found it uneconomic, like a 1988 woman with two children who was still on the retainer scheme: 'The retainer scheme is poorly managed and little thought about at present. The effect of the new contract on the scheme hasn't been considered yet. Childcare costs and defence fees and the new large education costs make it uneconomical to pursue. If this isn't sorted out then it isn't possible to continue. In the past it has been poorly paid, but manageable even if of low status...'

Another 1988 woman agreed: 'It's a good idea if you have a family, but nobody seems to understand how the system works. The pay of £155 for professional indemnity subscription and a journal is *laughable*. It should be much higher and increased in line with current payments...' (It should be noted that the current annual amount payable under the retainer scheme is £290.)

Around 5 per cent of doctors thought it useful for short periods of time, but a similar proportion thought it should only be contemplated if it was the only viable option. There was dissatisfaction among some doctors who felt restricted by the number of sessions allowed under the scheme, like this 1981 woman: 'Once a week is really not enough in general practice to follow up a lot of the problems that you start off investigating and treating. Lack of feed-back does not help the learning process. You rely on others to send patients back and keep you informed...'

Advantages and disadvantages of part-time GP principal posts

The question of part-time or less than full-time working in general practice as a principal is clearly of fundamental importance to the future of general practice. As the proportion of women in medicine increases, so does the proportion of women in general practice, and indeed there are many indications that general practice has become relatively more popular in recent years among women. It also appears to have replaced community health as a specialty in which part-time work is sought by women. Certainly, younger women interviewed in *Doctors and their Careers* were much less likely than their older counterparts to consider working in community health. It is also probable that there may be relatively fewer jobs in community health in future compared with general practice, as more traditional community health functions are taken into the primary health care team.

The implications for the future structure of general practice are far-reaching, particularly if women are to be fairly represented in practices. There will undoubtedly be a call for more, rather than less, flexible working patterns for women, so that part-time or less than full-time work can be more freely available. But there may well be more calls for more flexible working patterns for men GPs as well, since it is quite possible that men too might like to work less than full-time in general practice. We therefore asked all respondents, whether they had ever worked part-time or not, what were or would be the advantages and disadvantages of working part-time or less than full-time as a GP principal. We concentrated only on GP principal posts because they were regarded as much more important posts. We knew from our piloting of this study that the relative advantages of GP assistant posts related mainly to the fact that they offered a limited commitment in time and responsibility, while the disadvantages were seen to be the lack of status and continuity. Although women with very little available time found them useful, they were not considered a serious option by the vast majority of men or by most women who wished to make a career in general practice.

In addition to asking doctors about the advantages and disadvantages to them of working less than full-time as a GP principal, we also asked them about the advantages and disadvantages to other doctors of working *with* part-time GP principals. We were aware that many doctors, particularly men, might not see many advantages in working less than full-time themselves, but they might have strong views on the advantages and disadvantages of working *with* part-time principals.

Advantages and disadvantages of working as a part-time GP principal

There were some differences in views about the advantages and disadvantages of working as a part-time principal between those who had ever worked part-time in general practice and those who had never done so. There were also minor differences between those who had worked as part-time principals in the past and those who were doing so at present. There were also, not surprisingly, differences between men and women.

Overall, only one fifth of the doctors, 30 per cent of the men and 10 per cent of the women, could see no advantages to themselves of working part-time as a GP principal. Among the 763 doctors who had never worked part-time in general practice, 32 per cent of the men and 16 per cent of the women saw no advantages to themselves, while, among the 500 doctors who *had* worked part-time in general practice, the comparable proportions were 12 per cent of the men and 6 per cent of the women. The 1981 women were rather less likely to see any advantages than the younger women. It was interesting that as many as 5 per cent of the women currently working as part-time principals could see no advantages in doing so.

Nevertheless, it is striking that 70 per cent of the men and 90 per cent of the women *could* see advantages to themselves in working part-time as a GP principal. The main advantage was thought to be that it gave or would give more time for family or domestic commitments. Overall, this view was held by 71 per cent of the women and 25 per cent of the men. It was most firmly held by women with children, of whom 85 per cent saw it as an advantage, compared with 49 per cent of the women without children. It was also overwhelmingly held by the women who were currently working as part-time principals, of whom 83 per cent saw it as an advantage. One such doctor explained her reasons: 'I can have a family and look after my children most of the time. My husband comes home to a clean house with food on the table (most of the time!) I have had time to develop my interest in gardening and the WI and am an active member of our village community, as well as a doctor...'

Another part-time principal from the 1985 cohort described the advantages to her: 'I work four days a week but have a three day "weekend" when I'm not on duty. This enables me to run two homes and look after my two sons, husband and dependent mother while retaining my sanity...'

Women who had not had a part-time post in general practice were relatively less likely to see the advantages to them of working as a part-time principal, but there was no doubt that many of them, while not considering it at the moment, could see the advantages in the future. Others, who were working full-time could see advantages at present, like this 1988 woman: 'It would give me more time for childcare. There would be greater opportunity for extra-curricular interests and also organising life would be easier...'

The men who had not had part-time work in general practice were almost as likely as those who had to think that a part-time principal post would give them more time for family and domestic commitments. It was interesting that around a quarter of the male doctors, almost all of whom were full-time GP principals, thought that working part-time or less than full-time as a principal would be an advantage to them in that they could spend more time with their families. Many of them treasured this as a faint hope, but some would clearly have welcomed the opportunity.

There were other advantages to be seen by the doctors. Around 14 per cent of all respondents thought that part-time principal work gave or would give them more time for leisure interests, a similar proportion mentioned more time for other interests, while 13 per cent said that it had or would have the advantage of being less stressful than full-time principal work. These views were held in more or less equal proportions by both men and women and by those who had ever and those who had never worked part-time in general practice.

It was interesting that 11 per cent of the men, compared with 5 per cent of the women thought that part-time principal work would have the advantage of giving them more time to pursue other medical interests. Again this view was held by equal proportions of men who had had a part-time principal post and those who had not. The strong interest of many men GPs in keeping their hand in or maintaining a medical interest outside general practice was a marked feature of this study. A further 5 per cent of men specifically mentioned that it would give them more time for hospital work.

A wide variety of other advantages in part-time principal posts were named by doctors, and this question generated a lot of imaginative replies. These questions were deliberately kept 'open-ended', so that respondents did not simply tick a series of boxes, but were encouraged to write and think.

Some 5 per cent of women, but fewer men, said that an advantage was less on-call commitment. This factor was mentioned by 10 per cent of the women who were currently working as part-time principals, and was clearly an important factor in the decision to go part-time taken by women faced with the increasing tiredness which was said to come with an increasing work and domestic commitment.

Other doctors mentioned the advantages of having more time for studying, research or teaching. A number of men, but no women, said that it would give them more time for private practice. Some doctors thought it would be a good way of obtaining a full-time post, while others thought it had the advantage of being better than working as a part-time GP assistant or locum in terms of money and status. The flexibility of hours and time were thought to be an advantage both by doctors working part-time and those who had never done so.

Some doctors working outside general practice thought that it would help to keep them in touch with general practice, while a couple of women said that it would be better paid than their present work in hospital medicine. Three doctors said it would enable them to return to general practice, given the limitations of their present state of health.

What were the disadvantages to doctors of part-time or less than full-time working in GP principal posts? The main factor, mentioned by two-thirds of the men and 40 per cent of the women was said to be financial. Money became of increasing importance to the younger doctors, with 70 per cent of the 1988 men and nearly 50 per cent of the 1988 women mentioning it as a potential or actual disadvantage of part-time principal work. There was a striking difference between the women with children and those without, with nearly 60 per cent of the women without children citing less money as a disadvantage, compared with less than 30 per cent of the women with children. The women who were currently working as part-time principals were rather less likely than those who had done so in the past to mention the disadvantage of less money. It appeared either that the advantages of part-time working outweighed the disadvantages, or that they were prepared to put up with less money for the other advantages. Some were doubtful sometimes, like this 1985 woman: 'It is *very* tiring. Financially, after payment for childcare, it is unrewarding... However, it gives me time with my children and allows me to keep my career going. The fact that I have two separate roles during the week as GP and mother enhances both situations...'

A woman from the 1988 cohort agreed that there would be financial disadvantages in part-time working: 'I'd have a smaller income, and would have less availability for the patients. And I'd feel obliged to spend more time doing housework..' She intended to continue in full-time practice.

The question of losing continuity of care for patients was the second most important disadvantage to part-time principal work, and, interestingly, was mentioned by around a quarter of both men and women. It was clearly of importance to women since it was mentioned as a disadvantage by 30 per cent of the women who were currently working as part-time principals. The younger men were more likely to mention it as a potential disadvantage than the older cohorts.

Nearly a fifth of the women, but less than 10 per cent of the men, thought that part-time principal posts brought less status or authority within the practice. It was perhaps seen slightly more as a danger than a reality, since women who had worked as principals mentioned it rather less often than those who had not. It was clearly of more importance to the younger women, since a quarter of the 1988 women saw it as a disadvantage compared with 12 per cent of the 1981 women.

Nearly a fifth of the women, but only 2 per cent of the men thought that working part-time as a principal would have or had had an adverse effect on their careers. This was mentioned by over a quarter of the women who were currently working as part-time principals, and was obviously a worry to them. However, women who had had part-time principal work in the past were much less likely to mention it as a disadvantage, and it is possible again that it is more of a potential than a real danger. On the other hand, the women who were no longer working as part-time principals were usually those who had returned to full-time principal posts. Not all women were necessarily likely to be so fortunate.

Other disadvantages in part-time principal posts mentioned were less job satisfaction, the danger of working longer hours than the contract allowed, the fear that other doctors in the practice would consider part-timers to be less committed, general disapproval from colleagues, missing out on the full variety of skills and experience, difficulty or general fatigue in combining work and family and less job security.

There were few differences between men and women or between those who had worked part-time and those who had not in the extent to which these additional factors were mentioned. However, over 10 per cent of those who had worked as part-time principals in the past warned against working more hours than they were contracted for, and the advice given to those considering part-time work of checking their contract carefully was repeated in answer to this question by women who had worked as part-time principals. The problem of sticking to a set number of hours was often seen as almost insurmountable, as this 1985 mother of three and a part-time principal explained: 'Splitting myself between family and job is always a juggling act, and can get very stressful. It is impossible to remain "part-time" in any real sense, and work often encroaches on home – and occasionally vice versa...'

Advantages and disadvantages to other doctors of working with part-time GP principals

The vast majority of both men and women doctors could see advantages to working *with* part-time principals, and it was interesting that only around 10 per cent of doctors, rather more men than women, could see no advantages.

The main advantage was thought to be workload sharing and the provision of holiday cover and flexibility in hours for the other members of the practice. Around one fifth of both men and women mentioned this as an advantage, summed up by a 1985 women: 'They allow for flexibility since they are often able to become full-time intermittently to cover for absent colleagues and are better than a locum for that purpose...'

The second most frequently mentioned advantage was simply that part-time principals usually brought women doctors into the practice. Over one fifth of the women thought this an advantage compared with 13 per cent of the men. It was thought to offer a choice of having a woman doctor to patients, which was seen as beneficial both to the patients and to the practice. A 1981 woman summed up the views of many women: 'It allows the practice to have a second lady doctor, which is important in our multi-racial practice. Part-time ladies usually have children and are used to coping. They tend to be tolerant of their partners' and patients' foibles...'

Tolerance was thought to be an important characteristic, and the third most important advantage, mentioned by one fifth of the women, but only 10 per cent of the men, was that part-time principals led to happier and less stressed partners. It was difficult sometimes to see why this should occur, but it was often related to the fact that the part-timers were ready and available to step into the breach if problems arose. Some women were sceptical of the effect of this, like this 1985 woman: 'Someone to be used as a "dustbin" for unwanted chores – emergencies, troublesome patients, screening, programming, home visits...'

Nearly one fifth of women, but far fewer men, said that part-time principals often worked harder and longer than their full-time colleagues or than their contract stipulated. Women currently working as part-time principals were more likely to mention this than other doctors. And around 10 per cent of both men and women thought there were financial advantages to a practice in having part-time principals. A 1981 man pointed out the benefits: 'Up until recently a 20-hour principal would almost pay her salary in expenses and the practice would get a free doctor...'

The availability of a full basic practice allowance for doctors working 20 hours a week was removed under the terms of the new contract in 1990, and fears were expressed that this would adversely affect the prospects of women being able to work as part-time principals. A 1981 woman spelt out the other financial advantages of part-time principals: 'If this part-time partner is female, she attracts female patients, with the relevant contraceptive fees, cervical smears, child vaccinations etc., and increases the practice income disproportionately to her hours. Up till now she has brought in a full basic practice allowance although she only takes a fraction of a full-timer's profits...' Perhaps there was little wonder that some women were feeling worried about whether they would be able to continue to work part-time or to find a part-time principal post. Certainly the current part-time principals were aware of the financial benefit they brought to the practice, since one fifth of them mentioned this as an advantage to other doctors.

Around 10 per cent of doctors thought that part-time principals brought a variety of opinion into the practice. Some of the younger women were keen on an influx of 'new blood', like this 1988 woman: 'Part-time GPs may be fresher and more enthusiastic when at work. It's beneficial to have someone with outside interests. If it's a female with children, patients often appreciate a doctor who knows the problems...' Another 1988 woman agreed: 'You possibly get more input of fresh ideas from colleagues with a wider view of the world...'

Another advantage to partners of part-time principals was that a wider range of doctors and skills could be offered to patients, while around 5 per cent of both men and women thought that part-timers meant that there were more hands to do the routine work. A small number of respondents thought that part-timers allowed full-timers to keep up-to-date or to do work outside general practice.

Only 10 per cent of both men and women doctors saw no disadvantages to other doctors in working *with* part-time GP principals. This view was held by similar proportions of those who had worked part-time and those who had not. The main disadvantage, mentioned by just over one third of the men but nearly half the women, was a loss of continuity of care and the necessity for other partners to follow up the part-timers' patients. It was interesting that this view was held more or less equally by those who had worked part-time in general practice and those who had not. It was noteworthy that nearly 60 per cent of the 1988 women mentioned it as a disadvantage of working with part-time principals.

Women were also similarly more concerned than men about the potential disadvantage that part-time principals were not there when they were needed. Over one fifth of the women mentioned this, compared with only 10 per cent of the men. Again, there was little or no difference between those who had worked part-time in general practice and the rest.

Nearly one-fifth of the men thought that part-time principals might show less commitment or sense of responsibility, a view held by less than 10 per cent of the women.

Other possible disadvantages of working with part-time principals centred round communication problems when the doctors were not in the surgery and other administrative problems of a non-specific nature. Just over 5 per cent of the doctors thought there were disadvantages in that there were fewer partners to share the on-call commitment. All these factors were mentioned by roughly equal proportions of men and women.

An interesting disadvantage, mentioned by 3 per cent of the doctors, centred round the question of jealousy or resentment by the other partners of the part-timers' ability to combine work with other interests or responsibilities.

There were concerns about difficulties in delineating responsibilities and workload with part-time principals, while other doctors expressed concerns about less money coming into the practice, part-timers wanting more than their fair share of the income, problems with maternity leave and difficulties because of the new GP contract.

Although there were seen to be considerable advantages to other doctors in working with part-time GP principals, there can be no doubt that the respondents could think of many disadvantages. It must be remembered that we were asking them to list the advantages and disadvantages to other doctors of working with part-time principals, but we did not ask them to weigh the advantages and disadvantages. However, many of the comments they made indicated that part-time GP principals were not an undisguised blessing to their partners. It was interesting that those who were working or had worked part-time themselves shared the views of those who had never worked part-time.

There are clearly seen to be potential advantages in having part-time principals in the practice, particularly in offering flexibility and cover and easing the workload, as well as bringing women doctors into the practice. However, there does seem to be a very real concern about continuity of care and looking after other doctors' patients.

Should there be more part-time GP principal posts?

As a summary to this series of questions on the advantages and disadvantages to doctors themselves of working part-time as a GP principal, and the advantages and disadvantages to other doctors of working *with* part-time GP principals, we sought their views on the question of whether there should be *more* part-time or less than full-time GP principal posts.

Nearly 80 per cent of all respondents thought that there should be more part-time GP principal posts. Perhaps not surprisingly women were more likely to hold this view than men: 88 per cent of the women compared with 67 per cent of the men. Nevertheless, it is striking that over two-thirds of the male respondents thought there should be more part-time principal posts.

Table 6.8   Whether doctors think there should be more part-time GP principal posts

column percentages

	Total	Male 1981	Male 1985	Male 1988	Female 1981	Female 1985	Female 1988
Yes	79	61	69	74	86	90	89
No	15	32	25	21	9	6	6
Don't know/n.a	6	7	6	5	5	4	5
Base: all respondents	*1263*	*204*	*195*	*179*	*221*	*218*	*246*

Table 6.8 shows that, although the proportion of women thinking there should be more part-time principal posts was about the same for each cohort, the proportion of men increased from 61 per cent of the 1981 cohort to 69 per cent of the 1985 cohort to as many as 74 per cent of the 1988 cohort.

It was perhaps not surprising that those who were working or had worked part-time in general practice were more likely to think that there should be more part-time principal posts than those who had never worked part-time: 89 per cent compared with 72 per cent. But it should be remembered that this reflected the fact that the vast majority of doctors who were working or who had worked part-time were women, and indeed 92 per cent of the women in this category thought there should be more part-time principal posts. It was a view held most strongly by women who were currently part-time GP principals, 93 per cent of whom thought there should be more such posts.

It was however, notable that the 1981 women who had never worked part-time in general practice were rather different from all the other women, in that only 70 per cent of them thought there should be more part-time principal posts, compared with over 80 per cent of the 1985 women and nearly 90 per cent of the 1988 women who had never worked part-time in general practice. There were some indications, reinforced by other evidence in this study, that some of the older women who had always worked full-time were less than sympathetic towards women who wanted part-time working. But this view was by no means held by the younger women who had always worked full-time, many of whom were looking to see how they could find part-time principal posts in general practice, either at present or in the future.

There was an interesting difference among doctors who had qualified in the UK and those who had qualified in the Indian sub-continent, less than half of whom thought there should be more part-time principal posts, compared with over 80 per cent of the UK qualifiers. The difference was notable among both men and women, and indeed, over 70 per cent of the UK-qualified men thought there should be more part-time principals posts, compared with only 41 per cent of the men who had qualified in the Indian sub-continent. The comparable figures for women were 91 per cent of UK-qualified women and 55 per cent of women from the Indian sub-continent.

There was undoubtedly a strong tide of opinion among the doctors who responded to this questionnaire that there should be more part-time or less than full-time principal posts. Even though men were rather less likely to be of this opinion than women, there was still a definite majority view that more part-time principal opportunities should be provided. The fact that nearly three-quarters of the men who had received their vocational training certificate in 1988 held this view suggests that younger GPs are strongly in favour of such an increase. Certainly, if women are to achieve their potential in general practice, it seems to be the most sensible development. It also appeared that there was a substantial proportion of men who had their own reasons for thinking that part-time principal posts in general practice should be increased.

7 Factors affecting part-time work in general practice

We wanted to explore the extent to which doctors had considered working part-time as a GP principal if they had never had such a post. We were interested to see whether there were any particular constraints on doctors who were currently considering this or were thinking of doing so in future, and whether there were any reasons why people who had considered it in the past had abandoned the idea. We also wished to examine the reasons doctors gave for considering part-time principal posts and to ask them a range of questions about their preferences as far as part-time principal posts were concerned.

Consideration of part-time principal posts

As Table 6.3 showed, only around 6 per cent of the male respondents had ever held a part-time GP principal post, compared with around 50 per cent of the 1981 and 1985 cohorts of women and just under 40 per cent of the 1988 women.

Table 7.1   Whether doctors who had never worked as a part-time GP principal had ever considered doing so

column percentages

	Total	Male			Female		
		1981	1985	1988	1981	1985	1988
No	52	74	71	75	37	24	12
Yes - still considering it	14	5	6	6	16	30	31
Yes - will/may consider it in the future	26	16	18	18	28	37	48
Yes - have considered it in the past but no longer	5	3	3	3	16	6	5
na	2	3	1	1	2	3	4
Base: all who have never worked as a PT GP principal	*919*	*194*	*184*	*166*	*110*	*115*	*150*

We asked the 919 doctors who had never held such a post whether they had ever considered working part-time or less than full-time as a GP principal. Overall 72 per cent of the men and 23 per cent of the women said that they had never considered it. However, looking first at the men, as Table 7.1 shows, over one fifth of the 1981 men and a quarter of the 1985 and 1988 men were either currently considering it or said they would or might consider it in the future.

The three cohorts of women were rather different from each other. Over a third of the 1981 women who had not worked as part-time principals said they had never considered it, compared with a quarter of the 1985 women and only 12 per cent of the 1988 women. The answers were undoubtedly related to the age of the doctors, and their previous job histories. It is probable that the 1981 women who had never worked as part-time principals had different reasons from the 1988 women for not doing so. The younger women were less likely to have children and more likely to have been in full-time employment since qualifying. Essentially, up to the present, many of them had not considered anything other than full-time working because they had not needed to. However, even if they had not considered it before, many of them were certainly considering it at present or thinking of it in the future.

Nearly one third of the 1985 and 1988 women were currently considering working as a part-time principal, compared with 16 per cent of the 1981 women. And, in addition, nearly half the 1988 women said that they would or might consider it in the future, compared with over one third of the 1985 women and just over a quarter of the 1981 women. This is a very important factor to be taken into account when planning the future staffing of general practice.

Finally, 3 per cent of the men and 9 per cent of the women who had never worked as part-time principals said they had considered it in the past, but were no longer considering it. As Table 7.1 shows, as many as 16 per cent of the 1981 women who had never had such a post came into this category.

We asked these doctors why they had not proceeded to a part-time GP principal post, having considered it. The numbers of doctors involved were small, but they gave interesting reasons. Nearly half the men said that they had not taken the idea any further because they could not afford the drop in salary. Other reasons given by men indicated that they could not find a suitable post, that they were deterred by the attitudes of their partners or the potential effect on their partners. A 32-year-old man was still considering it, but summed up the experience of a number of men who had given up the idea: 'It was because of loss of power in the practice and not having a full say in the practice philosophy and direction...' There can be no doubt of the fear on the part of doctors that part-time partners are not really regarded as having as big a stake in the partnership as full-time partners, and that they may well lose power and influence.

Women had rather different and more varied reasons for not going ahead with their idea of seeking part-time principal posts. One fifth of them had been offered attractive full-time posts instead, one fifth had not been able to find a suitable part-time principal post locally, while nearly one fifth were like the men in finding that they could not afford a drop in salary.

Other reasons given by the women included a change in circumstances so that they no longer needed part-time work, difficulties with taking such a post because of family or domestic commitments, and being deterred by the on-call commitment of part-time principals. There were also individual mentions of problems because of race, the need for geographical mobility because of their spouse's job, problems with coordinating such a post with other work, fears of having to work longer hours than they were contracted for and problems with partners in the practice accepting them as part-time principals.

Reasons for considering part-time GP principal posts

We asked the 369 doctors who were currently considering working part-time as a principal and those who thought they might or would consider it in the future for their reasons. The overwhelming reason for considering part-time GP principal posts, given by over 80 per cent of the 244 women and 25 per cent of the 125 men in this category, was to give them more time for family or domestic commitments. The proportions for the men were similar for all cohorts, but the proportions of women increased from 71 per cent of the 1981 cohort to 85 per cent of the 1988 cohort.

There were clear signs among the 1988 women of the strain under which many of them were working full-time: 'It's difficult trying to look after a baby, husband and house. I'm unable to afford a full-time live-in nanny and I have no immediate family support nearby. It really precludes full-time work which includes on-call responsibility...' This theme was repeated many times among these young women, and it was not the only indication in this survey of exhaustion and fatigue among the 1988 women who were trying to combine full-time work in general practice with a young family.

However, male doctors were also concerned about the effects of full-time working on their family life, and it was by no means unusual for men to express the views of this 1985 male full-time principal: 'I am unhappy to continue a full working week and on-call. This is an unreasonable strain on my home and social life and prevents me developing other interests...'

The second most important reason for considering part-time principal posts was the desire for less pressure and fatigue in general. It was particularly interesting that this was mentioned by one third of the men who were considering part-time principal posts compared with 10 per cent of the women. Nearly 50 per cent of the 1981 men came into this category, and there was a strong sense of tired middle-aged men answering this question.

The third most important reason was also mentioned mainly by men. Over a quarter of the men and under 10 per cent of the women said that they wanted more time to pursue other interests, while a further 10 per cent of men said they wanted more time for leisure interests. Men also were more likely than women to say they wanted to pursue other medical interests, or to spend more time teaching, studying or doing research.

Essentially there was a fairly clear distinction between the men and the women who wanted part-time principal posts. The women were overwhelmingly interested in them so that they could spend more time with their families. Although this was the single most important reason given by the men, there were also a number of strands indicating that men would have liked part-time principal posts to give them a chance to get away from what they saw as the over-commitment of full-time general practice. Some of them were clearly seeking the opportunity for developing interests other than general practice, either in medicine, in other work, or simply in leisure or hobbies.

Time in career when part-time GP principal posts considered
We knew from our piloting that men and women might want part-time principal posts at different times in their careers, and we also knew that it was too simplistic to assume that doctors might want part-time working only when they had small children.

We asked the doctors at what period in their careers they would like to work part-time as a principal. Over 80 per cent of the women said this would be when they had small children, as did nearly one third of the men. Not surprisingly, this was the main time period given by the women, but not by the men.

We found it particularly interesting that 54 per cent of the men and 47 per cent of the women who were considering part-time principal posts said that they would like to have such a post towards the end of their careers. Nearly two-thirds of the 1981 men mentioned this.

Over one third of the men but less than one fifth of the women said they would like to have a part-time principal post while they developed another medical specialty. A 1985 woman thought there should be more room for manoeuvre: 'How nice if posts could be more readily adapted, and could be full or part-time or changeable. GP experience leads on to other specialties, for example psychiatry or psychotherapy...'

In addition, nearly one fifth of the men and 10 per cent of the women said they would like a part-time GP principal post while they worked part-time in a hospital specialty. This was an additional reflection of the strong undercurrent of boredom and dissatisfaction with general practice found among all cohorts of respondents, particularly among the men. They wanted to do more hospital work than they could manage while working as full-time principals, and there were indications that they wanted more responsibility than they had as clinical assistants.

Around 10 per cent of both men and women said they would like a part-time principal post throughout their careers, while other doctors wanted such posts while developing non-medical interests, while studying and as soon as they could afford a drop in income. There was a view among some doctors that more flexibility in opportunities for part-time working would be beneficial for both doctors and patients for a variety of reasons. Again, they felt that they were forced to choose between a full-time *or* part-time GP principal post and found this very restrictive.

Hours or sessions considered

We asked the doctors how many hours *or* sessions they would like to work as part-time GP principals. The distribution was similar to that found among doctors who had worked or were working as part-time GP principals. 20 per cent of the respondents (15 per cent of the men and 22 per cent of the women) said that they would like to work 20 hours a week, while 14 per cent of the men and 4 per cent of the women said they would like to work 30 hours or more a week. 25 per cent of the doctors (18 per cent of the men and 30 per cent of the women) said they would like to work 5 sessions a week, and 17 per cent of the doctors (equal proportions of men and women) said they would like to work 6 sessions a week.

Table 7.2   Hours or sessions wanted by GPs considering part-time GP principal posts

column percentages

	Total	Male			Female		
		1981	1985	1988	1981	1985	1988
Hours							
1-19	4	12	6	3	2	1	0
20	20	18	13	15	20	21	23
21-29	3	0	0	6	8	2	1
30 plus	8	18	18	8	6	3	4
OR							
Sessions							
1-4	7	3	0	0	16	8	9
5	25	15	13	25	27	31	30
6	17	10	22	15	14	19	16
7-10	14	20	16	22	6	10	15
Don't know	2	4	12	6	1	5	2
Base: all those who are considering/might consider GP principal post	*369*	*40*	*45*	*40*	*49*	*77*	*118*

Thus 70 per cent of the respondents wanted to work around half a working week as part-time principals. As Table 7.2 shows, only just over 10 per cent of doctors wanted to work fewer than 20 hours or 5 sessions a week, and, as might be expected, this was more true of women than men. Around a quarter of the doctors wanted to work more than 20 hours or 6 sessions as part-time principals. This represented over a third of the men and one fifth of the women.

This analysis shows that doctors contemplating part-time GP principal posts were not really thinking of just filling in a few hours or sessions. They were mainly considering half-time or more, and their comments indicated that they were fully aware of the need for a 'proper' commitment if they were to work part-time. Their main consideration appeared to be a desire not to be as over-committed as they felt themselves to be as full-time principals.

Range of general practice work considered

This desire to maintain a strong commitment to general practice while working less than full-time was reflected in their desire to maintain the full range of general practice work rather than a restricted range. We found that 94 per cent of the men and 92 per cent of the women preferred to have the full range of work if they had a part-time GP principal post. The only group who were less enthusiastic than the others about this were the 1981 women, of whom 86 per cent said that they would like the full range of work.

The main reasons given by two-thirds of both men and women for preferring the full range of work was because it offered more variety, interest and enjoyment. These were, of course, the main reasons given by those who had actually worked part-time in general practice. A further quarter of the men and women said they wished to maintain their breadth of skills and experience. 10 per cent of the doctors mentioned that they were keen to contribute as much as possible to the practice, which they felt could only be achieved by offering the full range of general practice work.

The women who were considering part-time GP principal posts were similar to those who had such posts in that they were worried that in some way they might be 'pushed' into a restricted range. There were many comments on the dangers of being seen as only suitable for 'women's problems' or routine work, as this 1988 woman said: 'I was trained for the full range of work and I would find a restricted range frustrating...'

Alternatives to part-time GP principal posts

It was apparent both from our piloting and from the main study that part-time or less than full-time GP principal posts were not always easy to find. We asked the doctors what they would do if no part-time GP principal posts were available.

The men and women differed in their responses, and the younger women differed from the older women. Around two-thirds of the men from all cohorts said that they would work full-time instead. But this view was taken by over 40 per cent of the 1988 women, by a third of the 1985 women and just over a quarter of the 1981 women.

On the other hand, nearly 40 per cent of the 1981 women said they would work part-time in another specialty, often community health, a possibility mentioned by only one in six of the 1988 women and hardly mentioned by the men.

10 per cent of the women and only one man said they would take a GP assistant post instead and 5 per cent of the women said they would continue on the retainer scheme. A wide variety of other possible moves were mentioned, including retiring early, stopping work altogether, working for a deputising service, taking other unspecified work, taking clinical assistant posts, working part-time in other jobs in or out of medicine or in medically related fields, trying to job share, working in private practice, continuing in the same medical specialty they were in (since this question was answered by some doctors not working in general practice), and working as a locum. A few doctors said they would keep looking for a part-time GP principal post, while an Indian woman doctor, who had had great difficulty in finding a post of any kind, said that she would 'become more philosophical...'

The very wide range of answers to this question suggests not only great resourcefulness on the part of the doctors who were considering part-time principal posts in general practice, but also indicates that there is a wide variety of jobs available to them. Most would not be unemployed if they could not get a part-time GP principal post, but many of them were not keen on the alternatives they put forward.

Return to full-time GP principal work

There is evidence that women who work part-time when their children are small often wish to return to full-time work when their children are older. There were certainly indications of this in *Doctors and their Careers,* and this kind of pattern of working has been found among other professional women (Silverstone and Ward, 1980). We asked the doctors whether they would intend to return to or take up full-time work as a GP principal in the future, if they obtained a part-time principal post.

Table 7.3   Whether those considering a part-time GP principal post would intend to return to full-time work as GP principal

column percentages

	Total	Male			Female		
		1981	1985	1988	1981	1985	1988
Yes	20	5	4	13	18	21	35
No	34	50	44	38	49	31	19
Don't know	46	45	51	50	33	48	46
Base: all those who are considering/might consider PT GP principal post	*369*	*40*	*45*	*40*	*49*	*77*	*118*

As Table 7.3 shows, there was a marked difference between the sexes in the response to this question, reflecting the different reasons put forward for considering part-time principal work. Over a quarter of the women said that they would intend to return to full-time principal work, compared with only 7 per cent of the men. The younger women were more likely to say that they would return to full-time work than the older women – 35 per cent of the 1988 women compared with around one fifth of the 1981 and 1985 women.

The men were more likely than the women to say categorically that they would *not* want to return to full-time principal work – 44 per cent of the men compared with 29 per cent of the women. Again, the older men were more likely to be quite sure that they did not want to return to full-time work than the younger men.

However, around half the men and just over 40 per cent of the women said they did not know whether they would intend to return to full-time work. The older women were less likely to be undecided than the younger women, showing their greater reluctance to consider returning to full-time work.

Advantages and disadvantages of part-time GP assistant posts compared with part-time GP principal posts

The main advantage in having a part-time GP assistant post, compared with having a part-time GP principal post was thought to be the smaller degree of responsibility - an advantage mentioned by one third of the women but less than one fifth of the men. A further advantage, mentioned by over 10 per cent of both sexes was the smaller amount of administrative work. The advantage of GP assistants in having no on-call commitment was mentioned by nearly 10 per cent of the women, but fewer men. Other factors cited included having less involvement in the management or administrative problems of the practice, having more flexibility, clearly defined hours and responsibilities and more free time. It was interesting that over 10 per cent of the 1988 women, but hardly any other respondents, said that there was a financial advantage in that assistants did not have to buy into the partnership.

However, nearly half the men and nearly one third of the women thought that part-time GP assistant posts had no advantages over part-time GP principal posts, while a further 15 per cent of doctors felt unable to comment on the advantages.

There was more agreement on the disadvantages of part-time GP assistant posts, with two-thirds of the women and nearly half the men saying that such posts lacked status or authority within the practice. Over 40 per cent of the women and one third of the men said that they paid less money. Over 10 per cent of both sexes thought they offered less job security, while nearly 10 per cent said part-time GP assistants risked exploitation by colleagues. Other disadvantages mentioned included less autonomy, less commitment to the practice, less job satisfaction and an adverse effect on career progress.

Only one doctor saw no disadvantages in part-time GP assistant posts, and there was an overwhelming impression that respondents felt that part-time GP assistant posts were much less attractive than part-time GP principal posts.

Careers advice about part-time work in general practice

The patchiness and inadequacy of careers advice to doctors at all stages of their careers was one of the most striking findings of *Doctors and their Careers*, and has been noted in other research reports. The problem is by no means confined to women doctors, but it has been argued that lack of careers advice, or inappropriate careers advice, is a more pressing problem for women than for men because of their more complicated career patterns. There is also the fact that they find it more difficult to follow traditional medical careers advice, given mainly by more senior doctors, which usually assumes a 'straight' career path with no deviations for interesting sidelines, including part-time working or having babies.

There is mounting evidence that advice about working part-time or less than full-time in medicine has not always been easy to obtain, with some notable exceptions among a few senior doctors who have made it their business to ensure that women seeking such advice are helped as much as possible. However, there has been an increasing interest in encouraging good advice about part-time or less than full-time working, both from the Department of Health (Department of Health and Social Security, 1986 – *Achieving a Balance*) (Department of Health, 1991 – *Women Doctors and their Careers*) and from postgraduate deans and clinical tutors.

We were interested to establish to what extent the respondents in this study had ever sought advice about working part-time or less than full-time in general practice. We wanted to know what had happened if they had sought such advice, from whom they had sought it, and how helpful, accurate and encouraging they had found it. We asked those who had sought it what general comments they had about such careers advice. We were keen to seek recommendations from the doctors themselves at every point.

We found that 3 per cent of the men (17 doctors) and 29 per cent of the women (199 doctors) had sought advice about working part-time or less than full-time in general practice. The proportions from each cohort were almost exactly the same, but, perhaps not surprisingly, 35 per cent of the women with children and 38 per cent of those on maternity leave had sought careers advice on part-time working compared with 20 per cent of the women without children. Women who had qualified overseas were almost as likely as UK-qualified women to have sought advice, but women who had qualified in Ireland were very unlikely to have sought advice.

Among those who had ever worked part-time in general practice, the proportions who had sought advice were, not surprisingly, higher than among those who had not: 38 per cent of the women and 13 per cent of the men, compared with 13 per cent of the women and 2 per cent of the men who had never worked part-time.

Again the younger women who had never worked part-time were rather more likely to have sought advice than the 1981 women, but, even so, fewer than one fifth of the 1985 and 1988 women had done so. They might have been considering part-time working but they had not usually pursued it very actively by asking anyone about it.

There was a difference between part-time GP principals (including the 20-hour a week principals) and part-time GP assistants. 44 per cent of the women currently working as part-time principals had sought advice compared with less than a quarter of those currently working as part-time assistants. The following analysis is mainly confined to the women doctors, since so few men were involved.

When careers advice on part-time working had been sought

The timing of seeking the careers advice was clearly of interest in this study. We found a marked difference between the three cohorts in the proportion who had sought advice on part-time work in general practice during their vocational training period. This ranged from 33 per cent of the 1981 women who had sought advice to 63 per cent of the 1985 women, to as many as 73 per cent of the 1988 women. On the other hand, the proportion who had sought such advice having completed their vocational training ranged from nearly 70 per cent of the 1981 women to just under 60 per cent of the 1985 women, to just over half of the 1988 women.

It looked as though the question of working less than full-time in general practice had occurred to the younger women at an earlier stage in their careers than to the older women. They had certainly sought advice at an earlier stage, but it is possible that other factors had affected the behaviour of the 1981 women. There is the possibility that they had been more worried about the consequences of seeking advice about part-time working in general practice, and, of course, they might not have considered seeking careers advice on the subject because they did not think any was available, whereas the younger women were operating in the late 1980s when the subject had been more widely discussed, not least after the publication of *Doctors and their Careers*.

Only a sprinkling of doctors mentioned other times at which careers advice on part-time work in general practice had been sought. Less than 5 per cent of doctors said that it was before they started their vocational training or after the birth of their child or children, while one doctor said it was when she returned from abroad and another said it was immediately she had qualified. Two doctors said specifically that they sought advice when they were working as full-time GP principals.

It is likely, however, that some of those who mentioned seeking advice after completing vocational training were referring to a period some time later, when they were working full-time in general practice. We did not ask them to specify how many years after they had completed their vocational training they had sought advice. However, it could not have been very long afterwards in most cases, because they had only received their vocational training certificates in 1981, 1985 and 1988.

Sources of careers advice on part-time work in general practice

The two most important sources of advice on working part-time in general practice were partners in the practice and the GP trainer. Overall, 53 per cent of the women who had sought advice had asked the partners in the practice, while 57 per cent had asked their GP trainer. However, there were differences among the cohorts, reflecting perhaps the different times at which advice had been sought by the different groups of women. Just over one third of the 1981 women had asked their GP trainer for advice on part-time working, compared with two-thirds of the 1985 women and 70 per cent of the 1988 women. On the other hand, around 50 per cent of the 1981 and 1985 women had asked the partners in their practice, compared with nearly 60 per cent of the 1988 women.

It looked as though the younger women who had sought advice had focused their attention on their immediate practice to a greater extent than the 1981 women. For example, nearly 40 per cent of the 1981 women had asked the regional adviser in general practice for advice, in comparison with around 30 per cent of the 1985 women and less than a quarter of the 1988 women. Nearly one fifth of the 1981 women had spoken to the regional postgraduate dean, compared with just over one in ten of the 1985 women. One in ten of the 1981 women had sought advice on part-time working from the BMA, compared with only one woman from the 1988 cohort. On the other hand, the 1985 and 1988 women were rather more likely than the older cohort to have sought advice from friends working part-time.

The more focused approach was probably partly due to the fact that the younger women's careers had been shorter, giving them fewer opportunities to cast the net wide, but there were also indications that they were making more active attempts to ensure part-time principal posts for themselves, thus concentrating on those who might be in a position to give them such jobs or who had up-to-the-minute experience.

A variety of other sources of advice were mentioned by the women doctors who had sought advice on part-time work in general practice, including clinical tutors (7 per cent, again mentioned more often by the 1981 women), the Medical Women's Federation (5 per cent), GP colleagues (5 per cent), the organiser of the retainer scheme (4 per cent), a women doctors' adviser at the Regional Health Authority (4 per cent), a consultant (3 per cent), the Family Practitioner Committee (FPC), or Family Health Services Authority (FHSA) as it now is, by 2 per cent, a college tutor by 2 per cent, and a female GP support group and 'literature' by 1 per cent.

What kind of advice was given?

The advice varied considerably, and divided fairly evenly between discouraging or cautious advice pointing out the difficulties and encouraging or positive advice including practical help.

Among the most frequently mentioned pieces of advice on the negative side was the strong advice to 15 per cent to look carefully at the partnership arrangement and the even more negative advice to 10 per cent that suitable posts were hard to find. Only around 6 per cent of the women had been advised simply not to consider it, but a further 6 per cent had been told to look carefully at the financial arrangements, 5 per cent to beware of exploitation, 3 per cent were told it was not a good move in career terms, and 2 per cent that it was not a good move financially.

On the other hand, over a fifth of the women were told to 'go for it' and persevere, 12 per cent specifically mentioned practical help or advice in applying for the retainer scheme (mainly 1981 women), plus a variety of other positive advice, including advice to start as a full-timer and decrease the hours when established, in contrast to other advice to start as a part-timer with the hope of getting a good full-time post.

There was no evidence that one particular type of source was more likely to offer positive or negative advice, although there was evidence that other women doctors had stressed the need to look carefully at the partnership agreements. They also gave a 'straight from the horse's mouth' perspective, as a 1988 woman explained: 'They said that part-timers ended up doing a full-time job in half the time; that the commitments were very difficult to fit in with personal commitments and that they were not treated as part of the team by other full-time partners...' She had decided to go into occupational medicine.

It was not infrequent for advice to be positive from one source and negative from another, as this 1988 20-hour a week principal pointed out: 'The GP trainer thought it a reasonable thing to do, but the postgraduate dean made me feel that I was asking to have my cake and eat it...' But sometimes the advice was simply negative, according to the women, like this 1981 woman describing her encounter with her GP trainer: 'He said that women should be glad of part-time posts with limited functions, like family planning etc.. I found this completely unacceptable and very sexist! What a waste of training...'

The problem was sometimes compounded by a number of factors, as this Indian woman doctor pointed out, speaking of the advice received from her trainer for whom she had nothing but praise: 'She said it's difficult to find a part-time post in your area. It's worse if you're a young mother. There's no chance if you're foreign...' She was currently working as a CMO doing family planning clinics, as a clinical assistant in general medicine, and doing sessions in a private clinic. 'My trainer – a delightful lady – has always hoped (and still does) that one day I might find a suitable partnership. She can't see any reason why not...'

There was evidence that some regional advisers in general practice were seen to be more negative than others, and there were references to regional advisers saying that it was more difficult in some areas to get part-time work in general practice than in others. A 1985 woman had sought advice from a number of sources: 'The BMA was fine, but had limited information. The regional adviser was very negative. I was told this was a very difficult area to get a part-time job...' This woman, like others, had also found it difficult to get information about the doctors' retainer scheme.

Assessment of advice about part-time work in general practice

We wanted to assess how helpful, accurate and encouraging the doctors had found the advice. We asked them for a composite picture, simply because we did not want to make the questionnaire even more complicated than it was already. The vast majority complied with this request, apart from a handful who had had completely different advice from different sources.

In terms of helpfulness, 40 per cent of the women doctors found the advice helpful, 43 per cent fairly helpful and 18 per cent unhelpful. The younger women had found the advice they had been offered rather more helpful than the 1981 women.

As far as accuracy was concerned, 39 per cent of the women doctors found the advice accurate, 46 per cent fairly accurate and only 8 per cent found it inaccurate, but 7 per cent felt unable to comment on the accuracy of the advice.

Therefore, although the women were not overwhelmingly impressed by the accuracy of the advice they received on part-time work in general practice, relatively few felt that they had received inaccurate advice. The question of helpfulness was different, in that although over 80 per cent found the advice at least fairly helpful, one fifth of the women found it unhelpful.

It was a different matter when it came to the question of whether the advice was encouraging. Only 25 per cent of the women doctors had found the advice on part-time work in general practice encouraging, 38 per cent had found it fairly encouraging, while 34 per cent had found it discouraging. Less than one fifth of the 1988 women had found the advice encouraging.

It is a matter of some concern that if women seek advice on working part-time in general practice, something that many women GPs want to do and have done, over a third of them have found the advice discouraging. Part-time working in general practice is here to stay, and it is clearly inappropriate that discouraging advice is given to women considering seeking part-time or less than full-time posts.

But this was the proportion of women seeking advice as a whole. Looking more specifically at the 40 women not working in general practice who had sought advice about part-time working in general practice, less than one in ten had found the advice encouraging and half of them had found it discouraging. Indeed 60 per cent of those working in other medical jobs had found the advice discouraging. It was perhaps not surprising that they were not working in general practice.

Even among the women currently working part-time in general practice, there were also differences, with the part-time GP assistants finding the advice they had been given more discouraging than those currently working as part-time GP principals.

Among the 17 men who had sought advice on part-time working in general practice, the proportion reporting the advice as unhelpful, inaccurate and discouraging was rather greater than among the women. There was no doubt that part-time working in general practice was not regarded as a good idea for men, and that they found it difficult to get good advice about it. Considering the interest many men showed in working part-time in general practice, as we saw earlier in this chapter, it does appear that advice could be tailored to their needs in a more positive way than most of them reported. However, perhaps the advice was too positive in some cases, as this 1985 man indicated: 'Most advisers said part-time work should be encouraged, but when I applied for part-time posts as a male doctor it seemed to be regarded with suspicion. Why is the enthusiasm in theory not borne out in practice?'

We were particularly interested in any comments or recommendations doctors had to make about careers advice on working part-time in general practice. Only about half the respondents who had sought advice added any comments, but the main thrust of their recommendations was that good advice was lacking at the moment, and it ought to be more readily available.

Other comments included the observation that the best advice came from doctors who were working part-time at present, that advice from other sources was often discouraging, that advice was needed on the proper choice of post, that positive advice did not always reflect realistic options, that job-share registers should be encouraged, that more advice was needed on the implications of the new contract on part-time working, and that more advice should be given at medical school.

Some doctors used the opportunity to give a little advice themselves, like this 1981 woman: 'A practice is a big financial and emotional investment. Our fellow doctors are not renowned for being honest when employing part-time doctors. Read the small print, don't despair, keep looking until you find a good practice that will value you and your contribution...'

It could be argued that, realistic as this advice might be, it is a sorry state of affairs when those seeking careers advice on something as important as part-time work in general practice, an aim of so many women doctors, can find that positive advice might not be applicable in the real world, and that the best advice to those seeking part-time work in general practice is to be as wary and suspicious as possible.

8 Geographical moves, career breaks and job-sharing

It has been clear for some time that women doctors find it more difficult than men to pursue a 'conventional' career in medicine. However, it has also become apparent that the question of what constitutes a 'conventional' career must be addressed, particularly when the proportion of women entering the medical profession is nearing 50 per cent. It is probable that only a minority of doctors in future will be prepared or able to pursue conventional careers in the traditional sense, and it seems sensible for the medical profession and those responsible for medical manpower planning to anticipate this change.

It has been recognised for some years that there are a number of constraints on the careers of women doctors. Foremost among these has been what has been termed 'domestic commitments'. But the research reported in *Doctors and their Careers* indicated that 'domestic commitments' was far too simple a term to use for the complicated constraints experienced by many women doctors, and, moreover, established that men doctors also suffered from a number of constraints inherent in the demands of the medical career structure which were by no means restricted to women.

Geographical moves

One of the most important constraints on doctors' careers identified in *Doctors and their Careers* was the necessity for doctors to move around the country during their postgraduate training. This was thought to have a potentially disastrous effect on personal relationships and the development of what many young doctors called 'a normal life'. The constant need to be thinking of the next job as soon as the present job had begun was also thought to have an unsettling effect on the doctors themselves, but one of the main problems was the actual physical movement around the country, especially if the doctor had to consider the career demands and prospects of their partner or spouse.

The need for geographical mobility might have been a less important factor in the past when the majority of doctors were male, with wives or partners who were not pursuing a serious career. But times have changed, not only in that nearly half the doctors entering postgraduate training are female, but also in that the wives and partners of young male doctors are increasingly unlikely to be prepared to abandon or modify their careers to follow their husbands round the country. Indeed, with the increase in dual career families and the reliance on two incomes for an acceptable standard of living, there may well be severe strains on marriages where frequent geographical movement is required.

It is not known to what extent a desire for less geographical mobility had had an effect on the choice of specialty of the doctors in the present study, but there can be little doubt that general practice, with its shorter period of postgraduate training, often combined with an organised vocational training period in one locality, is an attractive option to doctors who do not want to move around the country. There were indications in this study that the career choice of both men and women doctors had been affected by this factor.

There was evidence in Chapter 2 that the wives of GPs were much more likely to be working than not, often in managerial or professional occupations. Their careers were clearly important factors to be considered in the career moves of their husbands. But the evidence is that women are still more likely to adjust their careers to those of their husbands rather than the other way around, and it was this factor in particular that we wished to explore in this study.

We were interested to know whether the doctors had ever moved geographically for reasons other than their own career development since they had achieved full registration as a doctor in the UK, and if so, how many times, for what reasons, and what effect it had had on their careers.

Table 8.1 Whether doctors had ever moved geographically for reasons other than for their own career development

column percentages

	Total	Male			Female		
		1981	1985	1988	1981	1985	1988
Yes	36	20	16	19	57	55	44
No	64	80	84	81	43	45	56
Base: all respondents	*1263*	*204*	*195*	*179*	*221*	*218*	*246*
Yes	57	41	36	29	65	63	49
Base: all who have ever worked part-time in general practice	*500*	*17*	*14*	*21*	*152*	*148*	*148*
Yes	23	18	14	18	39	37	37
Base: all who have never worked part-time in general practice	*763*	*187*	*181*	*158*	*69*	*70*	*98*

Overall, 18 per cent of the men and 52 per cent of the women said that they had moved for reasons other than for their own career development. As Table 8.1 shows, the proportion for men was similar for all three cohorts, but among the women it ranged from 57 per cent of the 1981 cohort to 44 per cent of the 1988 cohort, probably reflecting both the longer careers of the 1981 cohort and also the fact that they were more likely to be married than the 1988 women.

Doctors who had qualified in the Indian sub-continent were less likely to have moved since full registration in the UK than all other doctors.

There was a marked difference between those who had ever worked part-time in general practice and those who had not, as Table 8.1 shows. 59 per cent of the women and 35 per cent of the men who had ever worked part-time had moved for reasons other than for their own career development, compared with 38 per cent of the women and 17 per cent of the men who had *not* worked part-time.

There was also a striking difference between those who were *currently* working less than full-time in clinical medicine, 62 per cent of whom had moved for reasons other than their own career development, and those who were currently working full-time in clinical medicine, only 25 per cent of whom had moved. Although this was clearly related to the fact that women were more likely to work part-time in clinical medicine, there was a strong association between moving and working less than full-time.

There can be little doubt that working part-time or less than full-time is strongly associated with geographical moves, but the extent to which it is a consequence of these moves is a moot point. It is probable that in many cases part-time working is not caused only by geographical moves but is associated with a number of other factors as well, most particularly marriage and children. Nevertheless, it appears that moving around for reasons other than one's own career development can well result in part-time working, whatever else has happened.

Some indication of the relationship between moving and part-time working and the inability to 'get on' was given by the fact that nearly 70 per cent of those who were currently working as part-time GP assistants and three-quarters of those currently on the retainer scheme had moved for reasons other than their own career development, compared with 56 per cent of those currently working as part-time GP principals, and less than a quarter of the full-time GP principals. It may be difficult to disentangle the causes, but the association was clear. Moving is not conducive to a successful career in medicine, unless the moves are made for the doctor's own career development.

The frequency of the moves was, not surprisingly, related to the length of the doctors' careers. There were also some differences between the men and the women.

Rather under half the men who had moved had done so once only, but under two-thirds of the 1981 men had moved once or twice, compared with nearly three-quarters of the 1985 men. The numbers were small, of course, but there were indications that there were some men who either had itchy feet, or who had moved for a variety of other reasons not connected with their career development. Certainly, a higher proportion of men than women from all cohorts had moved more than six times. Their reasons for moving, as we shall see, were rather different from those of the women.

A different pattern was found among the women. As Table 8.2 shows, the 1985 and 1988 women were more likely than their 1981 counterparts to have moved once only, and indeed, over 80 per cent of both these cohorts had moved

Table 8.2   Number of times doctors had moved since full registration for reasons other than their own career development

column percentages

	Total	Male			Female		
		1981	1985	1988	1981	1985	1988
Once	52	40	45	47	42	64	59
Twice	21	20	29	24	18	19	25
3 - 5 times	17	16	10	15	31	11	12
6 - 10 times	6	10	12	9	7	4	3
10 plus times	1	5	0	0	0	0	0
n.a.	3	9	3	5	2	2	1
Base: respondents who had moved for reasons other than own career	*459*	*40*	*31*	*34*	*126*	*119*	*109*

only once or twice, compared with 60 per cent of the 1981 women. Nearly one third of the 1981 women who had moved for reasons other than their own career development had moved between three and five times, and 7 per cent of them had moved more often. It was perhaps not surprising that some of the 1981 women had found it difficult to maintain a 'conventional' career in medicine.

Why had they moved? The overwhelming reason, given by 76 per cent of the women, was because of their partner or spouse's job, a reason given by only 10 per cent of the men. This reason was cited by over 80 per cent of the 1981 women, compared with just over 70 per cent of the 1988 women. It was given by nearly 90 per cent of the women doctors with children, compared with just over half of the women without children.

It should be remembered that 50 per cent of the married women doctors in this study were married to other doctors. The accepted need for geographical mobility among doctors during postgraduate training, can have far-reaching effects on the careers of both partners. It can present very real problems, since they may well find it difficult to find training posts in the same district. The problem does not go away if one partner has, for example, reached career grade as a principal in general practice while the other is still in a training grade and needs to move. It was undoubtedly associated with the high proportion of women doctors in this study who had moved for reasons other than their own career development.

The second most important reason for moving, given by one third of the men but only 10 per cent of the women, was because they wanted to work or go abroad. The proportions for each cohort were almost identical. There were clear indications among them of a group of doctors who had an insatiable wanderlust, like this 1981 man: 'I moved for interest, excitement and the education of my children. We moved to the Bahamas, Kenya, the USA, different parts of the UK and we're now in the South of France for the children's education...'

There were women too who liked moving around and seeing the world, like a 1988 woman who used her medical qualifications as a means to an end: 'I like travelling and working holidays. Then I met and married an Australian. Our priority was building and sailing a yacht around the world – not my career...'

There were a number of medical missionaries and other doctors with a strong religious faith among the respondents, who felt 'called by God' to pursue work abroad, like this 1988 woman: 'I moved abroad to fulfil my vocation as a missionary doctor...' In reply to the question of how it had affected her career, she responded: 'I am not concerned about the "normal" career routes in the UK...'

The third most important reason for moving was for personal or family commitments. This covered a fairly broad range, and was mentioned by a quarter of the men and 10 per cent of the women. In some cases the reason was to be near elderly relatives or for the children's education or to move to a job which offered more, rather than less, stability.

It was interesting that nearly one fifth of the men, but only 5 per cent of the women, said that they had moved because they wanted to live in a particular area. There were strong indications of men in particular choosing to live in a pleasant part of the country rather than 'develop' their careers. The numbers giving this reason were small, but there was evidence of men moving into general practice and away from hospital medicine because they wanted to settle down in a particular place and develop interests outside medicine.

Other reasons given by doctors for moving included financial reasons, such as the price of affordable property, forced relocation, for example through the armed services, and going where the jobs were available. There was a group of doctors who just fancied a change of scenery. 10 per cent of the men came into this category, and again reflected the views of a certain set of doctors who liked moving around and were not particularly concerned about 'developing' their careers.

How had the move or moves affected the careers of the doctors? Nearly 30 per cent of the men and one third of the women said that their careers had not been affected at all. Over one third of the 1981 and 1985 men reported positive benefits from moving around, particularly through the broadening of horizons and interests, but the 1988 men were less likely to be so enthusiastic about this and only around 10 per cent of the women had noticed benefits of this kind, although a small number said they had unexpectedly found a good part-time post or even a partnership, like a 1988 woman: 'It improved things, but some of this was luck and coincidence...'

On the whole, the women reported adverse effects, as did some of the men, like one who had gained his vocational training certificate in 1985 but had travelled around the world a lot in his earlier career and was finding difficulty in getting a full-time job: 'I now have a very long and unusual CV with multiple jobs in Australia, on the ships, in Saudi Arabia, the Emirates and Yemen, and I think people think I will not settle...'

Women who had moved because of their husbands' jobs often found it difficult to become 'known' in the areas to which they had moved, like this 1981 woman: 'I found it difficult at first to convince the clinical tutors, postgraduate dean and GP adviser of my seriousness. This caused a hiatus of about a year. Once I had worked and was known and got to know other doctors, things improved...'

This type of experience was frequently repeated, and, once again, shows the very 'personal' nature of medicine, and particularly general practice, in that personal recommendation or familiarity are very important factors in helping doctors to get jobs. It seems unlikely that there are many occupations in which it is so important to have a face that is known and accepted by the local professional network or to have contacts to ease entry into the local scene.

Over a quarter of the 1981 women and around one fifth of the other two cohorts of women said their career progress had been inhibited or delayed by their geographical moves, and 5 per cent of the women said they had had an enforced career break after their move because they could not find a job right away. A further 5 per cent reported that they had found it harder to get back into the system having had a career break combined with a geographical move. That the two things went together was not particularly surprising, considering the age of many of these doctors, who were having babies and moving around at the same time.

Around 5 per cent of the women said that their enforced moves had resulted in their changing from another specialty to general practice, while a small number said they had changed from general practice to another specialty – usually community health. Other effects of geographical moves included the need to take a job in a less suitable practice than desired, difficulties in changing jobs, having to take an assistant rather than a principal post, having to work full-time rather than part-time, and, in two cases, being obliged to stop working altogether.

The reaction of the doctors to what were often adverse effects on their careers often seemed to depend on the reasons for the geographical mobility. If they had chosen to move around, they often faced the consequences with at least some equanimity, like a 1988 woman who had travelled a lot: 'My friends who qualified in 1979 with me are now GP principals. I am not yet. However, I have seen a lot more of the world than them and have no misgivings...'

On the other hand, those women who had followed their husbands, sometimes to rather remote parts of the country, were not always so sanguine, and there was evidence not only of real resentment among them because of their decreased lack of opportunities but also irritation with the difficulty they perceived in getting advice and help with relocating and picking up their own careers.

Likelihood of geographical moves in future

Looking at the future, one quarter of the women and one in ten of the men thought they were likely to move geographically for reasons other than for their career development. As Table 8.3 shows, the younger women were more likely to be expecting a geographical move than the older women. However, a further quarter of the women respondents said they did not know whether they were likely to

Table 8.3   Whether doctors were likely to move geographically in future for reasons other than for their own career development

column percentages

	Total	Male			Female		
		1981	1985	1988	1981	1985	1988
Yes	18	8	9	12	20	23	30
No	60	71	73	73	60	50	42
Don't know	22	21	18	15	20	27	28
Base: all respondents	*1263*	*204*	*195*	*179*	*221*	*218*	*246*

move, with again higher proportions of younger women. It did appear that uncertainty about the future dogged the careers of a substantial proportion of the women doctors in this study.

It was interesting that there was little difference between those who had ever worked part-time and those who had not in the proportion thinking that they were likely to move in future for reasons other than for their career development. This was in marked contrast to the proportions who had actually moved in the past, among whom those who had worked part-time were much more likely to have moved than those who had not. One of the main reasons for this was related to age. The younger women were less likely to have worked part-time and less likely to have moved already for reasons other than their own career development. However, more or less equal proportions of the 1988 women, whether they had worked part-time or not, thought they were likely to move in future.

The overwhelming reason for expecting a geographical move, given by 82 per cent of the women, was because of their partner or husband's job. The main reason for moving given by the men was because they wanted to live in a particular area.

Other reasons for moving included family and personal commitments, to work abroad, forced relocation, a wish for more time to pursue other interests, to leave general practice, to improve the quality of life and on retirement.

Again, the men who were contemplating a future geographical move were more likely to think that it would have no effect on their careers than the women (24 per cent compared with 12 per cent). Nearly a fifth of them thought the effect would be positive, compared with just over 10 per cent of the women.

The women were more likely to think that it would have a negative effect in general, while around a fifth thought it would restrict or delay their career progress. Over 10 per cent thought it would make them unemployable, and this gloom was felt particularly acutely among the 1988 women.

Another particular concern expressed by 10 per cent of the women was the fear of difficulty in finding part-time GP principal posts in a new area. Again, there were clear indications that part-time principal posts were coveted posts which were thought to be more often available to 'known' people. Throughout these questionnaires there were constant references to the need for good contacts in order to be able to get part-time or less than full-time principal posts.

The need for geographical moves often came at crucial points in women's careers, as this 1988 woman pointed out: 'It will be disastrous. I will have just reached parity and I may have to move and look for another partnership...'

Other expected results of a future move included the possibility of an end to the doctor's career, a change from general practice to another specialty or a change from another specialty to general practice, a career break and financial difficulties.

Help to overcome constraints caused by geographical moves

There was little doubt that the likelihood of future geographical moves did not fill most respondents with enthusiasm. One of our main aims was to examine ways in which doctors could be helped to overcome constraints on their careers, so we asked those who thought they were likely to move what could help them in their career at the stage at which they moved.

The doctors offered a fairly wide range of possible types and sources of help. An increased availability of part-time posts in general practice was the most frequently mentioned factor, with nearly a quarter of the 1988 women saying this would help them most. 10 per cent of the women said that they would be helped by more information on job opportunities in different areas, and it was thought that FHSAs in particular could be more helpful and informative. However, a number of women felt that they needed both information and advice, and there were criticisms of both the standard and the type of advice given to women who were having to move because of their husbands' jobs. A 1985 woman went a little further than most in saying that she would helped by having 'a postgraduate adviser who is not suffering from Alzheimer's Disease...' There was a clear sense of frustration among many women answering this question.

Nearly 10 per cent of the women said that they would be helped by a more favourable and welcoming attitude on the part of GP principals to newcomers to an area. Others thought there should be a local support group for GPs new to the area, while some considered that they would be helped by doing locums in the new area to get to know the practices and for the practices to get to know them. There were again indications of the difficulty doctors found in 'breaking in' to an area where they were not known.

There were also fears about the future impact of the new GP contract, particularly on doctors who were thinking of moving for reasons other than career development. Nearly one fifth of the men and around 10 per cent of the women thought a change in government policy would help, and one part-time GP principal who was worried about getting a similar part-time post if she moved said tersely that she would be helped by 'the White Paper going up in flames...'

Other more positive suggestions included the establishment of a job-share register, an organised system for retainer scheme posts, greater availability of childcare facilities, the acquiring of more postgraduate qualifications or experience, having an extra qualification in a specialised field, retraining or refresher courses, and the recognition of overseas experience. This was mentioned by a number of women who felt that their desire to work in Third World countries could adversely affect their future careers, and a 1988 woman said: 'There should be a recognised career structure for UK doctors involved in overseas development work, both overseas and allowing them to return to work in the UK...'

Finally, 5 per cent of the women said that it would help if their husband could find a consultant post, which would mean that their travelling life was over and they could get settled in one place, thus allowing them to develop their own careers. There were some sad comments among these women, as well as some telling indications of the kind of lives they were used to living. A 1988 woman said she would be helped by '...my husband getting a consultant post within 30 miles of my practice...' Many of these women were *not* asking for unrealistic treatment and were prepared to make considerable sacrifices to remain working in medicine in jobs which they enjoyed and in which they felt they could make a contribution.

Career breaks

The conventional postgraduate career path of doctors assumes an unbroken series of posts leading to the achievement of certain grades by certain ages. It is clear that women doctors are less likely to achieve this than men doctors, in that most of them will usually take some time off to have babies, even if they have avoided the necessity to move geographically for reasons other than their own career development. In *Doctors and their Careers* the most frequently mentioned constraint on the older women doctors' careers was having children. Nearly 70 per cent of the 1966 qualifiers and 50 per cent of the 1976 qualifiers said that this had been a constraint on their careers. Few of the 1981 qualifiers had had children at the time we interviewed them in 1986, so it had usually not arisen for them.

Having children often meant a career break of some kind. Over one fifth of the 1966 women qualifiers interviewed in *Doctors and their Careers* said that a break of more than six months had been a definite constraint on their careers, although, of course, many women from that cohort had had a break without finding it a constraint. There were, however, indications in that study that the older women had found it rather easier to return to medicine and, indeed, to change specialty and to proceed to career posts after a break than the younger women thought would be possible in the climate as it was at the time of the research in 1986.

We were interested in looking at the experience of the doctors in this current study who had trained as GPs, and seeing how many had had a break of more than six months, for how long and what they considered to be the effects on their careers.

Overall, 14 per cent of the men and 41 per cent of the women said that they had had a break of more than six months at some time in their medical careers. As Table 8.4 shows, the proportion of men was not markedly different in any of

Table 8.4   Whether doctors had ever had a break of more than six months at any time in their medical careers

column percentages

	Total	Male			Female		
		1981	1985	1988	1981	1985	1988
Yes	29	11	17	15	51	43	31
No	71	89	83	85	49	57	69
Base: all respondents	*1263*	*204*	*195*	*179*	*221*	*218*	*246*

the cohorts, but the proportion of women ranged from over 50 per cent of the 1981 cohort to 43 per cent of the 1985 cohort to less than one third of the 1988 cohort, again reflecting both the shorter careers of the 1988 cohort and the fact that they were less likely to have children than the older women. Well over half the women who had qualified in the Indian sub-continent had had a career break of more than six months, compared with 40 per cent of the UK women qualifiers.

Again, those who had ever worked part-time in general practice were more likely to have had a break than those who had not. 47 per cent of the women who had ever worked part-time had had a break, compared with 30 per cent of the women who had never worked part-time. Comparable figures for the men were 31 per cent of those who had ever worked part-time and only 12 per cent of those who had not. Cause and effect were again difficult to attribute, and it seems likely that a combination of factors were related to part-time working and career breaks. The association was nevertheless strong.

It was clear that career breaks were related to children, at least among the women, since 52 per cent of the women with children had had a career break of at least six months, compared with 23 per cent of the women without children, which was, interestingly, almost exactly the same as the proportion of men without children. Only 11 per cent of the men with children had had a career break of more than six months. It looks as though children tend to keep men working but prevent women from doing so.

We asked the doctors their reasons for having a break of six months or more. Not surprisingly, the main reason was maternity, cited by nearly two-thirds of the women, ranging from over 70 per cent of the 1981 women, to 63 per cent of the 1985 women to 51 per cent of the 1988 women. It was the main reason given by over 80 per cent of the women with children who had had a break.

A further 40 per cent of women said they had had a break because of childcare, but again the proportions ranged from over half the 1981 women to 40 per cent of the 1985 women to a quarter of the 1988 women. Often maternity and childcare were given as joint reasons.

But if domestic reasons were the main reasons among women for having a break, they were by no means the main reasons among men. Working abroad was mentioned by nearly half the men, while travel was mentioned by nearly 40 per cent. The comparable proportions of women were 23 per cent mentioning working abroad and 17 per cent mentioning travel. It was again very noticeable, however, that exactly the same proportion of men and women without children who had had a break mentioned working abroad as a reason (55 per cent), while around half the men and women without children mentioned travel. It appeared that men and women doctors were not dissimilar in their attitudes and behaviour if they did not have children.

It should be noted, of course, that the number of men who had had a break was much smaller than the number of women (81 compared with 281). In fact, the actual number of women who had had a break for working abroad or for travel was half as great again as the number of men. There may have been quite a few men with a desire to travel the world, but they were outnumbered by the women. There was certainly evidence of some intrepid travellers among the women doctors responding to this survey.

The fifth most important reason for having a break was unemployment. This reason was given by a quarter of the men, but only just over 10 per cent of the women. It seemed particularly acute among the 1985 men, of whom over one third who had had a break attributed it to unemployment.

Other reasons for having a break included health reasons, to study, to pursue other non-medical interests, to help in the family business, other reasons connected with the family and to engage in medical journalism.

How long were the career breaks? A single break had to be more than six months to be counted, but we asked the doctors how long their career breaks had been altogether. In some cases the doctors were adding up a number of breaks, while in other cases they were referring to just one.

Almost exactly the same proportion of men and women who had had a career break – 42 per cent – said that it had lasted between 7 and 12 months, but, as Table 8.5 shows, the proportions varied between the cohorts, with the younger men and women more likely to fall into this category than their older counterparts. This was not surprising, given the fact that their careers were usually shorter in any case. Around 12 per cent of both men and women had had breaks of 13-18 months. Women were rather more likely to have had breaks of 19-24 months, but men were more likely to have had breaks of two to three years, while women were more likely to have had breaks of more than three years.

Care must be taken in comparing men and women who had had career breaks, not only because of the different numbers – 81 men and 281 women – but also because of the different reasons. Nevertheless it is interesting to note that there was not much difference between the average length of time spent on career breaks – 20.7 months for men and 21.7 months for women, and that the pattern was very similar for the three cohorts of both men and women, as Table 8.5 shows.

We asked those who had had a break what effect they thought it had had on their careers. Nearly 40 per cent of the women and 30 per cent of the men said it had had no effect on their careers. However, one fifth of the women and nearly half the men said the break had had a positive effect on their careers, either through broadening their interests, giving them experience in another field or

Table 8.5   Length of career break of those who had had a break of more than six months in their medical careers

column percentages

	Total	Male			Female		
		1981	1985	1988	1981	1985	1988
7-12 months	41	27	42	54	34	44	49
13-18 months	12	9	15	12	13	11	14
19-24 months	11	9	9	4	13	14	8
25-36 months	13	27	9	23	16	11	7
3 years plus	10	9	9	0	17	11	3
n.a.	12	18	15	8	8	10	20
Base: all who have had a break of more than six months	*362*	*22*	*33*	*26*	*112*	*93*	*76*
Average length of break in months	*21.5*	*27.4*	*20.6*	*16.0*	*26.0*	*20.8*	*15.7*

simply through refreshing their jaded spirits. A small number of women said the break had had a positive effect by giving them the opportunity to put their career and family commitments into perspective. Sometimes this opportunity was seen as a mixed blessing. As one 1988 woman said: 'It gave me time to reflect on the fruitless rat-race of hospital medicine...'

Interestingly, the women with children were rather more likely to say that the break had had no effect, while the women without children were more likely to say it had had a positive effect, often, it appeared, because the break was spent travelling or working abroad, both of which were usually seen as stimulating experiences. A 1988 woman thought her break had had positive effects: 'It was beneficial. I did an interesting variety of jobs abroad and travelled widely, and the sort of people that I wish to work with respect this. Plus it has been an entertaining topic at interviews...'

However, more than half the women thought the break had had a negative effect on their careers. The three main reasons were said to be difficulty in getting back into 'the system' after a break, loss of confidence, and a delay in their career progress.

The difficulty in getting back into the system was often related to a loss of contact with colleagues or others who might know of potential posts. This was clearly of great importance, particularly if the break was combined with a geographical move or the desire to work part-time rather than full-time after it. A 1988 woman summed up the problem: 'When you're not working it is difficult to keep in contact with other GPs and consequently you do not hear about jobs "on the grapevine"...'

Often the three main reasons appeared interrelated, with women finding that they had lost contact, lost confidence and fearing that their career prospects would be affected. A 1985 woman felt that her career had been affected by the break at first: 'But not now. Initially it was difficult to restart work and to convince colleagues that one could be serious and committed and not simply rushing home to breastfeed...'

The loss of confidence was more marked among women with children and was referred to by one doctor as being due to the 'brain rot of pregnancy – an unrecognised syndrome...' A number of women were concerned that they had found it difficult to maintain their skills and keep abreast of medical developments.

Other concerns among women who had taken a break included the fear that other doctors would be less likely to take them on because of their broken career, while a handful of women said that the main result had been a reduction in their superannuation benefit. Some women had changed from another specialty to general practice as a result of the break, while others had changed from general practice to another specialty.

Consideration of career breaks
We asked all the doctors who had not had a career break of longer than six months whether they had ever considered such a break.

It must be remembered that only 14 per cent of the men in our sample had actually had a break in their careers compared with over 40 per cent of the women. However, as Table 8.6 shows, among the doctors who had not had a career break, over a third had considered one – with almost exactly the same proportions of men and women, although among the 1981 and 1985 cohorts there were more men than women in terms of both numbers and proportions. In fact, the proportion of those working full-time in clinical medicine who had considered a break was higher than those of any other category. Again, the doctors who had qualified in the Indian sub-continent were much less likely than UK qualified doctors to have considered a break.

Why had the doctors considered a break? Perhaps surprisingly, the most frequently mentioned reason given by the women was to travel. This was mentioned by 42 per cent of women, compared with maternity, which was mentioned by 41 per cent of them, although nearly half of the 1988 women gave it as a reason. Working abroad was mentioned by 37 per cent of the women, childcare by 35 per cent and a sabbatical by 22 per cent.

The main reasons among the men were for a sabbatical (58 per cent), to work abroad (54 per cent) and for travel (50 per cent). Childcare was mentioned by only 3 per cent of the men. A sabbatical was sought in almost equal proportions by the three cohorts of men and women, but travel and working abroad were mentioned more often by the younger men and women.

It was interesting that so many of the men who had not had a break mentioned a sabbatical, compared with relatively few women. They were also keen on working abroad and travel. This reinforced evidence throughout the survey that

145

Table 8.6 **Whether doctors had ever considered a break of more than six months in their careers**

column percentages

	Total	Male			Female		
		1981	1985	1988	1981	1985	1988
Yes	35	32	35	41	26	28	45
No	65	68	64	59	74	72	55
Base: all respondents who had not had a career break	*901*	*182*	*162*	*153*	*109*	*125*	*170*

a substantial minority of men were finding full-time general practice arduous, if not boring, and that a change of scenery would not have come amiss. There were many indications that some male GPs were becoming increasingly concerned about spending the rest of their lives in full-time general practice without some respite.

Few other reasons for considering a break were given, but they included a desire to give up medicine altogether, to try a different career, to pursue other interests, for health reasons and a desire for alternative training or education.

The doctors did not want a very long break on the whole. Nearly two-thirds of the men and 60 per cent of the women said they had considered a break of 7 to 12 months. The average length of time considered was about a year for the men and 15 months for the women. The 1985 women tended to mention a rather longer period of time than the other women, mainly because they were more likely to be considering a break for maternity or childcare than the others.

Potential effect of career break on doctors' careers

What effect did the doctors think a break of more than six months would have on their careers? Nearly one fifth of the men and over a quarter of the women who had considered a break thought it would have no effect on their careers, while an additional one in ten of both sexes thought it would have no effect provided their GP partners agreed or it was taken 'at the right time'.

Nearly half the men thought it would have a positive effect on their careers, mainly because a break would have a refreshing effect on them or would help them retain an interest in medicine, while some thought it would have a positive effect because it would give them experience in other fields. The women were much less likely to think a break would have a positive effect on their careers, and, indeed, only one sixth of them thought it would have any kind of positive effect.

Around one third of the men but over half the women thought a break would have a negative effect on their careers. Indeed, a quarter of the women considering a break thought it would end their careers in general practice, and one fifth of them said their GP partners would disapprove, a view shared by over 10 per cent of the men who had considered a break.

There were not only differences between the sexes but also among the cohorts. The younger women were more likely to think that a break would have no effect on their careers or that it would have a negative effect. Over 40 per cent of the 1988 women thought a break would have no effect on their careers, but nearly one third thought it would end their careers in general practice. On the other hand the 1981 women who had considered a break were more likely to think it might have a positive effect on their careers. One third of them thought it might have a positive effect compared with less than one in ten of the 1988 women.

The older men too were more likely to think the break might be positive - over half the 1981 men compared with just over a quarter of the 1988 men. The younger men, like the 1988 women, were much more likely to think a break would have a negative effect on their careers.

One of the most important factors governing the responses of the women was, it appeared, whether they had children or not. One third of women with no children who had considered having a break thought it would have a negative effect on their careers, compared with 70 per cent of those with children. On the other hand, 50 per cent of those with no children thought a break would have no effect on their careers, compared with less than one fifth of those with children.

There can be little doubt that women with children were much more worried about the effects on their careers of taking a break than those without children. It also appeared that the younger women who had children were most worried about it. It looked as though doctors, whether male or female, who were considering taking a break to travel or to work abroad, were less likely to think the break would have a deleterious effect on their careers, while those who wanted a break to have a baby or to devote time to their children thought it would have a negative, if not disastrous, effect on their careers. There was a great air of despondency among some of these women, particularly if they were at the point when the decision on whether to take a break or not was imminent. It should be stressed again that the length of break considered by most doctors, whether male, female, young or older, was usually of less than one year.

Job-sharing

When doctors are asked to make recommendations about ways in which the medical career structure could be altered to help ensure that women doctors reach their full potential, one of the most frequently mentioned recommendations is an increase in job-sharing. However, one of the problems with job-sharing, particularly in the postgraduate training grades, is that it assumes two doctors at the same stage, in the same locality, in the same specialty who both want to job-share. This may well not occur outside the main centres and in the bigger specialties. Job-sharing is not easy even if all these requirements are fulfilled, because it also entails the need for the two doctors concerned to have at least some similarity in approach, and the ability to get on with each other and to organise the handover.

There have been some striking success stories in job-sharing, but it has not developed in the way that many had hoped. It is possible that it is easier in career posts such as consultant or GP principal posts. We were interested to know what experience the doctors in this survey had had of job-sharing, and to what extent they themselves wanted to job-share if they had not done so.

We found that only 1 per cent of the men (4 doctors) and 3 per cent of the women (19 doctors) had job-share posts at present, while less than 1 per cent of the men (2 doctors) and a further 3 per cent of the women (19 doctors) had had job-share posts in the past but no longer. This meant that 99 per cent of the men and 94 per cent of the women had no experience of job-sharing.

Among the women, 4 per cent of the 1981 cohort, 3 per cent of the 1985 cohort and 2 per cent of the 1988 cohort were currently job-sharing, and the proportions from the three cohorts of women who had job-shared in the past were 3, 4 and 2 per cent respectively. The overwhelming majority of women who had job-shared had children.

All the men had job-shared or were job-sharing as GP principals. The women were rather different. Around 80 per cent of the 1985 and 1988 women had job-shared as GP principals, but this was true of only half of the 1981 women. One woman had job-shared as a consultant, two as senior registrars, two as registrars, two as SHOs, one as a clinical assistant, one in the armed services and one as a GP assistant.

The length of time the doctors had job-shared varied, and was naturally related to their career lengths. For example, more than half the 1988 women had job-shared for less than a year, while over a quarter of the 1981 women had job-shared for more than two years.

How had it worked out for the doctors who had job-shared? All but one of the 1981 women said that it had worked out very well, but this view was shared by only around half the women from the other two cohorts. There had clearly been some problems, and three women said it had not worked at all well. There were thought to have been problems with communications, and one woman said it worked better if the two doctors were also sharing a nanny. The men were fairly equally divided between those for whom job-sharing had worked well and those for whom there had been some problems.

The evidence on job-sharing was obviously rather limited, with so few doctors involved. It was difficult to make out patterns, and it was perhaps not surprising that the comments from doctors were somewhat idiosyncratic. The very personal nature of the problems of job-sharing was illustrated by this 1981 woman who had had two different attempts at job-sharing. The current job-share worked well but the previous job-share had not: 'We have no major problems because we work at different hours. However, the previous doctor got very stroppy about the decoration of the room. For example, she hated any other pictures apart from her own, hated indoor plants, refused to allow photographs on show, did very few smears which meant I had to do most. Do you want to hear more?...Over the months it became quite upsetting. She felt the room was hers because she had been there for twenty years. She has left now...'

Job-sharing was clearly not without its problems, and it was difficult to see how a system could be evolved to make it work without full cooperation on almost every detail between the potential job-sharers. There is an obvious need for clear demarcation of duties and responsibilities, let alone a need for flexibility on other matters such as decoration and furniture, which might appear to be minor details, but can lead to a breakdown of trust and confidence.

We asked the doctors who had not job-shared whether they would like to do so, either now or in the future. It was a very popular option. 18 per cent of the men and nearly half the women said they would like to job-share. The proportions of men were similar for all cohorts, but the proportion of women increased from 35 per cent of the 1981 cohort, to 41 per cent of the 1985 cohort to as many as 57 per cent of the 1988 cohort.

Table 8.7   Whether doctors who had never job-shared would like to do so

							column percentages
	Total		Male			Female	
		1981	1985	1988	1981	1985	1988
Yes	32	17	17	20	35	41	57
No	66	83	80	77	64	57	42
Don'know/n.a	2	0	3	3	1	2	1
Base: all respondents who had never job-shared	*1219*	*201*	*194*	*177*	*207*	*203*	*237*

There was no doubt about the grade in which the doctors wanted to job-share. 96 per cent of the men and over 90 per cent of the women wanted to job-share as GP principals. Indeed, 96 per cent of the 1988 women who wanted to job-share expressed this wish. The only other grade mentioned by more than a handful of doctors was GP assistant, although over 10 per cent of the 1981 women said that they would like to job-share as GP assistants. Nine women and one man wanted to job-share as consultants, and a small number of women mentioned community health or clinical assistant posts.

Around 40 per cent of both men and women doctors said they did not know for how long they would like to job-share. Around 15 per cent of the men but very few women said they would like to do it for less than a year, while over 10 per cent of women but only a few men said they would like to do it for more than four years. However, it was noteworthy that one third of both men and women who wanted to job-share said they would like to do so indefinitely or for the rest of their working lives.

We asked the doctors if there was anything preventing them from job-sharing. Around a fifth of the men and more than 10 per cent of the women could not think of anything. The main constraint on the men who would have liked to job-share was clearly financial. Over 40 per cent of them said they could not afford to do so, a factor mentioned by one in ten of the women.

The main factor preventing women from job-sharing was lack of opportunities, mentioned by one third of women who would have liked a job-share post, compared with around one in six of the men. One fifth of the women could not find a job-share partner and one in ten of them said their partners or colleagues would disapprove of them job-sharing. Other factors mentioned by both men and women were the unsuitability of the set-up in their present practice for job-sharing, the disapproval of the FHSA, the fact that they were not ready to job-share because of family commitments although they wanted to do so in the future, and a desire to complete training in another specialty first.

Some of the women were rather bitter about the lack of availability of opportunities for job-sharing. One woman was on the GP retainer scheme and had run into administrative problems in Scotland: 'I was a limited commitment partner and my health board would *not* allow me to job-share. We only wanted one basic practice allowance between us and we were going to split my salary, but "it has never been done" was what I was told. I was going to job-share with one of my partners' wives. Both of us are now on the retainer scheme...'

Others were concerned about the lack of cooperation of partners or other GPs. A woman part-time locum who could not find a full-time post would have liked to job-share. She felt the main thing preventing her was '...the reactionary attitude of GPs in this area. They would prefer to employ a man while paying lip service to the idea of job-sharing...'

Some doctors thought that part-time working in general practice was going to be more difficult under the new contract, and a number said that job-sharing might be the only way of making sure of part-time principal work.

There can be little doubt that although the concept of job-sharing was popular, particularly among women, there appeared to be many obstacles put in the way of achieving it. It must be asked to what extent these obstacles are immutable and whether there could be more flexibility in general practice to allow for more job-sharing. It was difficult to determine to what extent the flexibility was needed on the part of the FHSA, or the potential partners in a practice, or whether a lead was needed from the Department of Health. This survey provides strong evidence that job-sharing is a favoured option and deserves to receive very serious consideration. An examination of the practical advantages and disadvantages of job-sharing in general practice should be carried out.

9 Assessment of careers in medicine and future plans

There were many indications in *Doctors and their Careers* that careers in medicine were not always as satisfactory as the doctors had thought they were going to be when they embarked on them at the beginning of medical school. There were clear signs of dissatisfaction and regrets among many of those interviewed, both men and women, with particularly high levels of regret among the younger doctors of both sexes. On the other hand, doctors working in general practice were less likely than those in hospital medicine to express regrets or to be as dissatisfied. In the final part of this study we wanted to explore the attitudes of our respondents towards their jobs and towards medicine in general. We wanted to look at their future plans and to ask them what advice they would give young people who were considering a career in medicine.

The current survey took place in the spring of 1990 at a time when the new GP contract was just about to be implemented. It would be fair to say that it had not been welcomed by doctors' representatives on the whole, and that there was great apprehension among GPs about the implications and future effects both of the new contract and of other changes in the NHS. This was the context in which the doctors were responding to questions about the level of their present job satisfaction and their future plans. Change was on the way, and there were uncertainties about it. However, if research only took place in a climate in which there was no change, there would not be much research. The following discussion reflects the situation as we found it.

Job satisfaction

How satisfied were the doctors with their present job or their status at the moment? There was a remarkable concurrence between men and women in response to this question, although, as Table 9.1 shows, there was quite a wide distribution among the respondents in terms of satisfaction. Overall, 51 per cent of both men and women said they were satisfied or very satisfied with their present jobs or status (23 per cent of the men and 21 per cent of the women were very satisfied; 28 per cent of the men and 30 per cent of the women were satisfied).

Table 9.1 shows that there was little difference among the cohorts, although the 1988 women were less likely to say that they were very satisfied than any

Table 9.1   **Doctors' satisfaction with their present jobs or present status at the moment**

column percentages

	Total	Male 1981	Male 1985	Male 1988	Female 1981	Female 1985	Female 1988
Very satisfied	22	22	22	24	24	27	14
Satisfied	29	28	26	30	28	27	34
Fairly satisfied	28	29	29	28	30	27	28
Not very satisfied	16	17	19	12	14	16	18
Not at all satisfied	4	3	2	4	4	3	5
Don't know	1	1	2	2	0	0	1
Base: all respondents	*1263*	*204*	*195*	*179*	*221*	*218*	*246*

other group. There were virtually no differences in the responses of doctors with or without children.

Among those who said they were fairly satisfied, there was again considerable similarity between men and women (29 per cent of men and 28 per cent of women), and no difference among the cohorts.

Similar results were found among those who were not very satisfied (16 per cent of both men and women), and among those who were not at all satisfied (3 per cent of men and 4 per cent of women).

Looking at the table as a whole, the 1988 men were marginally more likely to express satisfaction than other groups, while the 1988 women were marginally less likely to show overall satisfaction. However, the differences were not significant, and the picture was of a remarkably consistent distribution of levels of satisfaction among the doctors responding to this survey. Slightly over one fifth were very satisfied, nearly 30 per cent were satisfied and a similar proportion were fairly satisfied, about one in six were not very satisfied and under 5 per cent not at all satisfied, giving about one fifth of respondents who were dissatisfied, at least to some extent.

However, there were many critical comments, especially among those who were fairly satisfied. Even among those who were satisfied with their present jobs, there were rumblings of discontent and anxiety about the future, especially with regard to the new contract or the White Paper (Department of Health, 1989) and many expressed concern about the demands of general practice, particularly about the long hours and the on-call work.

The analysis which follows therefore relates to the reasons given by all doctors, whatever their response to the question on satisfaction. Doubts were expressed by many who had said they were satisfied with their present jobs or status, and it was quite clear that doctors often distinguished between their feelings about the job itself and their perception of the current state of general practice.

The main reason given for job satisfaction was, not surprisingly, the fact that the doctors enjoyed their work. This reason was given by over one third of both men and women who were satisfied with their jobs, even if they were worried about the future. A 1981 woman summed up the views of many principals, both men and women: 'As a GP partnership, mine is excellent. We work well together, have a good staff and I love medicine and the patients (most of the time!). But, especially with the new contract, I think what we are being expected to do is a retrograde step and will even increase the long hours I have...'

Her views were echoed by another 1981 woman: 'To date it has been a rewarding, stimulating but demanding job. I feel the new contract will make unrealistic demands and adversely affect my job satisfaction...'

The changes had clearly affected the answers of many women who said that their satisfaction was lower than it had been hitherto, like another 1981 woman who was working as part-time principal: 'Until the government's proposals I was very happy in my job. I work a lot of hours for half the income of my partners, and the government say this is still not satisfactory. They obviously want to get rid of part-timers...'

A good relationship with partners was the second most frequently mentioned reason for job satisfaction, and reinforces the evidence presented throughout this report of the very personal nature of general practice. In this respect, it seemed unlike hospital medicine. Partnerships in general practice were described in *Doctors and their Careers* as being like a marriage. They certainly appeared to demand greater contact and interdependence among doctors than hospital medicine did. If a partnership was working well, it made a great contribution to job satisfaction, but it was also clear that if it was working badly, the reverse was true.

In fact, the second most important reason for job satisfaction among women doctors was having a good part-time post. This was hardly mentioned by men, but a 1981 woman summarised the feelings of many women who were working as part-time principals after struggling with full-time work: 'I was very relieved to be free from rushing back and forth for child carers. Evening and weekend on-call was ghastly with small children expecting their mum to be with them then...'

A 1985 woman was very satisfied with her job because she had managed to establish a partnership in which both partners could work part-time: 'I have an excellent partner and we both work five sessions a week. We share all responsibilities and have equal power. We work also for the DHSS and pool the income. As a result our hours of work are very reasonable for a good income. This allows me plenty of time to spend with my daughter and I generally feel better because I'm not so tired as when I was full-time...'

But among the women who were happy with their part-time posts there were cautionary tales, reflecting the wariness many women expressed throughout this survey about the dangers of not negotiating terms and conditions properly and the warnings they gave about making sure the contract was reasonable. A 1988 woman pointed out the problems: 'I'm satisfied with my part-time principal post only after a lot of fighting for my own rights with regard to work-load and profit-sharing ratios. The initial contract offered was very unfair, but I've managed finally (over two years) to even things out. I do feel that someone with less insight or push may not have achieved the same...'

Another important reason for job satisfaction was simply that the doctors were doing what they wanted to do. There were doctors with a very strong vocation to help others, some of whom had a religious calling. Some were medical missionaries, like a 1985 woman - 'I believe that I am serving the Lord where he wants me to be. As a committed Christian, doing the Lord's will brings inner peace and joy...' - and this 1988 woman - 'My status represents the fulfilment of God's calling...'

However, most doctors were satisfied with their jobs for less spiritual reasons, and an important factor was living in pleasant surroundings. Some doctors, like this 1988 woman, were very satisfied with all aspects of their jobs: 'It is exactly what I trained for. I have a super bunch of partners and work in a beautiful area of the country. I think I have been very lucky...'

Other reasons for satisfaction included having good pay, good facilities, financial security and a flexible job and having good training.

However, as we have seen, around 20 per cent of all doctors were dissatisfied with their present jobs or status. The main reason, given by nearly one third of the men and nearly one fifth of the women who were dissatisfied, were the long hours and the on-call commitment. This was also frequently mentioned by those who expressed satisfaction with their jobs, and was clearly a major factor affecting job satisfaction among doctors. Indeed, one in ten of doctors who expressed satisfaction with their jobs mentioned their dissatisfaction with the long hours and on-call work. It was particularly irksome to the 1985 men and women, like this woman full-time GP principal: 'I work 70 to 80 hours a week. I work weekends and bank holidays and I get up in the middle of the night. I could surely have had an easier time with half the training...'

Among the men there were particular anxieties about the implications and demands of the new GP contract. Nearly one third of the men who were dissatisfied said they were concerned about the uncertainties of the new contract, while a further quarter said they thought the new contract would have a variety of negative effects, especially in the amount of bureaucracy and paperwork it involved. Again, it was mentioned by one in ten of those who were satisfied with their jobs. Women appeared to be less concerned about these implications of the new contract, but much more concerned about the potential effects on part-time opportunities, like this 20-hour a week principal: 'I feel like a lot of 20-hour a weekers – very disgruntled at the changes I will have to make to comply with the new contract, especially working five days a week. It defeats the whole principle of flexibility in general practice...'

Some women were concerned about the potential effects of the new contract not only on their part-time status but also on the general finances of the partnership with the withdrawal of the full basic practice allowance for 20-hour a week GPs. A 1981 woman summed up their anxieties: 'The current NHS changes have put a great deal of pressure on our practice, and this, coupled with very high interest rates, means I'm under financial pressure. Otherwise I would be very satisfied with my practice...'

Concern about money was expressed by around one in six of the dissatisfied doctors, as well as by others. A 1981 man drew comparisons with other occupations: 'Generally I feel that for the amount of hours I put into this practice the remuneration does not correspond. Sometimes I feel I might be better off as a salesman...'

The 1985 men were particularly concerned with finance, and were, in general, more vocal in their dissatisfaction than the other male cohorts. A full-time principal, who did an additional four hours a week in hospital medicine, articulated the complaints of a number of men from his year: 'Medicine as a career is not to be recommended – very long hours, too much red tape, patients' expectations unreasonable all too often, working in an inner city area is not fairly balanced compared with some rural practices, and I don't like the government's bully-boy tactics...'

Nearly one in ten of the dissatisfied women thought there were not enough part-time opportunities, while one in ten of the dissatisfied men and a smaller proportion of women could not find a job in general practice. This was particularly acute among the 1988 men, like this one: 'I'm not at all satisfied, because after repeated applications and interviews, and despite having good qualifications and the MRCGP, I am still not employed as a GP principal, but in a private hospital, two years after finishing my vocational training. The profession and Royal College do not seem to know or care about the numbers of doctors in my position. I have had a very expensive training which is being wasted. There is no job-finding service for vocational trainees and we have to battle it out on our own. May I suggest that this should be the subject for your next survey...'

His view was echoed, somewhat less eloquently, by a woman from the same year: 'I continue to be female and unable to find a job in this area...'

Although some women were dissatisfied because they said that part-timers were treated unfairly, there were few who said they were dissatisfied because they wanted to work part-time instead of full-time. However, nearly one in ten of the dissatisfied women said they would like to work full-time or to have a permanent job or partnership. Half of these were GP locums. And over 10 per cent of the dissatisfied women said they would like to work more sessions. Two-thirds of these were women on the retainer scheme who felt restricted by the rules. In fact, over 50 per cent of the women on the retainer scheme said they would like to work more sessions in response to this question about job satisfaction.

There were also dissatisfied women who were doing other work because they could not find work in general practice and a number of women who felt they were wasting their skills by working outside general practice.

A tiny number of doctors were dissatisfied because of alleged racial prejudice, while a small number of women doctors said they were dissatisfied because they were not working, but were looking forward to returning to part-time general practice.

Prospects in five years' time

What were the doctors' future plans? Did they intend to stay in medicine, or were there any signs that there might be an exodus from the profession? Did they intend to stay in general practice, or were they likely to try their hand at anything else?

Table 9.2   What doctors thought they would be doing in five years' time

column percentages

	Total	Male 1981	Male 1985	Male 1988	Female 1981	Female 1985	Female 1988
Working FT in clinical medicine	56	84	85	85	33	32	28
Working less than FT in clinical medicine	33	5	3	3	52	57	63
Working outside clinical medicine but in medicine-related occupation	3	3	4	3	3	6	1
Working outside medicine	1	1	2	1	2	1	0
Working both in and outside medicine	4	3	5	7	4	1	4
Not working	1	0	1	0	1	1	1
Don't know	2	3	1	2	5	2	3
Base: all respondents	*1263*	*204*	*195*	*179*	*221*	*218*	*246*

Table 9.2, which shows what doctors thought they would be doing in five years' time, should be compared with Table 2.19 which shows their present employment status. The results are not surprising, but the implications are important. Overall, there is a shift from full-time to less than full-time working, with 56 per cent of the doctors expecting to be working full-time in clinical medicine in five years' time, compared with 66 per cent at present, and 33 per cent expecting to be working less than full-time in clinical medicine, compared with 26 per cent at present. There is a marginal increase in the proportions who expect to be working outside clinical medicine but in a medically related occupation, from 2 to 3 per cent. There is also a marginal increase in those who expect to be working outside medicine, from less than 1 per cent to 1 per cent, and a slightly larger increase among those who expect to be working both inside and outside medicine, from 1 to 4 per cent. Fewer doctors expect not to be working – a decrease from 3 per cent at present to 1 per cent – and none of the

doctors were expecting to be on maternity leave, which accounted for 2 per cent at present.

The shift from full-time to less than full-time working was found, naturally, mainly among the women, but it was interesting that there was also a shift among the men. The proportion of men in all three cohorts working full-time in clinical medicine was well over 90 per cent at present, but this proportion declined to around 85 per cent who thought they would be doing so in five years' time. The proportion of men who thought they would be working less than full-time in clinical medicine increased marginally, as did the proportions who thought they would be in medically related occupations, working outside medicine and working both in and out of medicine. Among the 1988 men, none were working both in and out of medicine at present, but 7 per cent thought they would be doing so in five years' time.

The proportions of men moving into other work may have been relatively small for each category, but the potential shift away from full-time work in clinical medicine was quite marked, especially among the 1981 men, of whom 95 per cent were working full-time in clinical medicine at present, but only 84 per cent thought they would be doing so in five years' time.

Among the women the shift was, not surprisingly, more marked, particularly among the 1988 women, of whom 51 per cent were working full-time and 40 per cent less than full-time in clinical medicine at present, but only 28 per cent thought they would be working full-time compared with 63 per cent who thought they would be working less than full-time in clinical medicine in five years' time.

Among the 1985 women the shift was not quite so noticeable, but the proportion who thought they would be working full-time in clinical medicine dropped from 37 per cent at present to 32 per cent in five years' time, while the proportions working less than full-time rose from 49 per cent at present to 57 per cent who thought they would be doing so in five years' time.

The 1981 women showed a similar decrease in full-time working in clinical medicine, from 39 per cent at present to 33 per cent in five years' time, but only a marginal increase in less than full-time working, from 50 to 52 per cent.

Among all the female cohorts there was evidence of a rise in the proportion who thought they would be working outside medicine but in a medically related occupation, and a distinct interest in working outside medicine or working both in and out of medicine, compared with the tiny number of women who were doing so at present. The proportion of women who thought they would not be working at all in five years' time dropped sharply from the present position.

Looking at the figures another way, 89 per cent of the 539 men but only 60 per cent of the 293 women who were currently working full-time in clinical medicine thought they would be doing so in five years' time. It is noteworthy that one third of the women currently working full-time thought they would be working less than full-time in clinical medicine in five years' time.

On the other hand, 10 per cent of the 316 women currently working part-time in clinical medicine thought they would be working full-time in five years' time, although well over 80 per cent thought they would still be working less than full-time.

Two groups of women of particular interest were those who were not working at present and those on maternity leave. Nearly half of those who were not working thought they would be working part-time in five years' time, one fifth thought they would be outside clinical medicine but in a medically related occupation and only 10 per cent thought they would not be working at all. Well over 80 per cent of those currently on maternity leave thought they would be working less than full-time in clinical medicine, and all but one of these women thought they would be working.

Future jobs of doctors

What jobs did the doctors think they would be doing in five years' time, and how did this compare with what they were doing now? Table 9.3 should be looked at in conjunction with Table 2.21 which gives the present grade, job or status of the respondents.

Overall 50 per cent of the doctors (78 per cent of the men and 26 per cent of the women) thought they would be working as full-time GP principals in five years' time, compared with 56 per cent who were currently doing so (83 per cent of the men and 32 per cent of the women). 23 per cent of the doctors (3 per cent of the men and 41 per cent of the women) thought they would be part-time GP principals, compared with 17 per cent who were currently working as part-time or 20-hour a week principals (2 per cent of the men and 28 per cent of the women).

Table 9.3 confirms the drift away from full-time working expected over the next five years. This is not particularly surprising among the women, given the average age of the younger doctors, although it is notable that the proportion of women expecting to be full-time principals in five years' time drops for all cohorts, including the 1981 women, many of whom might be expected to have completed their families at the time of the survey.

But it was not only among the women that the proportion expecting to be full-time principals dropped. The same was true for the 1981 and 1985 men, with a drop of 10 per cent for both cohorts - from 87 per cent at present to 77 per cent expected in five years' time. On the other hand, the proportion of 1988 men who expected to be full-time principals rose from 73 per cent at present to 81 per cent in five years' time. This is not surprising, given that 7 per cent of the 1988 men were currently working as GP locums and 3 per cent as GP assistants.

The proportion of men expecting to be part-time GP principals was marginally more than at present, but among the women, it rose from 30 to 36 per cent of the 1981 cohort, 33 to 40 per cent of the 1985 cohort and 24 to 45 per cent of the 1988 cohort.

In addition, 4 per cent of the women and 1 per cent of the men thought they would be job share principals, a category not specifically pulled out in Table 2.21.

It is interesting that none of the women thought they would still be on the GP retainer scheme in five years' time and relatively few thought they would be

Table 9.3   What job doctors thought they would be doing in five years' time

column percentages

	Total	Male 1981	Male 1985	Male 1988	Female 1981	Female 1985	Female 1988
FT GP principal	50	77	77	81	26	28	23
PT GP principal	23	4	3	1	36	40	45
Job-share princ.	3	1	*	0	2	5	7
PT GP assistant	2	0	0	0	2	5	2
Consultant	2	3	2	3	1	3	*
Working abroad	2	3	2	2	2	1	3
Undecided but inc. GP	2	0	3	1	2	3	2
In & out of medicine	2	1	3	2	*	1	2
Other GP job	1	*	1	1	*	*	4
SCMO/CMO	1	0	1	0	4	2	*
Outside medicine	1	2	1	1	2	*	0
Public health	1	0	2	0	2	1	*
Hospital (other than consultant)	1	*	0	3	4	0	*
Other	3	5	1	1	7	5	3
Don't know at all	2	0	1	2	4	2	3
Not working	4	3	4	2	5	3	4
Base: all respondents	*1263*	*204*	*195*	*179*	*221*	*218*	*246*

GP assistants. Neither of these options was really popular among the women respondents. It looks as though they are positions which most women want to abandon as soon as possible, although 5 per cent of the 1985 women thought they would be part-time GP assistants in five years' time.

The proportion of doctors who thought they would be abroad was around 2 per cent for all cohorts. This proportion is an exclusive count and is not directly comparable with the figure in Table 2.19 which shows the overall proportion who were abroad at the time of the survey – 4 per cent of all respondents. They were included in the proportions given in the rest of Table 2.19 showing full-time or less than full-time working and so on. However, including the six doctors who gave a specific job as well as the information that they expected to be abroad, the overall proportion who expected to be abroad in five years' time remained at 2 per cent.

Essentially, Table 9.3 not only indicates a drift away from full-time general practice among women and older men, but also suggests a slight redistribution of work. In each cohort of women, rather more expected to be working as either full-time or part-time principals in five years' time than were doing so at present. Among men, the same is true only of the 1988 men. There is evidence that there is no single aim for the older men, and they expect to be in a variety of jobs.

We analysed the expected jobs by what the doctors were doing at the moment, and found that 81 per cent of those who were currently working as full-time GP principals thought they would still be doing so in five years' time. What about the others? We found that 10 per cent thought they would be part-time principals and 1 per cent job-share principals. The remaining 8 per cent who were currently full-time principals thought they would be doing a variety of jobs in five years' time, with 2 per cent undecided, 1 per cent outside medicine and 1 per cent abroad.

Of those currently working as less than full-time principals (the 20 hour a week and part-time principals), 17 per cent thought they would be full-time GP principals, 66 per cent part-time principals and 7 per cent job-share principals. Of the remaining 10 per cent, there were single mentions for a variety of jobs, both in and out of medicine, with 2 per cent undecided and 1 per cent abroad.

The noticeable drift away from full-time general practice among these doctors is a trend which should be taken seriously. Although the numbers among the men are not particularly large, they confirm the discontent with full-time general practice noted among a substantial minority of male full-time GP principals throughout this survey. It remains to be seen whether, in fact, they achieve their aim, but the fact remains that they wished to change direction, if only to add another string to their bow.

Among the women, although the intended move from full-time to part-time principal posts was probably more closely related to the intention to have children than to any other factor, it is also clear from the evidence presented in this report that full-time general practice was often found to be very tiring for both men and women, and that, in spite of the disadvantages of being a part-time principal, many women found it suited their needs in terms of combining a family and career.

Looking at the 134 doctors currently working in medicine other than in general practice, we found that 6 per cent thought they would be full-time GP principals, 10 per cent part-time GP principals and 1 per cent job-share principals in five years' time. If there was a drift away from general practice among the GPs, particularly away from full-time principal jobs, there appeared to be a slight trend in the other direction among doctors who had gained their GP vocational training certificate but were currently working in medicine outside general practice.

On the whole, however, although those who thought they were likely to be full-time GP principals were currently found among most types of other medical jobs, those who thought they would be part-time principals tended to be women and concentrated among SCMOs and CMOs.

Among the 61 doctors who were not working at the time of the survey, only 8 per cent thought they would be full-time GP principals in five years' time, but one third of them thought they would be part-time principals and 7 per cent thought they would be job-share principals. Over two-thirds of the doctors on maternity leave thought they would be part-time or job-share principals, but only one thought she would be a full-time principal. There was a lot of indecision among the other doctors who were not working, and it appeared that most of them were unable to predict with any certainty what they would be doing.

Same or different job or status in five years' time?

To what extent did the doctors think they would be doing something different in five years' time from what they were doing at present? Table 9.4 shows the anticipated changes in job or status among the doctors.

Table 9.4   Whether doctors' jobs or status would be the same in five years' time as now

column percentages

	Total	Male			Female		
		1981	1985	1988	1981	1985	1988
Yes	68	89	84	73	65	57	47
No	31	11	15	26	33	41	52
n.a.	1	0	1	1	2	1	1
Base: all respondents	*1263*	*204*	*195*	*179*	*221*	*218*	*246*

It can be seen from Table 9.4 that over two-thirds of the doctors thought they would be doing the same job in five years' time, but that nearly one third thought they would be doing something different. However, there was a big difference between the men and the women, with 82 per cent of the men thinking they would be doing the same thing, compared with 56 per cent of the women. The table shows clearly the tendency for the younger women to think that their status would change, with less than 50 per cent of the 1988 women thinking it would be the same as now, compared with nearly two-thirds of the 1981 women.

The main expected change in job or status, of course, was from full-time to less than full time work in clinical medicine. However, as we have seen, some women thought they would be changing from part-time to full-time work, while some doctors of both sexes thought they would be moving out of clinical medicine.

We asked the doctors whether the expected job or status in five years' time was what they would wish to be doing. 91 per cent of the men and 84 per cent of the women said that they were happy with what they were likely to be doing, but over 10 per cent of the women and 6 per cent of the men said they were not happy about it, while a small proportion of both sexes were unsure.

We asked those who were unhappy about their likely job or status what they would wish to be doing instead. The main response among the women was that they would prefer to be GP principals, mainly working part-time, with around one in ten preferring to job-share. Nearly one third of the men shared this wish. Nearly one fifth of both the men and the women who were not happy about their future likely jobs wanted to work in medicine outside general practice, while over a quarter of the men would have preferred to work outside medicine.

Regrets about decision to become doctors

In *Doctors and their Careers* our final question to the doctors interviewed was whether they had ever regretted their decision to become doctors. We had not originally intended to ask this question, but during the pilot stage of the study we were frequently told by doctors of their regrets that they had ever started medicine. We therefore incorporated the question into the interview and were struck by the extent to which doctors opened up at the end of a long interview with detailed accounts of how they wished they had done something else.

In that study, it was quite clear that the extent to which doctors had ever had regrets about their decision to become doctors increased dramatically among both men and women according to the year of qualification, with the younger doctors much more likely to express regrets. Among the men it rose from 14 per cent of the 1966 qualifiers to 26 per cent of the 1976 qualifiers to 44 per cent of the 1981 qualifiers, while among the women the comparable proportions were 19 per cent of the 1966 qualifiers, 30 per cent of the 1976 qualifiers and 49 per cent of the 1981 qualifiers.

These doctors were interviewed in 1986, approximately 20 years, 10 years and 5 years after qualification. We did not ask them if they still regretted their decision at the time of the interview, although many of them indicated that they did.

Some readers of *Doctors and their Careers* suggested that it was not surprising that younger doctors had regretted studying medicine in the immediate postgraduate training period, and that it was likely that older doctors would have answered in a similar fashion five years after qualification. The evidence presented in the report suggests that this was not so, particularly since the question asked was whether the doctors had *ever* regretted their decision to become doctors. The older doctors did not appear to have short memories about other parts of their careers, and there was strong evidence throughout the interviews that the younger doctors found many aspects of their careers less satisfactory than the older doctors had done. The trend towards less satisfaction among the younger doctors was quite clearly marked among both men and women in that study.

However, in designing the questionnaire for the present study we bore in mind potential criticisms, and, in any case, we wanted to explore the question of regrets rather more fully than we had done in the previous study. We also wanted to establish to what extent any regrets felt by the doctors were of a more permanent nature than 'ever' regretting a decision might be. We therefore asked the doctors to comment not only on the reasons for their regrets, as we had done in *Doctors and their Careers*, but we also asked them specifically whether they still regretted their decision to become doctors now.

Table 9.5 shows that nearly 50 per cent of the respondents in the present survey had regretted their decision to become doctors at some time. There was much greater similarity between the men and the women in this study than in the previous study, with 46 per cent of the men and 51 per cent of the women saying they had regretted their decision.

Table 9.5   Whether respondents had ever regretted their decision to become doctors

column percentages

	Total	Male			Female		
		1981	1985	1988	1981	1985	1988
Yes	49	40	43	57	43	45	63
No	48	57	54	40	55	51	35
Don't know	3	3	3	3	2	4	2
Base: all respondents	*1263*	*204*	*195*	*179*	*221*	*218*	*246*

Again, the proportions increased with each cohort, and, as we saw in Chapter 2, the later the cohort the later the likely date of qualification as a doctor. Thus, the majority of the 1981 cohort in this study had qualified between 1975 and 1977, the majority of the 1985 cohort had qualified between 1979 and 1981, and the majority of the 1988 cohort had qualified between 1982 and 1984.

Direct comparisons cannot be drawn with the cohorts in *Doctors and their Careers* for a number of reasons, not least because the doctors in the present study had all trained in general practice and because the study took place four years later. In addition, the respondents had generally been qualified for periods which were not directly comparable with the doctors in the previous study. Nevertheless, the pattern shown in *Doctors and their Careers* is repeated here. Moreover, there appears to be a higher incidence of regrets among the 1981 cohort in this study who qualified around 1976 than was found in the previous study among 1976 qualifiers. Similarly there appears to be a higher incidence of regrets among the 1985 cohort in this study who qualified around 1981 than among the 1981 qualifiers in *Doctors and their Careers*.

The 1976 and 1981 qualifiers from *Doctors and their Careers* have been followed up in a study carried out in 1991 which also looks at a new cohort of medical qualifiers from 1986, and their responses five years on are of particular interest (Allen, forthcoming).

Looking at the doctors in the present study, it can be seen from Table 9.5 that the proportion of men who had ever regretted their decision to become doctors increased from 40 per cent of the 1981 cohort to 43 per cent of the 1985 cohort to 57 per cent of the 1988 cohort. The comparable proportions for women ran almost parallel but rather higher at 43 per cent of the 1981 cohort, 45 per cent from 1985 to as many as 63 per cent of the 1988 cohort.

It must surely be a matter for concern that nearly two-thirds of the young women and nearly 60 per cent of the young men gaining their vocational training certificates in general practice in 1988 had regretted their decision to become doctors.

Looking at the present jobs of the doctors, we found that 50 per cent of the full-time GP principals reported they had ever regretted their decisions, compared with 47 per cent of the part-time GP principals (including the 20-hour a week principals). Full-time GP locums, perhaps not surprisingly, were more likely than other groups to express regrets. Those working outside medicine or in medically related occupations were much less likely than others to have regretted their decisions to become doctors, while doctors currently working in hospital medicine were more likely than others to have regretted their decision, with two thirds of the senior registrars and 10 of the 12 SHOs expressing regrets.

There was an interesting difference between those who had qualified in the UK and those who had qualified elsewhere. Whereas 51 per cent of UK qualifiers (50 per cent of men and 52 per cent of women) said they had ever regretted their decision to become doctors, this was true of only 28 per cent of the doctors who had qualified in the Indian sub-continent (26 per cent of men and 32 per cent of women). Only one third of the doctors who had qualified in Ireland had regretted their decisions and 42 per cent of those who had qualified in other countries, although this was true of one third of the men and over half the women qualifiers in this category.

Table 9.6   Whether respondents currently regretted their decision to become doctors

column percentages

	Total	Male 1981	Male 1985	1988	Female 1981	Female 1985	1988
Yes	20	24	19	23	20	17	20
No	76	73	78	75	75	81	75
Not sure/don't know	4	3	3	2	5	2	5
Base: all respondents	*1263*	*204*	*195*	*179*	*221*	*218*	*246*

But to what extent were the regrets transitory? Did the doctors still regret their decisions? We asked them whether they regretted their decision now. Table 9.6 indicates that one fifth of the total sample of doctors currently regretted their decision. Overall, 22 per cent of the men and 19 per cent of the women responding to this survey said that they still regretted their decision to become doctors. 24 per cent of the 1981 men and 23 per cent of the 1988 men regretted it, and so did 20 per cent of the 1981 and 1988 women. The 1985 cohort had marginally fewer present regrets, with 19 per cent of the men and 17 per cent of the women.

It was interesting that the 1988 men and women, who were much more likely than the other cohorts to have said that they had ever regretted their decisions to become doctors, were so similar to the others in the extent to which they still regretted it. It appeared that they might have had a tougher time during their training than the older doctors, but that their subsequent careers had made them as satisfied – or dissatisfied – as their older counterparts.

Full-time GP principals were more likely to regret their decision currently than part-time principals: 23 per cent compared with 16 per cent. The proportions were more or less identical for men and women. Other groups with relatively high levels of current regrets were those on maternity leave, over a third of whom regretted their decision, clinical assistants and doctors in hospital training grades.

Although part-time or less than full-time working was seen to have been a considerable constraint on the careers of so many doctors, particularly women, it was noteworthy that no difference was found between those who had ever worked part-time and those who had never worked part-time in the extent to which they currently regretted their decision to become doctors. It appears that regrets are usually related to factors other than the question of part-time working, and, indeed, from the evidence presented about the higher incidence of current regret among full-time principals compared with part-time principals, it is possible that long hours and on-call commitments may be more of a long-term constraint than working part-time.

Reasons for regrets

We asked the doctors for their comments on their answers. It was very clear that many doctors who had never regretted becoming doctors expressed the same views as those who had regretted it. We therefore present the most important comments both as a proportion of all doctors and as a proportion of those who had regretted their decision.

By far the most frequently mentioned reason for regretting their decision to become a doctor centred round the long hours, the on-call duties and the demands on their time. This was the reason given by around 50 per cent of both men and women who had regretted their decision and by over a quarter of *all* doctors, whether they had regretted it or not. It was given far more frequently by the younger doctors of both sexes, and, indeed around 40 per cent of the 1988 men and women, whether they had regretted their decision or not, expressed concern about this aspect of their work.

There was evidence of considerable fatigue and desperation among some of these young doctors, like this woman senior registrar: 'Since qualifying in 1984 I have spent the last six years either in a complete state of exhaustion or depression or feeling guilty because I have been working for a postgraduate qualification. My twenties have passed by, and all I have done is survive them because of my career in medicine. I have a string of broken relationships because I was too tired to make the effort. I am now 29 and am still working for exams. I would like to have children, but if I give up now it will make the last six years even more pointless...'

The young men from 1988 also showed signs of stress and fatigue, and complaints about the long hours were often combined with other factors, as in this case: 'Basically the job can often be too rushed, which is stressful. There is no mechanism to deter the chronic neurotic and timewaster whose main hobby is visiting or calling out the doctor. And my absolute bugbear, night duty (especially) and weekends. I think doctors should work shifts, like policemen, ambulance drivers, nurses, lorry drivers, train drivers and airline pilots. A tired, rushed doctor is liable to make mistakes...' This doctor still regretted his decision to become a doctor.

But it was not only the 1988 doctors who were concerned about long hours, since around half the 1985 men and women who had regretted their decision cited this as one of the main reasons, like this woman who had also left general practice for hospital medicine: 'I have regretted that medicine has necessitated forfeiting so many of my other interests. Looking back at my twenties and early thirties, I seem to have no memories except of work, chronic fatigue and being extremely resentful that junior doctors were the only people in the country working for less than £2 an hour overtime. I don't regret studying medicine, but I do regret the personal cost...'

Another 1985 woman, who had stayed in general practice, had a similar story: 'I spent probably the (potentially) best years of my life working 120 hours a week, and then found it hard to get a post at the end! When I did find a post, the recompense did not seem worth all the hours I had put in. Because of my life, we have found it difficult to keep friends outside medicine...'

And yet another 1985 woman who had gained her MRCPsych and a distinction in her MRCGP had regretted her decision to become a doctor in the past and still regretted it: 'My mid-twenties passed in a blur of physical and emotional exhaustion due to one in twos and one in threes. My life choices have been limited and altered by the rigid career structure and resistance to supporting the dual role of doctor and wife/mother in a positive way. The quality of my personal life and family life is significantly impaired by stress – both mine and my husband's...'

The commitment of on-call work was clearly of more concern to many doctors than the actual hours worked, as this 1985 man explained. He, like others who still regretted their decision to become doctors, had a number of reasons for his regrets: 'I hate being on-call. Much of my work is social, not medical. I am more interested in medical science than social problems. General practice is being slowly devalued by the public...'

The demands and expectations of patients in general practice were mentioned more frequently by men than women, and, indeed, nearly one fifth of the men who had regretted their decision to become doctors mentioned it, compared with 10 per cent of the women who had regretted their decision. It often appeared that some men had made the wrong choice of career, like this 1985 man - 'I'm disillusioned with people in general. I would prefer to work with machines...' - and another from the same year - 'I prefer working with the lower order of animals. I should have been a vet...'

Although only a small proportion of doctors said they had definitely made the wrong choice of career, they were found among men and women from every year, like this 1981 man who still regretted his decision: 'I wanted to be a scientist and was misinformed about what it would be like to be a doctor...' A woman full-time GP principal from the 1988 cohort was another doctor who regretted her decision for this reason: 'I found out too late, or rather admitted it too late, that, although academically and professionally competent, it does not suit my personality, aptitudes or skills. Also it does not pay well enough for the hassles that go with the job...'

There was no doubt that, even if the doctors liked the patients and did not feel they had made the wrong choice of career, many found their work emotionally draining, and this was the second most frequently mentioned reason for regrets, particularly by the women. Nearly 20 per cent of those who had regretted their decision and 10 per cent of the total respondents said they found their work emotionally draining.

The question of government policy or the effects of the White Paper on health or the new contract were also mentioned by nearly 20 per cent of those who had regretted their decision to become doctors, and by over 10 per cent of all respondents. The comments on this were lengthy and sometimes bitter. The doctors were often concerned about both the effects on them personally and the effects on the Health Service, like a 1981 woman, who regretted her decision now: 'The long hours worked, the immense responsibility at times, the government's introduction of the new contract and the extra *unnecessary* administration required. Also the recent health service cuts and the reduction in the quality of hospital services which can be offered to patients...'

The question of the future of the Health Service exercised many of those who expressed regrets, some of whom were particularly concerned about maintaining a 'free' service, like a woman GP from the 1981 cohort: 'I became a doctor because I believe passionately in free care for all. I can see this disintegrating...' Her views were shared by another 1981 woman: 'I am very worried about the White Paper and *money versus medicine*. We are not trained to think of money before patients. I hope I do not get disillusioned in future...'

The question of pay and hours was another cause for regrets among doctors. Over one in six of those who had regretted their decision mentioned this, but nearly one fifth of the men gave it as a reason, compared with just over one in ten of the women. The approach of the sexes was often different, with men tending to say the money was not good enough for the commitment and responsibility involved, while women were more likely to say it was not good enough to enable them to pay for the necessary childcare. A 1981 woman summed up these views: 'I expected hard work and long hours, but I also expected that I would be remunerated enough to provide good childcare for my children. This has not been the case – childcare is extremely expensive...'

It was noticeable that the younger doctors were more concerned about pay than the older doctors, and indeed a quarter of the 1988 men and one fifth of the 1988 women who had regretted their decision mentioned it. A 1988 woman, who had gained a distinction in her MRCGP, said doctors were '..underpaid and under-respected skivvies...', while a 1988 male full-time principal, married to another doctor, summed up the reasons for his regrets: 'Hours too long. Poor government attitudes to the profession. Too much management personnel in hospital sector. Pay grossly inadequate for the work. Family life ruined. High suicide rate. Enormous responsibility. Increasing litigation...'

Around one fifth of the doctors who had regretted their decision said it was mainly during hospital postgraduate training, and this theme was particularly noticeable among the women, who often stressed their total fatigue at the time, like this 1981 woman: 'Disillusion soon sets in when one becomes too physically and mentally exhausted to think about what one is trying to achieve...'

There were many references to the strain of hospital medicine, summed up by a 1985 woman who had regretted her decision in the past but not now: 'I like medicine and I like patients, but I resent being expected to work all hours and missing out on a time of my life when I could do so many things. I resent the learning by humiliation and fire rather than organised teaching and encouragement. The GP trainee year was not like that...'

The lack of advice and encouragement during training was mentioned by a number of women in particular, like a 1988 woman: 'I love my job most of the time, but sometimes I feel it takes too much out of me. I regret not having had any guidance – ever – on career matters, and feel I could have arrived sooner if I had been advised or knew where to go for advice...'

But it was not only women who complained about their hospital training posts. A 1988 man, who was now a full-time GP principal, no longer regretted his decision, but described why he had done so in the past: 'Because I suffered greatly at the hands of my seniors and the system when doing hospital jobs and honestly wonder how I survived. We were grossly overworked and greatly under-paid for it and the BMA didn't want to know and still don't...'

The strain on family and other relationships was a factor mentioned by around 10 per cent of those who had regretted their decisions. In some cases this was attributed to the hours, as in the case of this 1981 woman: 'It's difficult to gain the satisfaction of total patient care in general practice unless you are willing to do out-of-hours work and participate in partnership matters. Combining this with a family and a GP husband is very stressful. It would be easier if I had not married a doctor or if I had had a different career...'

In other cases, it was not only the hours but the demands of the medical career system. The problems encountered by doctors who marry other doctors were found to be an important factor in placing constraints on women doctors' careers in *Doctors and their Careers*. It is a problem which has important implications for medical manpower planning. A 1988 woman told her story, which was by no means unique: 'I married a doctor and we have a 2-year-old child. We are now living 120 miles apart – my husband is a senior registrar in London and I am a GP principal here. We see each other at weekends. We have an infertility problem which the stress of parting is not helping. I regret the fact that jobs are so competitive and it's so difficult to live where you want to. I have been divorced once – this is my second marriage. My first husband was a doctor also...'

There was no doubt that some doctors were concerned not only about the pay and the hours, but also regretted their decisions specifically when they looked at contemporaries with different lifestyles. Often the reasons merged into one, as a 1981 woman consultant explained about her regrets: '...when you have to do postgraduate study and research until you are 35 plus plus. I do envy friends who don't have to continue studying sometimes. Intellectually I found medical school dull. I enjoy the creativity of my present specialty...'

There were some interesting comments on the lack of privacy of GPs, as this 1981 woman explained: 'Because you have a label put on you and you are expected to live and act in a certain way, especially as a GP in a rural area. I don't like not being able to go about my life without the feeling that people are watching you and measuring you up...'

There were many other reasons put forward by doctors for regretting their decisions to study medicine, including worries about poor career prospects, especially among the 1988 men; difficulties in combining a career and family, only found among the women; discrimination against women, mainly found among 1988 women; lack of part-time opportunities, again mentioned mainly by women; being exploited and not respected, mainly mentioned by 1981 men; increasing litigation, mentioned mostly by men; poor job security; dissatisfaction with general practice; the inflexibility of the career structure in hospital medicine; the length of time needed in postgraduate training in medicine; and the unfair treatment of part-timers in medicine. All these factors were mentioned by between 1 and 5 per cent of the total sample.

Reasons for not regretting their decision

We asked doctors to comment on their answer to the question of whether they had ever regretted their decision to become doctors, but did not specifically ask them to give reasons for their answer. Although most of those who had regretted it gave reasons for their answers, nearly half of those who had never regretted it did not feel it necessary to elaborate. Women were more likely than men to give reasons.

The main reason was that they found their jobs interesting and stimulating, a response given more frequently by women. There was absolutely no doubt in the minds of some women, like this 1981 doctor working in community health: 'I had wanted to become a doctor since childhood. I feel I had a true vocation. I have never felt differently then or now...'

The strong sense of religious calling among some doctors was very noticeable in response to this question, and a 1985 woman's comments were typical of several of her counterparts: 'I believe the Lord called me into medicine. He provided for me as a mature student and wonderfully provided for all my financial and other needs as I was training. I have always found medicine an intellectually stimulating, challenging and rewarding career, and count it as a privilege to be able to help and heal others. It is not always easy, but the joys outweigh the difficulties...'

Although the 1988 women were more likely to have expressed regrets than other women, there were some who were very enthusiastic about their decision to become doctors: 'I *love* clinical medicine. I go to work for sanity to get away from the kids, but I enjoy being a mother too...'

Other reasons given for never regretting their decision included the comment that they had always wanted to be doctors, that it provided a lot of contact with people and a good standard of living, gave opportunities for working abroad, allowed women to combine work and family and gave many varied opportunities.

169

Around 7 per cent of doctors who had never regretted their decisions said the advantages outweighed the disadvantages, and a tiny handful said they liked it because doctors were respected in society.

Many respondents were not so sure that doctors were respected in society, and there was a strong undercurrent running through these questionnaires that doctors were prepared to make sacrifices in their personal lives if they thought they were appreciated by somebody. There were many indications that doctors were increasingly feeling rather beleaguered: both unappreciated by their patients and caught up in politics. Some of the comments were very outspoken, but many reflected the views of a woman from the 1981 cohort: 'On the one hand I do not regret it, as there are few part-time jobs which pay so well and which I can do to suit myself and my family. On the other hand, a medical career is not so satisfactory these days – there are limitations to what medicine can cure, the politics of medicine are depressing, the public view of medicine is to question everything. There is a lack of faith in doctors these days...'

10   A career in medicine

Since so many doctors had expressed regrets about their decision to become doctors, and a significant proportion still regretted their decision, we wanted to know to what extent they regarded medicine as an attractive career. *Doctors and their Careers* showed clearly that there were aspects of medicine as a career which were found unattractive by doctors in all specialties, although there were indications that those working in general practice were less generally critical than those working in hospital medicine or in other specialties. However, in the present study of doctors who had gained their vocational training certificates in general practice during the 1980s, we found considerable evidence of dissatisfaction with many aspects of medical careers. There appeared to be evidence of growing dissatisfaction with medicine as a career, even among general practitioners.

We were keen to present positive recommendations from this survey of doctors who were mainly working in general practice. There is now a body of evidence suggesting that medical careers advice and counselling are inadequate at all levels, but that they are particularly poor in relation to choosing medicine as a career. Certainly, the evidence presented in *Doctors and their Careers* indicated that few doctors had had realistic advice at school about a career in medicine, while most had had no real advice at all.

There is no doubt that a substantial minority of doctors regret their decision to become doctors, and that some feel strongly that they are in the wrong job. One of the big problems is that it is very difficult, for a variety of reasons, to abandon a career in medicine. Medicine is a more vocational course for a student than virtually any other, and doctors stress how difficult it is to change direction, particularly at the end of medical school. There is the feeling at that stage that they have invested so much of their lives that they have little choice but to continue, even though they may recognise that they might not have chosen a career in medicine if they were starting again. There were certainly indications in *Doctors and their Careers* that people had entered medical school with only a hazy perception of what being a doctor meant, and that many, particularly among the more recent qualifiers, had gone into medicine because they were good at science or because others had thought it a good idea. This was not necessarily the best foundation on which to build a lifetime career in a demanding profession.

We asked the respondents in this survey what advice they would give a 17-year-old who was contemplating a career in medicine, and then asked how their advice would differ depending on whether it was a girl or a boy they were speaking to. We hoped to compile a series of recommendations 'straight from the horse's mouth' - something which many of the doctors interviewed in *Doctors and their Careers* had said they would have welcomed.

Advice to a 17-year-old contemplating a medical career

The doctors were certainly only too willing to give 17-year-olds the benefit of their experience. Many wrote long and detailed pieces of advice at the end of a long questionnaire, and only 3 per cent of respondents failed to give an answer to this question. The following analysis shows that doctors were very anxious to show 17-year-olds that a medical career was not a bed of roses.

The question was left open-ended so that doctors could write as much or as little as they wanted to. Like all the open-ended questions in this survey, the answers were post-coded using a code-frame constructed from the responses given. They are presented here in tabular form, for ease of reference to the incidence of responses from the different cohorts and sexes. Some doctors gave a number of pieces of advice, while others restricted themselves to one answer, often sharp and short. The average was between one and two comments per doctor, and the percentages therefore add to more than 100 per cent.

As Table 10.1 shows, the most frequent piece of advice to 17-year-olds contemplating a medical career, given by nearly 30 per cent of doctors, was to be aware of the commitment involved. Over a third of the women said this, compared with just over one fifth of the men, and as the table shows, the younger doctors were rather more likely to stress it than the older doctors. A 1981 woman summarised the views of many doctors of both sexes: 'They should be *very* sure that there is really nothing else they want to do. The training is long and the hours are awful. Commitment to medicine is tested at every stage - throughout medical school and in house jobs and SHO jobs in hospital. Personal resourcefulness, boundless energy and physical fitness are very important. Lesser mortals run out of steam!'

The question of physical fitness and resilience to be able to cope with the long hours ran through a number of comments, and some doctors went further, like this 1981 man whose advice was terse: 'Get fit. Have psychoanalysis first...'

The second most common piece of advice was that the 17-year-olds should be completely dedicated and motivated and should think very carefully before taking the plunge. Around a quarter of both men and women mentioned this, and another 1981 woman summed up the advice: 'Think very carefully. It isn't as glamorous as people might tell you. Being a student is only the beginning. You have to be aware of the long-term effects on your home and family of rotating posts and anti-social hours. If you still want to be a doctor, good luck – it's a super job if you can survive it...'

Many doctors wanted to disabuse 17-year-olds of the idea that a medical career had any glamour attached to it, and a 1985 woman commented: 'My advice

Table 10.1   Advice to a 17-year-old contemplating a career in medicine

column percentages

	Total	Male 1981	1985	1988	Female 1981	1985	1988
Be aware of the commitment	28	24	18	26	32	30	36
Think carefully/ dedication needed	25	22	24	25	23	29	29
Hard work but worth it	14	13	14	8	17	17	13
Don't do it	13	12	19	16	11	9	13
Spend time with doctors first	11	9	10	15	5	16	13
Go for it/do it	11	16	12	10	14	9	6
Poor career prospects	7	5	9	11	6	5	8
Look at state of NHS/ new contract	7	6	6	7	7	8	6
Do something else	7	8	8	8	5	7	8
Be aware of length of training	5	2	5	6	7	8	5
Don't do it for the money	5	5	6	6	5	2	4
Take time out first	4	4	4	4	2	4	2
Don't specialise too early	3	4	2	3	2	3	2
GP better than hospital medicine	2	*	1	2	1	2	4
Big strain on family life	2	*	0	1	5	1	2
Base: all respondents	*1263*	*204*	*195*	*179*	*221*	*218*	*246*

would be to think hard. It's not as glamorous as they think. There is a lot of hard work for not a lot of money, although I think this is changing. Very few actually get to the top and become brain surgeons. Even for general practice, you now need more training and you need to take more exams. If you want children, they are going to interfere at some stage...'

The question of dedication was often stressed by the younger women, like this 1985 registrar : 'Think very hard about whether you want to work very long hours. Don't consider it unless you can envisage no other career, and don't consider it if you want to make money and have time to yourself. Medicine is beautiful and patients are great, but the politics and the system are very murky...'

The third major piece of advice, given by 12 per cent of the men and 15 per cent of the women, was that it was hard work but worth it. Those most likely to say this were the 1981 and 1985 women, but less than 10 per cent of the 1988 men agreed. The comments were often realistically phrased, like this from a 1985 woman: 'The job is demanding physically and emotionally and makes enormous inroads into one's personal life. The rewards are not good financially, but nevertheless it is a fascinating career and can be combined with parenthood...

The fourth most frequent piece of advice, given by 16 per cent of men and just over one in ten of the women, was the advice not to contemplate a career in medicine. Many doctors simply wrote 'Don't' in answer to the question. Others elaborated, like a 1981 man: 'Forget it! Become a stockbroker, go into computers, be a politician or some other parasitic mode of life...' His views were echoed by a 1981 woman for rather different reasons: 'Don't. I would discourage my children, especially girls. Working in the NHS is very demoralising. I'm sorry we didn't emigrate years ago. Medicine is a silly career for anyone who likes to *think*...'

Another 1981 woman was equally forthright: 'Take up an alternative career unless you truly can't resist doing medicine. The underfunding of the health service, "doctor bashing" by politicians, medico-legal aspects, media obsession with medical matters are all changing the face of medicine – mainly to its detriment...'

A 1988 male full-time principal spoke for many of his year, mixing his metaphors in his anxiety to deter potential followers: 'Avoid it with a barge-pole unless you are really crazy...'

Over 10 per cent of doctors gave the advice to spend time with or speak to doctors in different specialties first. A 1985 woman summarised their views: 'Go and visit various establishments of differing specialties and talk to those involved. Get a realistic view of what is involved and look into how available your likely specialty is and what is required. Do not commit yourself too early to a specialty – keep your options open...'

The same proportion of doctors gave the simple advice to 'go for it' or 'do it', but it was notable that this advice was given by 16 per cent of the 1981 men and only 6 per cent of the 1988 women.

Overall 7 per cent of doctors said that they would warn 17-year-olds about the poor career prospects in medicine, a view expressed by over 10 per cent of the 1988 men. It was also a view held by a number of overseas-qualified doctors, like an Indian doctor who had returned to India after applying for more than 50 posts. He had been interviewed in three places as a salaried doctor, worked for the deputising service while looking for work but had never regretted becoming a doctor. His advice was bleak: 'If you're an Indian citizen, don't look for your career in the UK. You will not get a good job in a white doctor's practice. You may get a job in the practice of Indian doctors where you will be exploited and humiliated. If you complain, no-one will listen to you...'

A further 7 per cent said the 17-year-olds should look closely at the state of the NHS and the terms of the new GP contract, and 7 per cent said they should look at what was involved in being a doctor and seek alternative careers. Some doctors were sad at having to give this advice, like this 1981 woman: 'My advice would be probably not to do it. There are more rewarding jobs (and better paid) with less hassle available. I'm really sorry to say this. I *always* wanted to do medicine since the age of five or six and was fairly idealistic about it till relatively recently...'

Young people were also warned about how long it took to train as a doctor and advised not to do it for the money. Other advice, like this from a 1981 man, was not to specialise too early: 'Get plenty of broad-based postgraduate qualifications and work overseas before you eventually decide what you are going to do...'

Other doctors thought it was better to take time off before medical school, possibly travelling round the world. Another 1981 man summarised the views of a number of doctors who thought that a bit of experience of life was necessary before starting medical school at all: 'Get out on the street, mix and work with all types and kinds of people. Postpone starting medicine as long as you can. If you still feel medicine is the best way to help people to be healthy, then carry on and study it...'

A number of doctors said that they would advise that general practice was better than hospital medicine. Women were more likely than men to say that medicine was a big strain on family life and that decisions on getting married should be postponed until medical training was complete.

There were a number of comments running through many pieces of advice which reflected a certain disillusionment among the respondents about the vocational nature of medicine. It appeared that many of them had entered medicine with a desire to help and heal people. A 1985 man wanted to make sure that young people were aware of what he saw as a changing scene: 'Forget it. I think most people go into medicine with the aim of helping and caring and have a need to do this. Unfortunately, the majority of work in medicine in the future will be dominated by the fear of litigation and attempting to deal with the impossible rush of the elderly...'

His views were echoed by a 1988 woman: 'If you don't expect too much from it, it's OK, but if you expect to find yourself doing the "saving suffering humanity" bit and being thanked for it, then you'll be disappointed...'

Advice to girls

We asked how the advice given to the 17-year-olds would differ, depending on whether it was a girl or a boy the doctors were speaking to. Nearly 70 per cent of the men but less than 50 per cent of the women said it would not differ. However, the 1988 men were much less likely than the older men to say that they would give the same advice to both boys and girls, while among the women it was the other way round, with the 1981 women more likely to give different advice to girls.

The main difference mentioned was the advice to girls that it was difficult to combine a career in medicine with a family. Around a quarter of the women from all years said this. It was interesting that nearly a fifth of the 1988 men said they would give this advice, compared with well under 10 per cent of the 1981 men. A 1985 man had thought out his answer in some detail: 'Girls make just as good doctors as boys. This is accepted by any rational person, so don't waste your time trying to prove it. It is not the issue. The issue is that there is great prejudice against any woman who wishes to have children. Any time taken off to have children or to look after them will make it almost impossible for you to get to the "top" of your specialty, and second best can be a long way down. If you don't want children, are you human enough to be a doctor?'

But another 1985 man gave the same advice from a very different perspective: 'I do not believe that a woman can practise full-time and raise a family satisfactorily. I would strongly dissuade a girl from studying medicine...'

Around 10 per cent of the doctors said that they would warn girls that women were discriminated against in medicine. Again, it was noteworthy that the 1988 men were more likely to say this than any other group of doctors, male or female. Some doctors were very concerned about what they saw as continuing discrimination of an unpleasant kind, like this 1981 woman: 'I would try to make both boys and girls aware of the sexism still rampant in medicine, both among doctors and the way some treat their patients. This might help them keep their eyes open and make more informed personal and professional decisions...'

Some of the advice about the discrimination against women was combined with advice on how to combat it, as another 1981 woman explained: 'I think women are badly discriminated against in medicine. They should be tougher, more vociferous in demands for part-time posts (both training and otherwise) to combine with a family life...'

There was certainly a strong view among women doctors in particular that girls should be warned about the difficulties in obtaining part-time work. Women doctors were also more likely to advise girls that they had to be better and more committed than men if they wanted to succeed. A 1981 woman summarised these views: 'If it was a girl I would recommend achieving higher qualifications and as high a grade as possible in full-time hospital medicine before needing part-time work, like I've done. I'd also say it beats teaching and nursing hands down!'

The doctors also advised girls that general practice was easier for women than hospital medicine, or to choose their specialty so that it fitted in with family or domestic life. Women in particular were likely to say that they would tell girls to finish their training before having children, and a few women said that they would warn girls that they were more likely to succeed if they did not get married.

The advice was not only cautionary, however, and some women said they would tell girls that the situation could only get better and to persevere, while others said medicine was an easier option for women than men because of the availability of part-time work.

Nevertheless, although the majority of men and nearly half the women said their advice would not be different to a girl, it should be remembered that a substantial proportion of doctors had said they would advise *any* 17-year-old against a medical career, and many had advised extreme caution to all young people contemplating a career in medicine. 'Be a lawyer or an accountant – or secretary of state for health...' was the advice of a 1988 man who regretted becoming a doctor. And this advice to do professional training other than medicine was repeated time and again by men and women from all years to both boys and girls.

If, after all this advice, they were still bent on a medical career, a 1988 man gave his recipe for a good life: 'Establish your own priorities in the life you wish to lead. Happily sacrifice the so-called "esteem" specialties in favour of a self-carved role in which you can be happy and comfortable. Medicine is ridden with conventionalists and conformists who may try to encourage the perpetuation of their kind in any following generation...'

Final comments on careers in medicine

The questionnaire ended with an invitation to the doctors to add any other comments they had on careers in medicine in general at the moment. Just over 40 per cent of both men and women had no further comments, but the rest had something to say, and many of them had a great deal to say.

The main comments concerned the White Paper on health, the new GP contract and other NHS changes. The older doctors were more likely to mention these, with around a quarter of the 1981 and 1985 men, nearly 30 per cent of the 1981 women and just over one fifth of the 1985 women expressing some concerns, either about specific aspects of the NHS changes or about the uncertainty caused by the changes. The uncertainty was more often mentioned than the actual changes themselves, but many reservations were expressed about the effect of the changes.

Some doctors were particularly concerned about what they saw as the underfunding of the Health Service and moves towards 'privatisation'. A 1981 woman summarised their views: 'The White Paper will make life harder, more commercial, less caring. The laboratory services will probably be privatised and the increasing influence of "private" commercial health care is bad for morale in the NHS...'

A 1985 man echoed her concerns: 'The drift is undoubtedly away from the NHS and towards private medicine with a consumer- orientated, aggressive style. The "ill" person will become a consumer of resources and have to accept the cost effective management. Like it or not, choice will be restricted, not increased...'

The implications of the GP contract were exercising the minds of many of the respondents. Some were critical of what they saw as 'unnecessary' screening, while others felt that the independence and professional integrity of GPs was under attack, like this 1985 man: 'The status of GPs to my mind is becoming more and more eroded. We now have to do more and more for comparatively less income. New general practitioners will have to be businessmen rather than pure clinicians. Our enviable status as self-employed doctors will, I feel, be removed. Recently, general practice has taken a backward rather than a forward step...'

A 1981 woman shared his views: 'We are called independent contractors, but more and more our freedom is being eroded. There is too much admin and paper work. Salaries are too low...' And another 1981 woman was also worried about increasing 'interference': 'Medicine should remain as an independent career and the government and politicians should not interfere with it as they have done with the NHS in this country...'

There were many comments on the increasing administrative load which GPs felt themselves to be bearing. Another 1981 woman spoke for many of her peers: 'The whole ethos is changing. I never liked the business side of general practice. This is now becoming more and more important and also affecting hospitals with the White Paper. Our relationship with patients is bound to change. I doubt if it will be for the better...'

The implications of the new GP contract for women were mentioned as a matter of particular concern: 'The new contract has enormous implications for part-time doctors. Sadly, it looks as though the government would like to see most women working as "assistants" and not as true partners. Whilst many women will gladly accept this role while they have young children, I feel ultimately they will become frustrated second-class citizens, and this will lead to the lowering of part-time doctors' status...'

Nearly 10 per cent of the doctors expressed the view that medicine was no longer an attractive career and that life was increasingly 'tough' for doctors. A 1981 woman felt very satisfied with her own career and was delighted that her husband had now achieved his ambition of becoming a consultant in a teaching hospital. However, she said: 'It has *not been easy*. My impression is that it is not getting any easier, and the quality of life in hospital medicine at a junior level is worse. And probably quality of life as a GP is set to go downhill...'

Another 1981 woman was not as satisfied with her own job, and was even more worried about careers in medicine in general: 'The stress levels in medicine at present are enormous and increasing. Out of hours work is increasing in volume, and patient expectation is also increasing, fuelled by attacks from the media and politicians. Many doctors, and therefore the health services in general, are near breaking point. Not a good time to enter the profession...'

And yet another 1981 woman agreed: 'Medicine is not for the faint-hearted, nor for those who do not relish hard work and problems to solve, or have no sense of humour...'

The fourth most frequent comment was the need for more careers advice and counselling in medicine. This was of concern to doctors of both sexes from all three years. In many cases, it appeared that the need was not only for advice about the actual specialty to be pursued and how to go about it, but also for help in developing a medical career. Some of the 1988 men were among the most critical of the medical career system in this respect: 'The NHS must be one of the worst employers in the country, offering only long hours at overtime rates one-third of normal time; inhuman hours per week; no assistance as regards careers advice or advancement, and interested only in getting as much work out of you for as little money as possible... The consultants are interested purely in getting you to do the work and are not interested in where you've come from or where you're going...'

Another 1988 man agreed that more interest on the part of more senior doctors would be helpful: 'When one finishes vocational training no attempt is made to find out what one is doing, whether you have a job or not and there is certainly no assistance given to you to find one. Established GPs care as little about this situation as the consultants, ie not at all...'

And another man from the same year confirmed the feeling of malaise and isolation expressed by so many of these younger doctors: 'The training is haphazard. The advancement is erratic. The overwhelming feeling is that your employer doesn't give a damn. This is very different from industry where "people" are seen as a valuable resource...'

A 1985 woman was concerned about both the lack of careers advice and the lack of counselling services for young doctors: 'Students do not realise the stresses and strains that hospital posts put on them and their relationships, and more advice and help are needed. Counselling groups should be available for young doctors. Perhaps young professionals should help each other more and avoid the tragedies of doctors committing suicide or dropping out. Hospital doctors should have a group they could go to for help and advice as they are scared to cross consultants and administrators. More emphasis should be put on career options during medical school...'

The perceived lack of flexibility in the medical careers system was the fifth most frequently mentioned concern. There were many criticisms of the postgraduate training structure by both men and women from all years. A 1985 woman was critical of the process: 'Postgraduate training in clinical specialties should be more structured, with more teaching and less apprenticeship. I believe this would lead to shorter and more efficient training. GP training, although variable, is the only time a doctor is a trainee first and a pair of hands second. How about teaching the teachers – the consultants – how to teach? They aren't all born with the skill...'

A 1981 woman was critical of the inflexibility of the system in allowing movement between specialties: 'It appears much more difficult now to change direction even at a very early stage. As a result I feel that some doctors are trapped in the wrong branch. In addition, although we end up with highly qualified consultants (for example), many have very little experience outside their very specific area. In many branches the career structure allows for a glut of SRs waiting for consultant posts and leads to low morale in these highly qualified people *who have no other outlet...*'

A 1985 man thought the training system was outmoded and inappropriate: 'I think the system is back to front. We train all our students to be hospital doctors, yet the majority will never reach consultant status. The undergraduates should be trained as general practitioners and after this, specialised training should be available for those who show an aptitude for a particular branch...'

A 1985 woman, like many of her counterparts, thought there should be a restructuring of the career system: 'The career structure in hospital medicine particularly needs to be reassessed. The hospital posts filled by GP trainees are often largely irrelevant to their chosen career, very little training is given and little thought to their specific needs. Those training for hospital careers are beset by the problems of too few senior posts sought by too many juniors...'

The effect of 'inflexible' postgraduate training programmes on women's careers was mentioned by 1988 women in particular: 'I think hospital medicine is more of a problem than general practice in its inflexibility, though both are bad. The degree of inflexibility seems indirectly proportional to the number of women succeeding in a specialty, which is summed up by counting the number of consultant women surgeons and the number of consultant women psychiatrists. Both men and women would gain by a change...'

Low morale among doctors was mentioned by 5 per cent of the respondents, and was expressed in a number of ways. It often appeared that respondents could accept hard work, long hours and even uncertainty about government policy, but they found it very difficult to accept all this *and* what they saw as a lack of appreciation by their patients. An Indian male full-time principal spoke for a number of respondents: 'Under the present government, the GPs are expected to do too much for the public, without respect and finance. The patients are demanding and taking undue advantage of poor hard-working general practitioners...'

A similar proportion were concerned about the plight of junior hospital doctors, particularly the long hours and weight of responsibility they had to bear. A 1981 woman gave a long and thoughtful reply: 'House officers should not have to cope with acute admissions alone. Lack of experience puts the public in danger, and in medicine one should not ever learn by one's mistakes. This means that there should be more staff at all grades to cope with the workload and cut the hours of work which are excessive for junior staff. There should be more part-time posts akin to clinical assistants where one can gain experience and do a useful job of work without having to climb the ladder of seniority towards consultant posts...'

This question really brought the 1981 women into their own, and many of them wrote short essays on the questionnaire: 'The hours are too long. They're ridiculous. My husband is exhausted working 80 hours a week as a GP. The NHS is very demoralised. It probably needs to be thoroughly reorganised and sacred cows cleaned out – especially in the hospital services. No-one seems to have the vision, the courage and the negotiating skills to undertake it. We have a service which was designed for 19th century medical needs. We need to link medical needs *now* and design services accordingly...'

Concern about the length of the hours worked by both GPs and hospital doctors was expressed by 5 per cent of the 1981 men and women, like this male full-time GP principal: 'Medicine is a vocation, and this is a good ethic when applied to the doctor-patient interface. But the idea of "vocation" meaning "working all hours" is no longer realistic. Every doctor should have the option to work a 40-hour week (to include on-call to the general public) without feeling that he or she is letting the side down...'

And a 1988 man echoed the views of many of his contemporaries: 'I think far more jobs in medicine should be of a sessional nature, paid per session. The same doctors should not be expected to work day and night, and, if forced to, should have the next day off...'

Over 6 per cent of the women said that there were not enough part-time opportunities in medicine, and a 1981 woman stressed the need for such posts: 'I believe every effort should be made to keep women working – even part-time – as this would save a lot of woman-power. Not enough incentives are given to help them continue in their careers once they are married with a family. It's only a waste of expensive training...'

There were concerns that patronage and the 'old boy network' were too influential, views expressed not only by women. A 1985 male full-time principal said: 'It's not what you know, it's who you know that counts for most career advances. The very gifted will make it regardless. The rest of us are much of a muchness, except who we know in the right places...' Another 1985 man agreed: 'A successful career seems to depend on too many factors other than medical ability, for example how much grovelling you do to get your star house-jobs, how good you are at rugby, how much you project an image at medical school...'

Five per cent of the women stressed the difficulties in combining a family and career, and thought there should be more help from a number of sources in recognising the problems women have. A 1985 women said; 'Attitudes to women in medicine are changing, but not fast enough. Heads of Royal Colleges have turned a blind eye for too long. There are many bright, ambitious women who are not satisfied with part-time general practice. Male GPs are particularly unsympathetic...'

A 1988 woman full-time GP principal thought more practical measures were needed from the top to help women doctors: 'If the government really want to encourage more women in general practice, please could they take practical steps to do so, rather than empty words...'

A 1981 woman summarised the views of many women doctors: 'I still feel it's a reasonable career for women, *but* difficulties with lack of security, short contracts, long hours, and the feeling that families are not important, have often made me feel that I was less than human. I have envied housewives and shop assistants on occasion. I also feel that it is difficult for married doctors to each consider their own careers and foster appropriate family life...'

There were general worries about increasing competition for jobs, particularly among the 1988 men, some of whom, as we have seen, tended to be experiencing more difficulties in getting principal posts than their older counterparts had done. But some women thought that men had an unfair advantage in this competition, like a 1981 woman who was working outside general practice: 'Medicine has ruined my life basically. I did not enter general practice because I was being discriminated against at interviews because I was single and female. At several interviews I was specifically told that the married applicants needed the job more than me...'

A few overseas-trained doctors commented on what they saw as racial discrimination, but on the whole their views closely reflected those of all other doctors, except that none commented on the long hours of junior doctors, the inflexibility of postgraduate training schemes or any difficulties for women in combining a family and career.

Other observations made by doctors covered a variety of views, including the comment that medicine was never an easy option but most people could not give it up or found it attractive despite everything, that the financial rewards were poor for the amount of work expected, that there was too much paper-work now, that improved training schemes were needed in general, and that there were much better career alternatives to medicine anyhow. There were also concerns that career progress in medicine depended more and more on postgraduate qualifications and passing examinations, and worries about the need for geographical mobility to 'get on' in medicine.

A few doctors said there was a need for counselling and support for doctors under stress, but, considering the incidence of stress coming through many of these questionnaires, it appeared that doctors were not very good at prescribing solutions or treatment for themselves. It was, in fact, surprising that so few doctors put forward practical suggestions for relieving the stress so many of them were clearly under.

In many respects, the final questions in this survey portrayed a catalogue of woe. There were many indications of a high proportion of doctors feeling unsure, anxious and generally overworked and underappreciated. Most of the respondents were working in general practice, most had entered the specialty during the 1980s and most of them were in their thirties. There can be little comfort for those following them in reading the accounts of their careers given in the last two chapters.

11 Discussion of findings

The aim of this study was to look at the factors affecting the demand for part-time training and part-time career posts in general practice. The resulting report has shown that the factors are complex and the demand is great, particularly for part-time GP principal posts, the career posts in general practice. The demand does not only come from women doctors, and there are many indications in this report that there is a rising tide of demand for a more flexible approach to the organisation of work within general practice.

The data on which this study is based were collected in 1990, just as the new GP contract was being introduced. The doctors responding to the survey were aware of the terms of the contract, and the completed questionnaires contained many references to its potential impact, although no specific questions were asked about the contract as such. But it was clearly a subject which was exercising the minds of many of the respondents, and it is necessary to remember the timing of this survey and the context in which it took place.

We have commented that much of the material covered in the final chapters of this report portrayed a catalogue of woe, as doctors wrote about their stress, overwork, anxiety and apprehension. We found it a matter of concern that this was so widespread among these respondents, most of whom were doctors in their thirties working in general practice who had mainly entered the specialty during the 1980s. The extent to which they were encouraging role models for younger doctors of both sexes was, in our view, doubtful.

In the light of subsequent reports that the number of young doctors entering general practice vocational training schemes has been falling in the last year or so, the findings from this study are clearly of crucial importance in exploring and assessing the reasons for this. Something has clearly changed since the last study we carried out in 1986 interviewing medical qualifiers from 1966, 1976 and 1981, when there was evidence of young doctors, both men and women, flocking into general practice for a variety of reasons, not least their disenchantment with the demands and prospects in hospital medicine (Allen, 1988a). This evidence was reinforced at the time by deans of medical schools speaking of the 'brightest and best' of their students opting for general practice. Now the situation seems to have gone a little sour, and there is plenty of evidence in the medical press and from the recent survey conducted by the General Medical Services Committee (GMSC) to suggest that morale among young general practitioners is not high (Electoral Reform Ballot Services, 1992).

And yet, as this report has shown, the situation is more complex than this. Many of the respondents in the present survey were happy in their work, satisfied with their lives, successful in their careers and had no real complaints. Others were relatively satisfied, had made a success of their careers, but made frequent comments on how the organisation of work both in general practice and in medicine in general could be improved. Among these were women who had managed to achieve the part-time GP principal posts which were in such great demand, who felt they had managed successfully to combine the twin demands of family and career, but still had a great deal of criticism of the difficulties they had experienced. But there were many doctors, including a substantial minority of men, who were clearly dissatisfied with their own individual achievements, worried about their future prospects and critical of a structure which they saw as imposing constraints, not only on their own progress but also on the future development of general practice.

This research has reported the views and experience of a wide variety of doctors. The analysis has been complicated, and we warned in Chapter 1 about the dangers of treating the doctors from the different cohorts as one homogeneous group for statistical purposes. The report has indicated that, although the 'majority' of doctors may have a certain view or experience, the most important indicator for the future may be found among a group or cohort of doctors. We have tried to draw attention to the main implications of the views and experience of these doctors, who may represent a minority or a number of different minorities, but who may well make all the difference to the future development of general practice. It should also be remembered that 'satisfaction' is a notoriously difficult concept to measure, and that those doctors who expressed satisfaction with their present jobs often made critical comments about other aspects of medical careers. Similarly, among those who were dissatisfied with their present situation or the present structure, there were doctors who could never envisage doing anything other than work in medicine, a career for which they had a real vocation.

This discussion of the findings from the present study is designed as part of the more general debate about careers in medicine and the future organisation and staffing of general practice, as well as looking specifically at the question of part-time training and part-time career posts. There can be little doubt that the issues are intertwined.

It should also be remembered by those who may feel that this discussion of findings is concerned mainly with negative, rather than positive, findings, that we were asked to identify and analyse the factors which might prevent doctors from achieving part-time training or part-time career posts in general practice, with particular reference to the extent to which women doctors might have special problems. We have reported the constraints perceived by doctors on their careers, and we discuss them accordingly. Our findings may not fit in with the pre-conceptions of all readers, but they are a faithful reflection of the views and experience of the doctors who responded to this survey.

Women doctors and general practice

We have seen that the proportion of women as entrants to general practice has been rising steadily over the past 15 years, and, indeed, that women will shortly account for 50 per cent of those entering general practice. The importance of making the best use of half the potential labour force in general practice cannot be overemphasised.

But it has become more and more evident that women doctors, although they have a very high participation rate in medicine, usually wish to spend at least some of their careers working part-time, or less than full-time. Failure to recognise this, and failure to attempt to meet the demand for part-time posts, has serious implications, as a cursory glance at the figures shows.

It should also be emphasised again that references to 'part-time' working in medicine can be very misleading. 'Part-time' working can range from part-time training posts in hospital medicine, involving 60 hours a week or more, to posts which account for less than five hours a week. We have stressed time and again that 'part-time' working in medicine can often amount to the equivalent of more than full-time working in other occupations. The hours spent by doctors in 'part-time' posts in general practice, described in Chapter 6 of this report, certainly indicate that 'less than full-time' working would often be a better description of the post. However, the phrase is lengthy and we have usually used 'part-time' in this report, with the understanding that it covers a wide variety of hours, including those which add up to a nearly full-time commitment.

In the present survey, we found that just under half of all the women GP principals were working full-time, although the proportion varied among the three cohorts, with rather higher proportions of the women from the 1981 and 1988 cohort working full-time than we found among the 1985 women, who were, of course, the group most likely to have very young children. But, looking to the future, a high proportion of the 1988 women thought they would be working part-time in five years' time, and it is important to recognise that this pattern is likely to be repeated for future generations of women doctors.

But, of course, not all the doctors responding to this survey were working in general practice, and not all the women in general practice were GP principals. Before we discuss our findings in detail, it would be useful to summarise briefly the present employment status of the doctors. Much of the ensuing discussion can only be fully appreciated against the background of what the respondents were actually doing at the time of the survey.

What the doctors were doing

Nearly 100 per cent of the men doctors were working, compared with 92 per cent of the women doctors. If the women on maternity leave were included among the working doctors, the proportion of women who were working rose to 96 per cent of respondents. This is a very high participation rate among women doctors.

The doctors were mainly working in clinical medicine. Excluding the women on maternity leave, we found that 95 per cent of the men and 89 per cent of the women were working in clinical medicine. The big difference between men and women lay in the proportions who were working full-time and those who were working less than full-time in clinical medicine: 93 per cent of the men and 43 per cent of the women were working full-time, while 2 per cent of the men and 46 per cent of the women were working less than full-time.

Our main remit was with general practice. We found that 90 per cent of the male respondents and 79 per cent of the women were currently working in general practice. If the 4 per cent of women who were on maternity leave from general practice and intended to return were added, we found that 83 per cent of the women were in general practice.

Looking only at the doctors currently working in general practice, and excluding the women on maternity leave, we found that 92 per cent of the men in general practice were full-time principals, compared with 40 per cent of the women. 3 per cent of the men were part-time or 20-hour a week principals, compared with 37 per cent of the women.

It can be seen, therefore, that 95 per cent of the men and 77 per cent of the women working in general practice were principals, but the major difference lay in the fact that nearly half these women were working less than full-time.

We have noted that the 1988 men in general practice were less likely to be working as principals than their older counterparts, and that the 1988 women, although they were more likely to be working in general practice than the older women, were similarly less likely to be principals than their older counterparts.

Women doctors were more likely than their male counterparts to be working as part-time GP assistants or locums, or to be on the retainer scheme. Over one fifth of all the 1988 women had jobs in these categories.

11 per cent of all the doctors had their main job working in medicine outside general practice, and it was noteworthy that nearly one fifth of the 1981 women came into this category. Only 1 per cent of the doctors were working outside medicine altogether. 2 per cent were on maternity leave and 3 per cent were not working for some other reason.

We found that the working doctors had complicated 'packages' of jobs, particularly those working in general practice. Overall, 99 per cent of the men and 50 per cent of the working women said they had jobs which added up to a full-time commitment, but these were made up of three different types of 'package': full-time posts with no part-time work, full-time posts with one or more part-time posts, or a package of part-time posts. Only 1 per cent of the men, but the other 50 per cent of women said they had jobs which added to a part-time commitment: either a package of posts or one part-time post only.

These packages are analysed in some detail in the report, because they throw an interesting light on the ways in which the doctors worked. It is clear that women doctors tend to have more complicated packages of work than men doctors and that the profile of women GPs' participation in medicine is more complex than that of the men. However, there is also plenty of evidence that a relatively high proportion of GPs, whether working full-time or part-time, do additional work outside general practice.

Type and location of vocational training in general practice
This research was designed to examine part-time training and part-time career posts in general practice and to look at the extent to which there were factors preventing doctors from achieving such posts. Before we could analyse this material, we had to have some knowledge of the vocational training patterns of all the doctors and the factors affecting these patterns.

The data show that GP vocational training packages were by no means simple, even among the doctors who gained their vocational training certificates in 1988, by which time it might have been thought that conventional patterns would have been well established.

Rather over one third of the doctors had been on an organised vocational training scheme, just under a fifth had had part of their training on an organised scheme, while just over 40 per cent had organised the whole thing themselves. There were differences among the cohorts, but the trend was towards organised schemes, although these had become more competitive, with younger doctors making more applications for schemes than those from the earlier cohorts. There were definite indications that doctors qualifying in the Indian sub-continent were more likely to have put together their own vocational training packages and to have made more applications for organised schemes than those qualifying in the UK or Ireland.

Although over 80 per cent of all doctors had done all their vocational training in one region, women were more likely than men to have trained in more than one region, and, indeed, nearly a quarter of the 1988 women had done their vocational training in two or more regions.

The question of constraints caused by geographical movement or geographical ties for reasons other than the doctors' own career development was central to this study. There was a strong association between geographical movement and part-time working in medicine, demonstrated in a number of different ways in this report. One of these was connected with the vocational training period.

Nearly 50 per cent of the women, compared with just under one third of the men, said that the question of geographical ties had affected the type of vocational training they had gone for. The main reasons given by men were connected with a desire for geographical stability, while women were more likely to say that they were constrained by the demands of their partner's or spouse's job. If this partner or spouse was another doctor, and 50 per cent of the married women doctors in this study were married to other doctors, the problem was particularly acute. The plaint of the 1988 woman doctor who said - 'I wanted to work somewhere reasonably near my husband...' - was repeated many times in this research.

Length and composition of vocational training
We found that the length and composition of GP vocational training described by the doctors in this study covered a very wide spectrum. It was clear that many respondents were hazy about the actual composition of their vocational training,

in terms of which of their posts were actually approved by the Joint Committee on Postgraduate Training for General Practice for their vocational training certificate. It was interesting that only 50 per cent of the doctors said that their vocational training was composed of the expected pattern of twelve months as a GP trainee and two years of SHO posts, of which at least 12 months were spent in prescribed specialties.

There was evidence of doctors starting their careers with the clear intention of pursuing a career in another specialty and then converting their experience into GP vocational training. There was also evidence of doctors adding experience to their prescribed vocational training for a variety of reasons which were not stated.

Many of the GPs responding to this survey had had much more varied careers before gaining their vocational training certificates than might have been expected, given that the vocational training regulations have required three years training since 1982. This evidence was reinforced by the length of their careers since full registration as doctors in this country. There can be little doubt that, although general practice was evidently an increasingly popular career option among the younger doctors, it was still not the first choice specialty for many of the respondents from all three cohorts.

Part-time postgraduate training

The extent to which the doctors had done any of their GP vocational training part-time was very limited indeed. 3 per cent of respondents (1 per cent of the men and 6 per cent of the women) said they had spent some or all of their GP trainee posts working part-time. Nearly 3 per cent of respondents (2 per cent of the men and 3 per cent of the women) said they had spent any part of their SHO vocational training posts working part-time.

Overall, some 9 per cent of women and 2 per cent of men reported any part-time postgraduate training in medicine, but the 1988 women were less likely to have had any part-time training than earlier cohorts, and there was a strong sense of these younger women feeling a need to get on with their careers by training full-time if at all possible. They, like the 1988 men, had also tended to opt for general practice at an earlier stage in their careers, and to have gained their vocational training certificates at an earlier age and stage in their careers than earlier cohorts.

The main reasons given by women for training part-time were to be able to fit in with domestic or family commitments. There were many indications that they saw this as the only way of saving their marriages, or sanity, or both. Few doctors thought that their part-time training had had an adverse effect on their careers, although some thought it might have slowed down their progress.

Over 10 per cent of women but less than 5 per cent of men who had not had part-time training had considered it, but more than half of these doctors had not pursued the idea because there had been no available jobs.

There can be no doubt that some of the women respondents had been lost to hospital medicine because they had been unable to find a part-time training post in a hospital specialty. A quarter of the women respondents from each year said they would have wished to make a career in hospital medicine if part-time postgraduate training had been more readily available.

The most common specialties mentioned were paediatrics, obstetrics and gynaecology and general medical specialties, and there was clear evidence of regret among women who would have preferred to work as consultants in these specialties rather than work in general practice. The fact that a quarter of the women entering general practice in these years in the 1980s would have preferred to continue in hospital medicine but were prevented by lack of opportunities must be a cause for concern. There was no doubt that the lack of part-time postgraduate training posts at crucial times in their careers and domestic lives had deprived the public of the services of women doctors in specialties where their skills and attributes might appear to be particularly needed.

The overwhelming majority of women, and three-quarters of the men, thought there should be more opportunities for part-time training in general practice. There was no doubt that it was considered vital for the future prospects for women doctors, and for all those with domestic or family responsibilities, that such opportunities should be available. However, it was indicative that a substantial minority of respondents thought that part-time training should be more readily available to all doctors, in order to alleviate some of the stress that so many doctors referred to in the course of this survey. There was also evidence that some doctors were thinking of part-time training in another specialty to help them get out of general practice. As we shall see, alternatives to general practice were being actively considered by some respondents.

In and out of general practice

Over half the male GPs and nearly two-thirds of the female GPs said they had only one post, with virtually all the men having one full-time post, whereas the women were almost equally divided between those having one full-time post and those having one part-time post.

But this meant that around half of the men working in general practice and nearly 40 per cent of the women had more than one post, and most of the additional posts were outside general practice. Although a small number of these respondents were only doing general practice as a minor addition to their main jobs, most of them were mainly in general practice and doing some other kind of additional job. The majority of them had one other job only, usually for between three and five hours a week. The most common type of work was as a clinical assistant, although work as medical officers or in occupational health was common among men, and community health posts were more frequently found among women.

It was interesting that around one third of the men and one fifth of the women who held additional jobs wanted to increase the amount of work they did outside general practice. Nearly 40 per cent of the men and one fifth of the women who did *no* work outside general practice would have liked to do some. What was the reason for this desire for more work, particularly since so many of these doctors, as we have seen, were so overwhelmed with their responsibilities in general practice?

The main reasons were to add interest and variety to their work and for financial reasons. There was plenty of evidence in this report of GPs finding general practice rather restricted, and both men and women indicated that they needed more stimulus in their working lives than they received in daily general practice. There was little doubt that a substantial minority of doctors would have preferred to be in hospital medicine, and many GPs felt their skills and knowledge were not being fully extended and utilised in general practice. The interest in clinical assistant work in hospitals was related to this, but, for some, the one or two sessions a week they worked as clinical assistants was not enough.

Not all GPs, however, really wanted to increase the total number of hours they worked. There were undertones throughout this survey of doctors wishing to increase their work outside general practice while wishing to decrease the amount of time they spent in general practice. The desire for part-time or less than full-time work in general practice was not necessarily confined to women, and certainly not confined to those who wanted more time for domestic or family commitments.

There were certainly many indications of dissatisfaction with general practice, combined with fears of what the future would bring when the new contract was fully in force, which was making some doctors look around for other options in career terms. The developing of new lines of work, while continuing in general practice, was certainly one of these, and, in some cases, particularly among the 1981 women, there were many signs that their disillusionment with general practice was strong enough to encourage them to take active steps to diversify their interests, in some cases out of medicine altogether. The 1981 woman who said, 'The hours are too long in general practice. I have lost my enthusiasm and am burnt out... I wish to be normal again and have a normal life. I wish to see my children. I wish to cook them their meals, help them with their homework, bath them and tell them bed-time stories...' was by no means unique.

Potential returners to general practice

Over 200 doctors, 16 per cent of the total, were not working in general practice at the time of the survey. We found that the most frequent reason for this was the non-availability of suitable GP posts. This was mentioned by both men and women, and although we often found that men had found it difficult to get full-time posts, while women were finding problems in getting part-time posts, there was also evidence that some women were finding it difficult to obtain full-time principal posts in general practice as well.

However, the reasons among the women for not working in general practice were often complex and related to geographical moves and the need to follow their spouse or partner, whose job requirements were regarded as more pressing, particularly if they were working in hospital medicine. There was no doubt that lack of opportunities in part-time general practice was a major source of irritation to an important minority of women doctors in this survey, and the retainer scheme was by no means regarded as an answer to this problem, with many comments on the inadequacy of the scheme in terms of time allowed and the 'trivial work' involved.

The question of returning to general practice centred round the reasons for leaving it. If doctors were happily settled in another specialty which they preferred, the question did not arise. However, for others, for example, many of those abroad or those who had just returned from abroad, the likelihood of returning was strong. Nevertheless, it appeared that many of the women who wished to return to general practice would only do so if they could find suitable part-time work, most usually as part-time principals. The challenge of how to arrange this, especially when so many of the women concerned were relatively mobile, was of crucial importance in this study.

Part-time working in general practice

There was evidence that part-time working in general practice was largely a female occupation. Five hundred doctors, representing 40 per cent of all the respondents, had worked part-time, or less than full-time, at some time in general practice, and 90 per cent of these were women.

Nearly two-thirds of the women doctors had ever worked part-time in general practice: 39 per cent as a part-time GP principal, 20 per cent as a part-time GP assistant, and 6 per cent had held both types of post at one time or another. The comparative proportion of men was 9 per cent, fairly equally divided between part-time principal and part-time assistant posts. Women with children were much more likely than other women to have worked part-time.

Around one third of all the women respondents were currently working part-time in general practice, while just under one third had worked part-time in general practice in the past. Most of those currently working part-time were working as principals rather than as assistants.

Just over one-fifth of the women working as full-time principals had held part-time principal posts in the past, indicating that the availability of such posts helps to keep women in general practice. This was certainly the view of those who held them.

But part-time in general practice, particularly in principal posts, was hardly a limited commitment, and most of the part-time principals were working more than 20 hours or around six sessions a week. Part-time GP assistants worked less, but this was often accounted for by the fact that some were on the retainer scheme which only allowed for one or two sessions, much to the annoyance of some of the women doctors who wanted more work.

There was no doubt at all that the vast majority of doctors working part-time in general practice wanted to cover the full range of general practice work, and there was scathing criticism of practices which wanted to push part-time doctors into a restricted range, which was described as 'frustrating and demoralising'.

191

There is a continuing question over whether part-time working has an adverse effect on the careers of doctors, and many women doctors have expressed suspicion that doctors with 'unconventional' careers, which includes those who have worked part-time or moved around a bit, might be regarded as 'unsound'. Overall, just over a quarter of the doctors who had ever worked part-time thought it had had an adverse effect on their careers, with those who had worked as part-time assistants more likely to hold this view than the part-time principals.

There was concern that part-time working gave a doctor less status in the practice and among patients, and anxiety was expressed that people might not think that a part-time doctor was a 'real' doctor.

This fear of a loss of status through working part-time pervaded much of the discussion among both men and women of the advantages and disadvantages of working part-time or less than full-time. There was plentiful evidence of a clearly recognised pecking order in general practice, in spite of the fact that, on the face of it, it appeared to be much less hierarchical than hospital medicine.

There were some angry and frustrated women doctors among those who thought their career prospects had been adversely affected by working part-time, and their advice to other doctors contemplating such a move was often precise and direct. Strong words were used to tell others that they should make absolutely sure that they negotiated clear-cut partnership agreements or contracts, that their contract was watertight, that they could not be exploited, and that the financial arrangements were foolproof.

There was clear evidence of women whose experience as part-time principals or assistants had been less than satisfactory. The role models they were offering young women leaving medical school were hardly positive and the main advice given by many was to beware.

But advice stressing caution and the need to scrutinise every word of a contract or agreement in general practice was by no means restricted to women doctors who had had unhappy experiences, and there appeared to be a need for increased advice, counselling and information for all doctors, whether male or female, contemplating part-time or less than full-time working in general practice.

However, thoughts about part-time or less than full-time working in general practice were not confined to women with domestic or family responsibilities. Only one third of the men and one in ten of the women could see no advantages in working as part-time or less than full-time GP principal. Although, as might have been expected, most women thought such posts would give them time for family or domestic commitments, a quarter of the men too thought they would like more time with their families. As we noted, many of them treasured this as a faint hope, but some would clearly have welcomed the opportunity.

There was a strong undercurrent among male respondents in this survey of a desire to do something other than full-time work in general practice. Many expressed a wish to diversify their medical interests, often with the hope of developing an expertise they already had, while others were keen to develop interests outside medicine in order to relieve the stress of full-time general practice.

The main factor preventing the doctors from working less than full-time in general practice was, not surprisingly, financial, with money of particular importance to the younger doctors. However, there were indications that older doctors of both sexes were beginning to weigh up the advantages and disadvantages of working full-time in general practice. Although many were anxious not to lose the continuity of patient care which they thought an important part of full-time general practice, there was evidence that a more flexible set of arrangements for sharing patient care was high on the list of priorities for many doctors.

The advantages and disadvantages of working *with* part-time principals were carefully assessed by the respondents. The main advantage of workload sharing and flexibility of cover for the other members of the practice was reinforced by the observation that the contribution of part-time principals usually brought a woman doctor into the practice, a feature which was said to be increasingly desirable for patients. Some women doctors thought it was increasingly desirable for partners too: 'Part-time ladies usually have children and are used to coping. They tend to be tolerant of their partners' and patients' foibles...'

But 'part-time ladies' were not universally popular, and reservations were expressed about the contribution of part-time principals, not only in terms of continuity of care of patients but also with regard to work-sharing, particularly the contentious question of on-call work, and the distribution of roles, responsibilities and money within the practice.

However, nearly 90 per cent of the women thought there should be more part-time GP principal posts, a view shared by over two-thirds of the men, most interestingly by 74 per cent of the 1988 male cohort. It was notable that doctors of both sexes who had qualified in the Indian sub-continent were much less likely than the UK qualifiers to think there should be more part-time GP principal posts.

There was undoubtedly a strong tide of opinion among doctors that there should be more part-time or less than full-time GP principal posts. If women are to achieve their full potential in general practice, this seems to be the most sensible development. It was particularly interesting that, although men were rather less likely than women to advocate more part-time principal opportunities, there were clear indications of an increasing interest in such opportunities, and it appeared that a substantial proportion of men had their own reasons for favouring such a development.

Although most men who had never worked as a part-time principal had never considered doing so, around a quarter had considered it, compared with three-quarters of the women in the same position. It should be noted that nearly 90 per cent of the 1988 women who had never had such a post were actively considering working as a part-time principal. Many of them were juggling their domestic commitments with a full-time job and were finding the burden overwhelming. There were many indications of exhaustion and fatigue among the 1988 women who were working as full-time principals: 'It's difficult trying to look after a baby, husband and house. I'm unable to afford a full-time live-in nanny and I have no immediate family support nearby. It really precludes full-time work which includes on-call responsibility...' And it was undoubtedly the on-call responsibility on top of a full-time job which tipped the balance for many of these young women into considering part-time work.

The main reason for considering part-time principal posts was, not surprisingly, for family or domestic reasons, but, again, we found a substantial proportion of both men and women expressing a desire for less pressure and fatigue in general. Nearly half the 1981 men who were considering part-time principal posts came into this category, and we noted that there was a strong sense of tired middle-aged men among those answering this question, even if the average age of men from this cohort was only 39.

There was a distinction between the reasons offered by men and women seeking or considering part-time or less than full-time principal posts. The women were mostly interested in gaining time to spend with their families, while the men were more interested in developing other interests and getting away from what they saw as the over-commitment of full-time general practice.

There was evidence, especially among the 1981 cohorts, of doctors wanting to change to less than full-time work in general practice towards the end of their careers, while younger doctors of both sexes often wanted to develop other work or leisure interests. Doctors did not usually want to cut their hours dramatically, but simply appeared to want a lighter workload and time to do other things. They certainly did not want to be restricted in the range of general practice work they did, and again expressed the fear of being 'pushed' into 'women's problems' or routine work.

One of the most interesting aspects of this part of the survey was the concurrence of the views of both men and women that more flexibility in work patterns could benefit doctors of both sexes, and that one of the main problems at present was the perceived need to choose between *either* a full-time *or* a part-time GP principal post. There was virtually no enthusiasm for part-time GP assistant posts, which were not considered a serious option by any doctors other than those who wanted only very limited hours.

The men usually said they would not want to return to full-time general practice if they took a part-time post, but a substantial proportion of the women said they would, particularly the younger women, reflecting the fact that older doctors had rather different reasons for wanting to work part-time. There can be no doubt that many younger women doctors wanted part-time work only for a limited period, and, if the full potential of a steadily increasing proportion of general practitioners is to be realised, and patients are to be offered a good service, part-time opportunities must be increased to allow these doctors to keep up their expertise so that they can return to full-time work with confidence.

Careers advice, counselling and information

The patchiness and inadequacy of careers advice to doctors at all stages of their careers was one of the most striking findings of *Doctors and their Careers*, and has been noted widely before and since publication of that report. The pressing need for more comprehensive and focused careers advice and counselling has been underlined by the increasing numbers of women in medicine. There is general agreement that the former system of ad hoc advice on the job from 'patrons' and senior doctors, backed up by a loosely organised system of advice for doctors with problems, was insufficient to meet the demands of doctors with more complicated career paths than the more traditional 'straight' career paths assumed to be the norm for 'sound' doctors.

Advice about part-time working in medicine has not always been easy to obtain, with notable exceptions among some senior doctors who have gone out of their way to develop systems for helping individual doctors. The recommendations in *Doctors and their Careers* with regard to careers advice and counselling have been encouraged by the Department of Health, but there is undoubtedly a long way to go before the universal application of good careers advice and counselling is observed.

In this study, careers advice and counselling about part-time working in general practice were found to be as patchy as most careers advice and counselling in medicine. Less than one third of all the women and only 3 per cent of the men had sought advice about working part-time in general practice, although, as we have seen, a much higher proportion had actually worked part-time or had considered doing so.

A clear impression was given in previous research that seeking careers advice in medicine was not without its dangers, in that fears might be aroused that the doctors concerned were in some way inadequate or were contemplating a course of action, for example, part-time work, which might jeopardise their careers as ambitious doctors. This impression was reinforced in this survey. It appeared that doctors contemplating part-time work were very sure that this was the only thing they wanted to do before they consulted others.

The advice was most usually sought from partners or GP trainers, not all of whom were thought to have given helpful or accurate advice. The advice varied considerably and divided fairly evenly between discouraging or cautious advice and encouraging and positive advice. It was notable that, although most doctors who had had advice thought it more or less helpful and accurate, far fewer found it encouraging.

There was a demonstrated need for better careers advice and counselling on part-time work in general practice, but many doctors observed that the best advice came from those who had experienced it themselves. Much of this advice was to operate very cautiously, to beware of exploitation and to be as wary and suspicious as possible. We found this to be a sad reflection on the development of part-time working in general practice, which is so clearly the main channel through which women are to be retained and encouraged in general practice. There is obviously a very real need for a realistic appraisal of the way in which such careers advice and counselling is given, and a definite need for the development of a data base of information on part-time opportunities. Without such basic facilities, it is highly unlikely that women can develop their potential in general practice.

Geographical moves, career breaks and job-sharing

It has been recognised for some years that there are a number of constraints on the careers of women doctors, but *Doctors and their Careers* produced evidence that many of these constraints were shared by men doctors. One of the most important was the need for young doctors to be prepared to make frequent moves around the country during their postgraduate training. This was thought to be adding an increasing strain on doctors, particularly those in dual career families, since their domestic lives were disrupted in a way which many found unacceptable. It was found especially difficult by young doctors whose spouses or partners were also doctors, since the likelihood of finding two training posts of the necessary grade and specialty in one location was not always strong.

We found in this survey that the wives of GPs were more likely to be working than not, often in managerial or professional occupations, and there can be little doubt that their careers were important factors in their husbands' choice of career moves and specialty. However, since women usually adapt their own careers to meet the demands of their husbands' careers, we were particularly interested in looking at the constraints imposed by the need for geographical mobility.

There was a strong association between part-time or less than full-time working and geographical movement. Nearly 60 per cent of the women and 35 per cent of the men who had ever worked part-time in general practice had moved for reasons other than their own career development, compared with 38 per cent of the women and less than one fifth of the men who had *not* worked part-time.

Although part-time working in general practice and geographical movement were both more frequent among women, the two were associated among men as well. In many cases, of course, part-time working is related to a number of factors, most particularly family responsibilities, but it does appear that moving around for reasons other than one's own career development can make it difficult for doctors to retain or acquire full-time posts, or, for that matter, suitable part-time posts.

There was no doubt in the minds of many women that general practice was difficult to break into at principal level, whether full-time or part-time, particularly in a new area. The 'personal' nature of general practice, with caution on the part of a partnership in taking on a new partner who was an unknown quantity combined with worries on the part of a potential woman principal of being exploited without a watertight contract, was not always thought to offer the most welcoming work opportunities for women GPs who had had to move geographically mainly because of their partner's or spouse's job.

Of course, not all geographical moves were made for this reason, and there were many sunny stories told by adventurous doctors who had travelled the world and by dedicated missionary doctors who had followed God's calling. However, there was evidence of a real problem among a substantial proportion of women in continuing or establishing a career in general practice because of the difficulties caused by geographical movement caused by the demands of their partner's job. The moves often came at critical times in their own careers and were often compounded by difficulties experienced in getting advice and help with relocating and picking up their careers.

Even if they had not yet moved, many doctors were expecting such a move, and some of those who had moved already knew they were likely to move again. These moves did not fill most of the doctors with much enthusiasm because they feared the consequences. The most frequent solution offered to the problem of career constraints caused by geographical movement was the provision of more part-time principal posts in general practice, but there were also calls for more advice, counselling and information and a more welcoming attitude from GP principals to newcomers to an area.

The calls for more flexibility in the structure of general practice pervaded this study, arising in one form or another throughout. The lives led by many of the women respondents often appeared to lack qualities which most people would consider normal. When a young woman doctor has to say that she would be helped by '...my husband getting a consultant post within 30 miles of my practice...' and another speaks of the problems caused by living 120 miles away from her husband whom she only sees at weekends, perhaps it is time for the profession, and those planning medical manpower, to think very seriously about the implications of leaving unchanged a system which has such adverse effects on the quality of life of a not inconsiderable number of young doctors.

The potential problems caused by career breaks are well-known, and, not surprisingly, most career breaks of more than six months were caused by women having babies and looking after children. Again, those who had worked part-time in general practice were more likely to have had a career break than others, and there was a clear association between part-time working and career breaks. But what is interesting is that most of those who had had career breaks were working again. As previous research has shown, women doctors do not stay out of medicine for very long, and, as we found in *Doctors and their Careers*, the length of the career breaks taken by women was similar to those taken by men. The main difference, of course, was that the proportion of women having a break was considerably greater.

Few doctors saw the break as a really positive experience in career terms, although one young women thought it gave her time 'to reflect on the fruitless rat-race of hospital medicine...' The three main reasons for finding the career break a negative experience were the difficulty of getting back into the 'system', the loss of confidence and a delay in career progress.

A marked feature of this study was the disillusion and fatigue found among a substantial proportion of men doctors, and it was noteworthy that over one third of both men and women who had not had a career break had considered one, with particular interest shown by men from the 1981 and 1985 cohorts. Their main desire was for a sabbatical or to travel, and it reinforced the evidence found throughout our investigations of a substantial minority of men becoming increasingly concerned at the thought of full-time general practice for the rest of their working lives. Nevertheless, women contemplating a career break were usually concerned about the potentially adverse effects it would have on their careers, and it was certainly regarded with apprehension by the majority of these women.

Job-sharing, although a very frequent recommendation among doctors, is not widespread in medicine. This study was no exception, with only 1 per cent of the men and 3 per cent of the women currently in job-share posts, while even fewer had had job-share posts in the past. The experience had not always been happy and, although the evidence was limited and necessarily anecdotal, there are clearly problems in organising successful job-sharing which may not have been sufficiently explored.

The idea of job-sharing was a very popular potential option among both men and women, with nearly one-fifth of the men and nearly half the women saying they would like to job-share, mainly as GP principals. One third of both the men and women who wanted to job-share wanted to do so for the rest of their working lives. This, combined with the evidence or the proportion of doctors who wanted to work less than full-time as GP principals, must be taken as a serious indication of dissatisfaction among both men and women with the demands of full-time general practice.

However, caution should be expressed about the actual organisation of job-sharing. It may not be the undisguised blessing that so many doctors seemed to think it was, and may not be the best solution to the needs of men and women doctors who want to work less than full-time. Lack of opportunities to job-share were the main factors put forward by doctors when asked what was preventing them from job-sharing. But there are reasons for the marked shortage of opportunities, and these must be examined. There certainly appears to be a need for an exploration of the potential for job-sharing in general practice, and an assessment of the factors affecting its more widespread introduction, particularly in the light of the new GP contract.

Assessment of careers and future plans

Although just over half of the doctors said that they were satisfied or very satisfied with their present job or status, this assessment concealed a great deal of worry and unhappiness among many doctors. Even among those who were satisfied with their jobs there were rumblings of discontent and anxiety about the future, especially regarding the new GP contract, and many expressed concern about what were seen as the increasing demands of general practice, particularly relating to long hours and the on-call work.

Many doctors distinguished between their own job satisfaction and their views on the future of general practice and, although they may have enjoyed their jobs, there were indications that they were not satisfied with the state of general practice or medicine as a profession.

One of the most important factors affecting women's satisfaction with their present jobs was whether or not they had a good part-time post. Some of the women had evidently had to negotiate long and hard to achieve the status they wanted, but most thought it worth it, and there can be little doubt that getting a part-time or less than full-time principal post is a major factor in inducing job satisfaction among women doctors who have trained in general practice.

In *Doctors and their Careers* there was plenty of evidence of general practitioners describing how the quality of their lives was preferable to that experienced by hospital doctors. This enthusiasm appeared to have waned among the respondents in the present survey, but there were still indications of satisfaction among doctors who were living in pleasant parts of the country, with time to follow chosen leisure pursuits. On the other hand, there were also indications to the contrary, of doctors who had entered general practice to get away from hospital medicine, only to find that the demands of general practice had increased and were preventing them from enjoying life. There were strong criticisms from both men and women of increasing administrative demands, bureaucracy and what many saw as interference in clinical judgment.

Much of the dissatisfaction among women was related to the difficulties they experienced in finding satisfactory part-time work as principals in general practice. There were also dissatisfied women who wanted to work more hours than the limited sessions available under the doctors' retainer scheme. But there was also evidence of both men and women being unable to find full-time principal posts in general practice, and it did appear that the matching of doctors to posts left much to be desired in the present system of organising general practice.

It is possible that the doctors who had difficulties in getting jobs were unsuitable for compelling reasons, but the fairly widespread difficulty experienced by the 1988 men in finding principal posts at the time of the survey did suggest that some kind of 'job-finding service for vocational trainees', as suggested by one dissatisfied doctor, might be a good idea. It should cater for those seeking full-time and less than full-time principal posts, and might also meet the demands of those who thought that setting up a job-share register was a top priority.

The future plans of the doctors did not make encouraging reading. The implications of what they intended to be doing in five years' time are far-reaching, and have important messages for medical manpower planners. The expected shift from full-time to part-time working was not particularly surprising, given the age profile of the women doctors, but it was significant that this expected shift was not only found among women. The expected decline in full-time working was most marked among the 1981 men, of whom 95 per cent were working full-time in clinical medicine at present, but only 84 per cent thought they would be doing so in five years' time. There was a drift among doctors of both sexes not only towards working less than full-time in clinical medicine but also towards working outside clinical medicine, at least for some of the time.

Essentially, the analysis suggested not only a drift away from full-time general practice among both sexes, but also a redistribution of work. Although two-thirds of all the doctors thought they would be doing the same job in five years' time, nearly one third thought they would be doing something different. There were, of course, differences between the men and women, with the men more likely to think they would be in the same job, but nevertheless the findings have important implications for the future.

The profile of general practice is fluid, and much more account should be taken of the shifting pattern of jobs and demands. Times are changing, and it cannot be assumed that the traditional structure with most general practitioners working full-time as principals in one practice for their entire working lives is going to continue. But if it does not continue, adjustments need to be made, to satisfy not only the demands of the doctors working in general practice, but also the demands of the public they serve.

Regrets and concerns

Around 50 per cent of the doctors responding to this survey had regretted their decision to become doctors at some point in their careers. But this overall statistic conceals an important trend. It is important to note that the proportions rose among both men and women with each successive cohort; indeed, 57 per cent of the men and 63 per cent of the women who had gained their vocational training certificates in 1988 said they had regretted their decision to become doctors. The proportions of doctors expressing regret were consistently higher than those found in *Doctors and their Careers* where the same question was asked.

The doctors were less likely to regret their decision currently, but nevertheless around one fifth of doctors from all three years still regretted it, with rather higher proportions of men from 1981 and 1988 expressing current regret than other doctors. Most noticeably, nearly a quarter of the full-time GP principals regretted their decision at present, reflecting the discontent shown among this group of doctors throughout this report.

The most frequent reasons for regretting the decision to become doctors, whether in the past or at present, centred round the long hours, the on-call duties and the demands on their time. It was expressed more frequently by younger doctors of both sexes, and, again, reinforces recent evidence from other sources of younger GPs being less willing than their older counterparts to commit their lives to the demands of general practice as it has traditionally been organised, particularly with all the other duties which have been perceived to have been added to the job.

Many doctors felt that the accumulation of long hours and personal sacrifice had been too much to bear, and the sad comments from these doctors in their thirties who felt their youth had disappeared in overwork and fatigue should be carefully noted by those who feel that there is too much whingeing among young doctors today. We remind readers again of the young woman of 29 who spoke of spending 'the last six years in a complete state of exhaustion or depression or feeling guilty because I have been working for a postgraduate qualification. My twenties have passed by, and all I have done is survive them because of my career in medicine. I have a string of broken relationships because I was too tired to make an effort... I would like to have children, but if I give up now it will make the last six years even more pointless..'

Her comments were echoed many times in the course of this research, and there was no doubt that there was much bitterness about the demands on young doctors in postgraduate training among many of the respondents in this study, even if they now enjoyed their work and found their jobs satisfying.

There was cumulative evidence of doctors feeling under siege, neither appreciated by patients whose demands and expectations were rising, nor in tune with politicians and managers by whom they felt threatened and misunderstood. The woman doctor who reflected unhappily on the 'lack of faith in doctors these days...' was speaking on behalf of many of the respondents in this research.

Careers in medicine

There was absolutely no doubt that a career in medicine was not something which many doctors were prepared wholeheartedly to recommend to a 17-year-old contemplating such a move. The advice given by the respondents, both men and women, was laced with caution and scepticism.

The main stress was on the need to consider very carefully the commitment and dedication needed by anyone thinking of a medical career. Young people were advised to be *quite* sure there was nothing else they wanted to do, while a substantial minority of doctors strongly advised any young person against considering such a career.

Advice to girls was even more cautious, with both men and women stressing how difficult it was to combine a career in medicine with a satisfactory family life. Women doctors were particularly keen on telling young girls how difficult it was to obtain suitable part-time work in medicine, and this recurrent theme only underlined the need to increase such opportunities, not only to satisfy the needs of women already in medicine, but also to encourage young women to enter the profession.

Again, it should be stressed that caution was expressed not only by doctors who were dissatisfied or who thought they themselves had had relatively unsuccessful careers. This research, as we have noted before, was characterised by the extent to which we had to take into account a complex series of views which were not necessarily related to the extent to which the doctors themselves had had successful careers in general practice.

The future

Many of the doctors responding to this survey looked forward with gloom, and there were many concerns about the uncertainties surrounding the future of general practice, let alone the future of the Health Service. The perceived 'erosion of freedom' of general practitioners, increasing bureaucracy, 'interference' from politicians and the implications of the new GP contract were all factors exercising the minds of many respondents, both men and women.

It could be argued that the timing of the survey, which coincided with the introduction of the new contract, might have picked up evidence of greater anxiety and concern than would have been found at a later date, if only because doctors were apprehensive about the unknown effects of the contract on their lives and careers. This is, of course, quite possible, but, without conducting a further survey, it is difficult to say to what extent it is true. However, it should be stressed that there were many findings in this survey on which the new contract had little or no bearing. It would be wrong to assume that many of the causes for concern uncovered in the course of this research have disappeared in the period since the new contract has been in operation.

The lack of opportunities for part-time work as principals in general practice was seen as a major problem by many women, while many men were clearly suffering from overload and over-commitment. Both men and women bemoaned the lack of flexibility in the medical careers structure, in which little movement between specialties was feasible, and in which movement between full-time and part-time working was regarded with suspicion, even if part-time posts carrying responsibility were readily available, which they were not.

These complaints were compounded by what was seen as a lack of careers advice, counselling and information for all doctors, and a lack of interest in the plight of doctors whose career or personality did not readily fit into a conventional mould. There were, perhaps more of these around than is often thought, or perhaps the anonymity of a survey of this kind brings them out of their shells.

One of the most striking features of these responses was the extent to which so many doctors gave evidence of needing help in dealing with the stresses of their working lives, but appeared to be getting little support. The relatively few respondents who actually recommended the development of more counselling and support structures for doctors might not have been aware of how widespread the need appeared to be. Doctors are notoriously reluctant to seek help, but there did appear to be a strong need for some more positive channelling of the concerns expressed in this research. There was a sense of isolation among many of the respondents, and perhaps it should be remembered that general practice can be a lonely profession, and that doctors need support and care, like everybody else.

The GMSC report, *Your choices for the future*, (Electoral Reform Ballot Services, 1992), indicated that 'doctors want to lead normal lives, which seems to conflict with patients' expectations of them...' (Hayden, 1992). The present report has underlined the difficulties and constraints that so many doctors experience in leading 'normal lives'. It is to be hoped that further debate will take place in response to the recent cumulative evidence of disquiet with the present structure of general practice, particularly since it appears to have led to some recruitment difficulties.

This discussion of the main findings of the research has not only summarised the most important factors affecting the demand for part-time working in general practice, but has emphasised throughout the importance of looking at the demand in the context of the present structure of careers in general practice, and, indeed, of medicine in general. There is every indication that, unless there is a readiness to consider whether changes might be necessary in the organisation of general practice to accommodate the demand for more part-time working, there might be increasing difficulty in maintaining the high standard of general practice in this country. There certainly appears to be a need to look at the factors affecting job satisfaction and morale in the profession, if medicine is to recruit and retain the 'brightest and best' of succeeding generations of young people.

12 Policy implications of key findings

This study investigated the views and experience of nearly 1300 doctors who received vocational training certificates in general practice in 1981, 1985 and 1988, most of whom entered general practice during the 1980s. They were therefore fairly recent entrants both to the medical profession and to general practice. The overwhelming majority were in their thirties, and few were at a stage in their careers when they would enjoy the benefits that accrue through seniority of service. However, the three cohorts studied in this report represent an important section of young doctors, whose experience and attitudes are of importance in informing the debate on the future direction of general practice and its manpower arrangements.

The policy implications of the key findings of the research are outlined below.

The profile of doctors in general practice

The proportion of unrestricted GP principals who are women has risen from 16 per cent of the total in 1980 to nearly 24 per cent in 1990, while the proportion of women GP trainees has risen from 32 per cent to 47 per cent over the same period. It is well recognised that women doctors are likely to have different career patterns from men doctors, although they maintain a high participation rate in medicine. Failure to address the implications of the markedly changed balance between the sexes in the profile of general practitioners may have serious consequences both for the future of general practice itself and for those working in it.

Part-time working in medicine

It should be recognised that the phrase 'part-time' can be very misleading in relation to less than full-time working in medicine. The range of hours covered by doctors working 'part-time' in medicine is very wide and, in some instances, can amount to the equivalent of full-time hours or more in other occupations. Every effort should be made to ensure that less than full-time working is recognised as being of equal value and is accorded the same status as full-time work in medicine.

Part-time working in general practice

At present, the main demand for part-time, or less than full-time, working in general practice comes from women. Two-thirds of the women respondents in this survey had worked part-time in general practice. There is every indication that the demand among women for part-time work in general practice for at least some period during their careers will continue, and will probably increase as more young women enter the specialty. On current trends, women will soon account for 50 per cent of those entering general practice. There is a clear need for a reassessment of the way in which general practice is organised if their talents are to be fully utilised.

Increased opportunities for part-time training in general practice

There is a need for an increase in part-time training posts in general practice. The overwhelming majority of women and three-quarters of the men thought there should be more opportunities for part-time training in general practice. Only a tiny proportion of respondents of either sex had had any part-time training posts during their GP vocational training period. Both men and women who had considered part-time training had found it difficult to arrange because of a lack of available jobs. There was strong evidence of an unmet demand for such posts.

Increased opportunities for part-time postgraduate training in hospital medicine

The question of more part-time postgraduate training posts in hospital medicine is closely linked to the question of increased part-time training posts in general practice. If the number of women consultants is to be increased there is a need for increased opportunities for part-time postgraduate training in hospital medicine. Few respondents to this survey had held such posts, but 25 per cent of women from each cohort said they would have wished to make a career in hospital medicine if part-time postgraduate training had been more readily available. Their main preference was for paediatrics, obstetrics and gynaecology and general medicine, specialties in which the skills and attributes of women doctors might be particularly needed. But there was evidence that the potential demand from men was greater than generally recognised and part-time training opportunities in hospital medicine should not be confined to women. However, the implications for general practice of increasing the supply of part-time training posts in hospital medicine, with the possible decrease in the numbers of women entering general practice, should be examined.

Increased opportunities for part-time principal posts in general practice

Nearly 90 per cent of women respondents and over two-thirds of the men thought there should be more part-time GP principal posts. Three-quarters of the youngest cohort of men shared this view. There was strong evidence in this report that women, like men, prefer to be GP principals rather than GP assistants. There was a demonstrated need for an increase in the number of part-time principal posts, which were said to be more difficult to arrange than full-time principal posts. There were anxieties that such posts were accorded less power, status and money within a practice, and fears that holding such posts had affected or would affect career prospects. There was a call for advice and guidance on partnership agreements and contracts for doctors working less than full-time. A restricted range of general practice work for part-time principals was rejected by most respondents.

Greater flexibility in the balance between full-time and part-time working
Doctors of both sexes called for more flexibility in work patterns in general practice and it appears that the present balance of work between full-time and part-time principal posts should be examined, with particular reference to ease of movement between full-time, less than full-time and part-time working. It should not be assumed that part-time or less than full-time GP principal posts are sought only by women. There was clear evidence of male full-time GP principals who wanted to reduce their work commitment in general practice, either to increase other medical work or to pursue other interests, and indications that men wanted to reduce their full-time commitment towards the end of their careers.

Work outside general practice
The extent to which GPs work outside general practice should be assessed. This study showed not only that a relatively high proportion of full-time GPs did other work, but that there was a desire to increase this work, while a substantial proportion of those with no other work wanted some. Although it was not perhaps surprising that financial reasons were an important motivating factor, there was strong evidence of GPs wishing to maintain medical expertise and to add interest and variety to their work. The extent to which general practice as at present organised might fail fully to satisfy the talents and aspirations of young GPs should be examined.

Geographical moves
The strong association between part-time working and geographical moves for reasons other than career development should be recognised, and the problems it causes should be addressed. It was clear that women doctors were more likely than men to suffer constraints on their careers because of geographical mobility related to the demands of their husbands' or partners' jobs. This problem is particularly acute since a high proportion of the spouses of women doctors also work in medicine, a profession in which frequent geographical moves during postgraduate training are expected. The adverse effects on quality of life caused by prolonged separation or constant travelling in order to maintain both a medical career and marriage should be examined.

Career breaks
The effects of career breaks on careers in general practice should be assessed. There was a clear association between career breaks and part-time working in medicine. It should be recognised that career breaks, whether taken by women for domestic reasons or by men for other reasons, are usually of short duration, although women are more likely than men to have a career break. Career breaks should not be regarded as a reason for discriminating, either directly or indirectly, against women. The desire by a substantial minority of men for career breaks was indicative of a general underlying fatigue and disillusionment among full-time male GP principals which was a notable feature of this research.

Job-sharing
There should be an exploration of the potential for job-sharing in general practice. Nearly one-fifth of the men and nearly half the women said they would like to job-share, mainly as GP principals. However, there was little evidence of successful job-sharing and the potential problems have not been fully examined. An assessment should be made of the factors affecting its more widespread introduction. The question of offering support to help facilitate job-sharing should be examined both at a local and at a national level.

Potential returners to general practice
The extent to which general practitioners are not working in general practice at present should be assessed. Some have taken a positive decision to choose another specialty, but there was evidence that a significant minority had found it difficult to obtain either a full-time or part-time post in general practice for a variety of reasons. The establishment of job-registers was thought to be a priority by some doctors, and it appears that more attention should be given to helping GPs find suitable posts. There was evidence that doctors sought careers advice only as a last resort, particularly since many were concerned about appearing in need of help or 'difficult' to place.

Careers advice, information and counselling
There was overwhelming evidence of a need for more careers advice, information and counselling in general practice. The case for more careers advice at all stages in medicine before choosing a specialty has been well-documented, but there is a clear need for advice, information and counselling for GPs contemplating part-time work, at the time of geographical moves, when considering a career break, and, not least, at a time of personal or job-related stress. General practice was frequently described as an isolated profession and suitable support systems were not always easy to find. The generally accepted 'ad hoc' nature of careers advice, information and counselling in medicine may not be the most suitable arrangement for doctors seeking advice on circumstances which are outside the mainstream. It should be recognised that an increasing proportion of general practitioners are likely to have a variety of career patterns and demands in future.

This is related not only to the fact that half of them will be women with their special needs for part-time work, but also to the fact that men GPs also wish to develop different work patterns.

Future plans

The study indicated a potential drift away from full-time working in general practice among both men and women respondents when asked about their plans in five years' time. Evidence of regret and disillusion with medical careers is presented in the report, even among those who were satisified with their present jobs and remained strongly motivated by a vocation to help people. There was cumulative evidence of a dissonance between the desires of general practitioners to lead a 'normal life' and their perceptions of increasing demands and expectations on the part of patients, managers and politicians. Dissatisfaction with the 'on-call' requirements of general practice were apparent among all groups of general practitioners, reflecting other recent evidence.

Appendix

Sampling and methods

The sampling of the doctors

1. The study was designed to achieve completed questionnaires from 200 men and 200 women from each of three cohorts of doctors who had been issued with vocational training certificates by the Joint Committee on Postgraduate Training for General Practice (JCPTGP). The selected years for sampling were 1981, 1985 and 1988. Table A.1 gives the total number of certificates issued by the JCPTGP in those years.

Table A.1   Number of certificates issued by JCPTGP in 1981, 1985 and 1988

Year	Male	Female	Total	Percentage female
	Nos	Nos	Nos	%
1981*	1552	1010	2562	39
1985	1341	700	2041	34
1988	1319	879	2198	40

* certificates first issued 15 February 1981

Source: *Report on the Work of the Joint Committee on Postgraduate Training for General Practice, 1991*

2. Agreement was reached between the Department of Health, Policy Studies Institute and the JCPTGP that the sampling frame for the research should be the records held by the Joint Committee of doctors to whom they had issued certificates in the three selected years.

3. Agreement was also reached with the General Medical Council (GMC) that they would supply the up-to-date addresses of the sampled doctors who were still registered with the GMC on labels to be sent to the JCPTGP.

4. A sample of 300 male and 300 female doctors who had received certificates from the JCPTGP in each of the three years was selected by randomising the full list for that year using the central digits of their General Medical Council (GMC) registration number. The sample selection of certificated doctors was carried out by a member of the Joint Committee's staff in three stages:

   (a) the full list of certificated doctors for each year was selected from the full data base of certificated doctors held by the JCPTGP and was sorted into male and female doctors, giving six individual data bases. These were arranged in alphabet and date order within each year;

   (b) each of the six data bases was randomised by sorting the list. The method was to use the central digits of the doctors' GMC numbers (ie ignoring the first three digits of the GMC numbers);

   (c) the first 300 names from each randomised list were selected to give the sample for the relevant year and sex.

   This method of sampling gave a full cross-section across the surname list and through the date of certification list. It also gave a cross-section of doctors with prescribed and equivalent experience certificates.

5. The lists of selected doctors were sent to the General Medical Council which supplied the up-to-date address for each doctor from its own data base.

6. The list was scrutinised for those who were no longer registered with the GMC. Some addresses were found in the records of the Royal College of General Practitioners. However, 12 doctors who were no longer registered with the GMC could not be traced at all, while 6 doctors were known to have died. The total eligible sample was therefore 1782 doctors.

7. The GMC generated four sets of labels for the doctors who were still registered. One was kept as a record by the JCPTGP, and the other three sets were for use in the three stages of the mailing to the doctors. Labels for the other doctors were supplied by the JCPTGP.

8. The names and addresses of the doctors were known only to the JCPTGP and the GMC. Each doctor was given a serial number from 1 - 1800, and a key was kept by the JCPTGP, so that non-responding doctors could be sent follow-up reminder letters.

Contact procedures

9. Each doctor for whom an address was available was sent a package from the JCPTGP, enclosing a letter from PSI inviting them to take part in the research, together with a letter from the JCPTGP, a questionnaire, information about PSI and the background to the study, and a reply-paid envelope. Doctors with overseas addresses were sent an additional letter requesting them to reclaim the costs of postage incurred by returning the

questionnaires. The letter from the JCPTGP endorsed the research and stressed that the name and address of the doctor remained confidential to the Joint Committee.

10. The first mailing was sent in January 1990. A reminder letter was sent a month later to those who had not responded, and a further reminder with the full package, including another questionnaire, was sent a month later to the remainder. Some questionnaires were returned literally by return of post after the first mailing, but questionnaires were still being returned in July and August 1990, and one questionnaire was returned in 1991, too late to be included in the analysis.

Response

11. Table A.2 shows the response rates from the selected samples of 300 from each cohort of men and women. As noted in paragraph 6 above, 12 doctors who were no longer registered with the GMC could not be traced at all, and six doctors were known to have died, leaving a total eligible sample of 1782 altogether. We received completed questionnaires from 204 men from the 1981 cohort – a response rate of 70 per cent; 221 women from the 1981 cohort – 75 per cent; 195 men from the 1985 cohort – 66 per cent; 218 women from the 1985 cohort – 73 per cent; 179 men from the 1988 cohort – 60 per cent; and 246 women from the 1988 cohort – 82 per cent.

12. The response rate for the men was lower than that of the women in each of the cohorts. The differences were not notable apart from the 1988 cohort, where the response rate for women was particularly high – at 82 per cent. It is difficult to explain why the responses of men and women differ more in the 1988 cohort, and, indeed, why the 1988 men's response is the lowest of all. It cannot be explained by a high level of post office returns, since these were relatively uniform for all cohorts, nor by definite refusals, since these were very low throughout. We can speculate that the high response among the 1988 women was related to the fact that many of these women were in their late twenties or early thirties and were making decisions about having families and working part-time. The subject matter of the survey was of particular relevance to them, and undoubtedly gave many of them a welcome opportunity to express their views. It is possible that men in the same cohort did not feel as motivated to respond. We also thought it might be possible that a number of the 1988 cohort might be abroad at the time, or that they had moved from the last known address but that the questionnaire had not been returned by the post office. We recognised that this cohort was the most likely to have moved since completing their vocational training. However, this would not explain the difference between the men and the women, and we record the lower response rate while emphasising that it does not detract from the representativeness of the responses within the sample.

13. We received 56 replies from doctors who we knew were abroad at the time of the survey (4 per cent of the total respondents), and Table 2.19 in the main report shows the breakdown between the cohorts. We sent questionnaires to 102 doctors at overseas addresses, (divided fairly equally among the cohorts and men and women), and received responses from 59 of them. We knew that five of those to whom we sent questionnaires abroad had returned to this country. However, it was unclear from their responses where a further nine doctors from this group were working. On the other hand, we received a number of replies from doctors abroad to whom we had sent questionnaires in the UK.

The response rates from doctors with known overseas addresses varied from over 70 per cent of the 1988 men, to 60 per cent of the 1981 men and women and 1988 women, to around 50 per cent of the 1985 men and women. Some of the responses were among the longest and most detailed in this survey, and included some dedicated medical missionaries and doctors working in the third world who gave graphic accounts of their work and motivation.

14. We received 13 replies from doctors who were of the 'wrong sex', in that they had been sampled as men or women, but were of the opposite sex. The numbers cancelled each other out in the relevant cohorts and so we ignored this slight discrepancy. There were two cases where we suspected that spouses had filled in the questionnaires sent to their husband or wife who had received certificates in the same year. (There were also some husband and wives who told us they had both been sampled and both responded.)

15. We have noted in Chapter 2 that 5 per cent of the men and 10 per cent of the women claimed to have received a vocational training certificate before 1981. We have commented that they were probably referring to some other certificate, although some were adamant that they had never received a vocational training certificate. They have all been included in the cohort from which they were sampled.

Questionnaires

16. The questionnaires were fully structured, in that the exact wording of each question was specified and questions were asked in a predetermined sequence. A fairly high proportion of questions allowed for an open-ended response, with the respondent being invited to write as much as they liked, within space limitations.

Table A.2   Response

	Total	1981 Male	Female	1985 Male	Female	1988 Male	Female
Total sample	1800	300	300	300	300	300	300
Dead	6	5	0	1	0	0	0
No longer registered with GMC and untraceable	12	2	4	5	1	0	0
Questionnaires not sent	18	7	4	6	1	0	0
Total eligible sample	1782	293	296	294	299	300	300
Response	1263 *(71%)*	204 *(70%)*	221 *(75%)*	195 *(66%)*	218 *(73%)*	179 *(60%)*	246 *(82%)*
Gone away/ PO return	52 *(3%)*	8 *(3%)*	8 *(3%)*	8 *(3%)*	9 *(3%)*	8 *(3%)*	11 *(4%)*
Sick/retired/wrong year	4 *(*%)*	1 *(*%)*	3 *(1%)*	0	0	0	0
Refused/returned blank	10 *(*%)*	5 *(2%)*	0	2 *(1%)*	2 *(1%)*	0	1 *(*%)*

References

Allen, I. (1988a) *Doctors and their Careers*. Policy Studies Institute

Allen, I. (1988b) *Any Room at the Top?* Policy Studies Institute

Allen, I. (forthcoming) *Doctors and their Careers: a Follow-up Study*. Policy Studies Institute

Day, P. (1982)*Women Doctors: Choices and Constraints in Policies for Medical Manpower*. King's Fund Centre

Department of Health and Social Security. Health Circular 1980, HC (FP)(80) 1

Department of Health and Social Security. National Health Service (Vocational Training) Regulations 1979, SI 1979 No. 1644

Department of Health and Social Security (1986) *Hospital Medical Staffing: Achieving a Balance*. DHSS

Department of Health (1989) *Working for Patients*. HMSO

Department of Health (1991) *Women Doctors and their Careers. Report of the Joint Working Party*. Department of Health

Department of Health, Medical Manpower and Education Division (1991) 'Medical and dental staffing prospects in the NHS in England and Wales 1990' *Health Trends* Vol. 23 No. 4, 132-41

Electoral Reform Ballot Services (1992) *Your Choices for the Future. A Survey of GP opinion. UK Report*. Electoral Reform Ballot Services

Elston, M.A. (1980) 'Medicine: half our future doctors?' in *Careers of Professional Women*, ed. Silverstone, R. and Ward. A. Croom Helm

Hayden, J. (1992) 'A team future for general practice', *British Medical Journal* **304**, 728-9

JCPTGP (1990) *Report of the Joint Committee on Postgraduate Training for General Practice 1990*, JCPTGP

JCPTGP (1991) *Report of the Joint Committee on Postgraduate Training for General Practice 1991*, JCPTGP

Richards, C. (1991) 'General Practice as a career', *British Medical Journal* **303**, 827-8

Silverstone, R. and Ward, A. (eds) (1980) *Careers of Professional Women.* Croom Helm

Ward, A. (1981) *Careers of Medical Women.* Medical Care Research Unit, Department of Community Medicine, University of Sheffield

Part-time Working in General Practice

The Policy Studies Institute (PSI) is Britain's leading independent research organisation undertaking studies of economic, industrial and social policy, and the workings of political institutions.

PSI is a registered charity, run on a non-profit basis, and is not associated with any political party, pressure group or commercial interest.

PSI attaches great importance to covering a wide range of subject areas with its multi-disciplinary approach. The Institute's 40+ researchers are organised in teams which currently cover the following programmes:

Family Finances – Employment Studies – Information Policy – Social Justice and Social Order – Health Studies and Social Care – Education – Industrial Policy and Futures – Arts and the Cultural Industries – Environment and Quality of Life

This publication arises from the Health Studies and Social Care programme and is one of over 30 publications made available by the Institute each year.

Also available from PSI

DOCTORS AND THEIR CAREERS by Isobel Allen

The major survey of the views and experiences of over 600 men and women doctors who qualified in 1966, 1976 and 1981.

210 x 144 mm, 400 pages, hardback, ISBN 0 85374 344 4, £29.95

ANY ROOM AT THE TOP? by Isobel Allen

A paperback containing the main results of the *DOCTORS AND THEIR CAREERS* survey.

210 x 144 mm, 96 pages, paperback, ISBN 0 85374 445 9, £7.95